Integral Community Enterprise in Africa

At a time of global economic crisis and disillusionment with capitalism, Adodo offers refreshing and positive insight into a more integral way of business management, enterprise and community development as well as holistic healing in Africa. For over three decades, Africa was the recipient of billions of dollars in aid funds that were meant to catapult the continent from undeveloped to developed status. Yet the more the aid poured in, the poorer African countries became.

The devastating effect of western economic models in Africa that followed is well documented. *Integral Community Enterprise in Africa* exposes the limitations of existing theories, such as capitalism, socialism and communism, and shows how western theories were imposed on Africa. Such imposition of concepts and ideas is not only demeaning but also unsustainable, serving only the interest of the elite.

Father Anselm Adodo argues for the need to have a southern theory to serve as an alternative to western theories. The majority of African intellectuals and activists, while criticizing existing theories, often do not provide alternative theories to address the prevalent inadequacies entrenched in conventional social, political and economic systems. This revolutionary book aims to address this lapse and proposes the theory of communitalism as a more indigenous, sustainable and integral approach to tackling the social, political, economic and developmental challenges of today's Africa. There is an African alternative to capitalism, socialism and communism – a surer path to sustainable development in and from Africa.

This is a book that is positioned at the very core of a much needed African Renaissance. A profoundly new approach to development in Africa, this is essential reading for anyone concerned with authentic development in Africa and in the world.

Anselm Adodo is the founder and director of Nigeria's foremost herbal research institute, the Pax Herbal Clinic and Research Laboratories. He is a prominent advocate of African herbal medicine research, indigenous knowledge systems, rural community development, health policy reform and transformation of education in Africa.

T0321032

Transformation and Innovation
Series editors: Ronnie Lessem and Alexander Schieffer

This series on enterprise transformation and social innovation comprises a range of books informing practitioners, consultants, organization developers, development agents and academics about how businesses and other organizations, as well as the discipline of economics itself, can and will have to be transformed. The series prepares the ground for viable twenty-first-century enterprises and a sustainable macroeconomic system. A new kind of research and development, involving social as well as technological innovation, needs to be supported by integrated and participative action research in the social sciences. Focusing on new, emerging kinds of public, social and sustainable entrepreneurship originating from all corners of the world and from different cultures, books in this series will help those operating at the interface between enterprise and society to mediate between the two and will help schools teaching management and economics to re-engage with their founding principles.

For a full list of titles in this series, please visit www.routledge.com/business/series/TANDI.

Integral Renewal
A Relational and Renewal Perspective
Ronnie Lessem and Alexander Schieffer

Integral Advantage
Revisiting Emerging Markets and Societies
Ronnie Lessem

Integral Ubuntu Leadership
Passmore Musungwa Matupire

Integral Innovation and Technology Management
A Worldview
Odeh Rashed Al-Jayyousi

Community Activation for Integral Development
Ronnie Lessem

Integral Community Enterprise in Africa
Communitalism as an Alternative to Capitalism
Anselm Adodo

Integral Community Enterprise in Africa

Communitalism as an Alternative to Capitalism

Anselm Adodo

Routledge
Taylor & Francis Group

LONDON AND NEW YORK

First published 2017 by Routledge

2 Park Square, Milton Park, Abingdon, Oxfordshire OX14 4RN
52 Vanderbilt Avenue, New York, NY 10017

Routledge is an imprint of the Taylor & Francis Group, an informa business

First issued in paperback 2019

British Library Cataloguing-in-Publication Data
A catalogue record for this book is available from the British Library

Library of Congress Cataloging-in-Publication Data
A catalog record for this book has been requested

ISBN: 978-1-138-63679-8 (hbk)
ISBN: 978-0-367-88726-1 (pbk)

Typeset in Bembo
by Apex CoVantage, LLC

Contents

Figures

Tables

About the author

Anselm Adodo is a member of the Benedictine order of the Catholic Church. He was ordained a priest in 1997. He had his initial philosophical training at the studium of philosophy in St Benedict Monastery, Ewu, Edo State, Nigeria. Father Anselm Adodo is the founder and director of Nigeria's foremost herbal research Institute, the Pax Herbal Clinic and Research Laboratories, popularly called Paxherbal. He is a prominent advocate of African herbal medicine research, indigenous knowledge systems, rural community development, health policy reform and transformation of education in Africa. Anselm holds a BA in religious studies from University of Nigeria, Nsukka, Nigeria, and master's degrees in systematic theology from Duquesne University, Pittsburgh, USA, and in medical sociology from University of Benin, Nigeria. His doctoral degrees are in management of technology and innovation from Da Vinci Institute, South Africa, and also in medical sociology from University of Benin, Nigeria. He has authored a number of books, which include: *Herbs for Healing* (1997), *Healing Radiance of the Soul* (2003), *New Frontiers in African Medicine* (2005), *Herbal Medicine and the Revival of African Civilization* (2010), *Disease and Dietary Patterns in Edo Central Nigeria: An Epidemiological Survey* (2013) and the bestselling *Nature Power: Herbal Medicine in Tropical Africa*, first published in 2000 and reprinted eight times. Anselm is an adjunct professor at the Institute of African Studies, University of Ibadan, Nigeria, where he teaches African transformation studies and traditional African medicine. He is a fellow of the Nigeria Society of Botanists and director of Africa Centre for Integral Research and Development (ACIRD), popularly called Pax Africana.

Foreword

You are holding in your hands the important work of Father Anselm Adodo titled *Integral Community Enterprise in Africa*, which describes how business and enterprise should build genuine communities rather just individuals. The word community originates from the medieval Latin *communia*, the neuter plural noun of the Latin adjective *communis*, literally 'that which is common'. Adodo proposes a *communitalist* perspective and theory, built on the four paxes (4Ps), addressing the four key dimensions of development, which he termed community (*communis*), sanctuary (*spiritus*), university (*scientia*) and laboratory (*economia*). In Adodo's integral model there are four worlds: North (science or knowing), West (economics and enterprise or doing), South (nature and community or being) and East (culture and society or becoming). He argues this the world of academic research has been dominated by the West (economics). As a result, there has been a 'one-sided methodology that is heavily biased towards the West, and systematically neglects the South and East, if not also the North.' He argues that the foundation and origin of civilization lie in the south that of community and relationships with nature.

Adodo wisely argues that the only way forward is for humanity and research to reconnect with the foundation story of humanity through a truly integral research that integrates and embraces the four worlds of South, East, North and West, each with its own distinctive strengths and weaknesses.

The communitalist theory is consistent with North American indigenous understanding of the four key dimensions of the person (spiritual, mental, emotional and physical). The so-called medicine wheel of indigenous peoples of North America is based on the North (mental: thoughts), the South (emotional: feelings), the East (spiritual: values that direct behaviour) and the West (physical: body language). This indigenous understanding of four aspects in four directions is a key architectural structure for developing a more sustainable and flourishing economy at the local, regional and national levels. In my own work with indigenous people in North America I have learned the wisdom of the medicine wheel – that is, seeing the person, the community and the world through the integrated lens of the four aspects of the person and the four directions. The individual as well as the community is flourishing to the extent that all four dimensions are in harmony driven through time by coalition (free will).

Indigenous wisdom counsels that without the balance of the four aspects of the person and the four directions, the world is in a state of dis-ease and imbalance. Some would argue that the economic order of our world has been in a state of dis-ease and imbalance at least since the Industrial Revolution and the formative work of Adam Smith's *Wealth of Nations*. The current economic order is dominated by the North or the domain of the mind and reason. Adodo's important work points out the wisdom of community of knowledge, bridging the gap between community, Spirit, nature and reason. Too long have we been preoccupied by a search for knowledge (*gnosis*) when we have forgotten that the roots of genuine wisdom (*Sophia*) can be found only through lived experience.

I appreciate the importance of Adodo's work as a new model for genuine community 'economic' development using an integral approach. As an economist it has taken me an entire lifetime of professional work to have come to my own realization that the language we have been using in economics and business is flawed or rather its true meaning has been lost in translation. In my 2007 book, T*he Economics of Happiness: Building Genuine Wealth*, I pointed out that the word 'economy' comes from the Greek words *oikos* (house-hold) and *nomia* (management or sharing according to needs) and happiness (Greek: *eudai-monia*) means 'well-being of spirit.' Most importantly the word *wealth* comes from the thirteenth-century Old English words *wela* (meaning 'well-being') and *th* (meaning 'the condition of'); therefore, genuine wealth is about the conditions of well-being of com-munities. As a former business professor my favourite teaching to students was the true meaning of the word *competition*: from the Latin *competere*, meaning 'to strive together.' The etymological root of the word *education* is the Latin word *educare*, meaning 'to draw out' what is already within. Genuine education is about discovering the gifts within each one of us. For Adodo, 'education takes place in full embeddedness in the real life-world of one's community.' It is an openness to new ideas and concepts, for 'there is not one but many ways of knowing, doing, seeing and being.'

Adodo's work brings me hope for a wise and more well-being-focused economic model for genuine community development in Africa and in all other places in the world. It builds on the forgotten wisdom of indigenous understanding of the world. Indigenous peoples have long seen the world through a balanced, harmonious and integral lens.

From my own research into the happiest communities and nations, they tend to be ones that are already resonating with the revealed wisdom that Adodo points to, found in villages in Africa, as I have found in First Nations communities in Canada. The happiest places in the world tend to be less focused on money and material wealth and more on relationships, reciprocity, autonomy, harmony with nature, physical and mental well-being. Indeed, the happiest places on earth are not necessarily the most financially prosperous. Happiness research in Canada has found that the happiest communities tend to have a high sense of belonging, have high levels of physical fitness and high levels of perceived mental well-being, have meaningful employment and have strong and enduring loving family relationships.

Economists and world leaders would be wise to consider adopting an integral com-munalist approach to decision making and governance that would make well-being the ultimate aspiration of economic policies. Taking an integral approach to decision making would make decision makers ponder 'what is the well-being impact of our decisions on the four aspects of the human being and the four dimensions of development?' This inte-gral approach that sees the world through the eyes of natural ecosystems would continu-ally seek to achieve harmony or flourishing conditions of well-being. From an accounting perspective, this would mean considering how the five capital assets of a nation (human, social, natural, built and financial) are integrated to achieve not only a net positive financial outcome (GDP, profits) but also a well-being return on investment to all five assets of a community or society.

For the research world of academia, particularly in the area of community develop-ment, Adodo's work is important in pointing out the value of practical research into the lived experience of indigenous communities that have understood the need for balance and harmony for thousands of years. This important emerging field of integral research as developed by Ronnie Lessem and Alexander Schieffer addresses the shortcomings of conventional social research. One of such shortcomings, according to Adodo, is that 'social research tends to remain a mere intellectual exercise with no measureable social impact' and no tangible transformation of communities or societies.

Adodo's work is important as a pragmatic roadmap and tool for community economic development. His focus is the practicality of his research in the lived experience of the people or practice of application. As he points out, 'my final transformative practical contribution is geared towards a new model of business and enterprise based on nature, community and humanism, and finally, the foundation of a communiversity where authentic community-based participatory action research and knowledge creation rather than mere accumulation of theoretical knowledge are the focus.'

Enjoy this important book and renew your hope for a more sustainable future.

Mark Anielski
Author of *The Economics of Happiness: Building Genuine Wealth*
Ontario, Canada, 2016

Acknowledgements

I wish to acknowledge the numerous people who have been part of this research journey for the past twenty years. I joined the Benedictine community of Ewu, Edo State, in 1987 and I have enjoyed the love, companionship and affection of so many members of the community. I am grateful to the monastic community of St Benedict Monastery for giving me the space and freedom to grow and bloom. The local Ewu community has been warm in their relationship with the monastic community, from the village king to the chiefs, elders and the local people. This book is about them and their struggles. I have enjoyed working closely with them and I am grateful for the many ways in which they have shaped my views and helped me to grow. I appreciate the support and contributions of those friends and collaborators, too numerous to be mentioned, who made this work possible. I appreciate the efforts of the staff of Pax Herbal Clinic and Research Laboratories who were involved in the different stages of this research work, especially Anthony Ojo and Austin Obi. I owe the successful completion of this research work to their dedication and cooperation.

My academic mentors, Professors Lessem and Schieffer, founders of the Trans4m Centre for Integral Development, headquartered in Geneva, Switzerland, were involved in every stage of my research journey. Their endless probing questions and queries have helped me to sharpen my methodologies and arguments.

I thank my friends, collaborators and well-wishers for their support and companionship. At difficult times, one often needs the encouragement of such friends and colleagues to keep going.

Finally, I appreciate the love and support of my family members: my mother, Omodun, and my siblings: Funke, Dele, Tola, Damilola, Bunmi, Tope, Yomi and Wonu.

Abbreviations

ACIRD	Africa Centre for Integral Research and Development
AIDS	Acquired Immune Deficiency Syndrome
ANC	African National Congress
ARI	Africa Research Institute
BCM	Black Consciousness Movement
CI	Cooperative Inquiry
CISER	Centre for Integral Socio-Economic Research
CNN	Cable Network News
DSTV	Digital Satellite Television
EDEMCS	Ewu Development and Educational Multipurpose Cooperative Society
ICT	Indigenous Contagion Theory
IMF	International Monetary Fund
MRCS	Member of Royal College of Surgeons
NAFDAC	National Agency for Food and Drug Administration and Control
NNMDA	Nigeria Natural Medicine Development Agency
PAR	Participatory Action Research
PHCP	Pax Health Care Providers
TIAA	There Is An Alternative
TINA	There Is No Alternative
UNESCO	United Nations Education Scientific and Cultural Organization
WHO	World Health Organization

Introduction

The topic of this text is motivated by the neglect of indigenous African knowledge, most especially indigenous medical knowledge in Nigeria. This preference for a one-sided western exogenous knowledge system leads to an identity crisis and a loss of interest in traditional culture and values among the rural populations of Edo State and Nigeria, as well as to economic and political poverty. This work demonstrates that the journey to physical, mental, social and economic-and-enterprise health must follow the reverse order – that is, must start from the village and grow outwards towards the city. In other words, integral healing, which I also call *Pax Africana*, biologically and metaphorically starts with nature and community.

I used integral research in this work. The integral worlds model puts emphasis on a holistic way of research and social innovation built on the dynamics of the symbolic four worlds of South, East, North and West. It helps us to understand the strengths and weaknesses of each world and what each can learn from the other. Each of the four worlds reflects more concretely a certain part of the world. Thus, the South is linked with Africa, the East with Asia, the North with Europe and the West with America. The four worlds are metaphorically present in every society, in every organization and in each person. There is in each society, organization and person a southern relational world of nature and community, an eastern holistic world of culture and spirituality, a northern world of systems, technology and structure and, finally, a western world of enterprise, economics and continuity. Each world has its own preferred and authentic research methodology. In the action research–oriented level of each research path, the South would apply participatory action research (PAR), the East cooperative inquiry (CI), the North socio-technical design and the West action research.

The methodology I employed in this work is emancipatory feminist critique, leading to a new home-grown, contextual theory called communitalism or Pax Africana, which can also be applied globally. Although my research path followed the southern relational trajectory, I chose to combine *participatory action research* (PAR) and *cooperative inquiry* (CI) as my action research methodologies. In the research process, I employed the tenets of PAR to activate the local community of Edo State to engage in regular dialogue to identify their challenges, and find a common ground to effectively proffer their own solutions rather than outside solutions. This led to the creation of *Ewu Development and Educational Multi-purpose Cooperative Society* (EDEMCS). From a local group of marginalized and underrated people, EDEMCS is becoming a voice powerful enough to challenge the status quo, and force a change in power relations in Edo State and Nigeria. In the CI group, I followed John Heron's (1996) four epistemologies, or 'ways of knowing' – namely, experiential knowing, presentational knowing, propositional knowing and practical knowing. One of the practical transformative contributions of the CI group is the creation and continuous evolution of the *Africa Centre for Integral Research and Development* (ACIRD). It aims to institutionalize knowledge creation in and for Ewu village, Edo State, Nigeria and Africa as a whole via a new theory called communitalism. Communitalism, originating from the South, demonstrates that an institutionalized model of business and enterprise based on nature, community, spirituality and humanism, integrally so to speak, is a better driver of social and technological innovation in Africa.

The emancipatory critique method used in this work revealed some of the limitations of existing theories, such as capitalism, socialism, neo-liberalism and communism, and how Africa has been a testing ground for such externally imposed western theories. Such imposition of concepts and ideas are not only demeaning but also unsustainable, and serve only the selfish interest of the ruling elite. One of the major defects of such exogenous theories is they are not built on nature and community, and are not related to the people's culture and worldview. What, then, is the way forward? Violent revolutions? Guerrilla warfare? Civil wars? History has shown none of these has really produced sustainable outcomes. This research work argues for the need to have a southern theory to serve as alternative to the conventional theories. The majority of African intellectuals and activists, while criticizing existing theories, often do not provide alternative theories to correct the prevalent inadequacies entrenched in conventional social, political and economic systems.

My research work proposes the theory of communitalism as a more indigenous, sustainable and integral approach to tackling the social, political, economic and developmental challenges of today's Africa. Such a communitalist perspective, built on the four paxes (4Ps), addresses the four key dimensions of development, which I term Community (*Communis*), Sanctuary (*Spiritus*), University (*Scientia*) and Laboratory (*Economia*). The 4Ps are expressed concretely in the Ewu rural community of Edo State, Nigeria, through four corresponding local institutions – namely, EDEMCS for Pax Communis, St Benedict Monastery for Pax Spiritus, ACIRD for Pax Scientia and Paxherbal for Pax Economia. The four pax dimensions, then, are brought together as a community of knowledge, bridging the gap between community, spirit, nature and reason.

The chief characteristic of conventional universities, or Mode 1 universities, is their preoccupation with fundamental research with little or no interest in the application of the knowledge. Mode 1 universities are built on the concept of research as an objective search for truth, independent of nature, community and the environment. This research work suggests a return to the Mode 2 way of knowledge production, which is transdisciplinary. It is a return because Mode 2, or context-driven research, was the dominant way of knowledge creation until the nineteenth century.

The focus of ACIRD is the generation of community-based knowledge through Pax Africana (the four paxes). The community development association, EDEMCS, is specifically formed to introduce an emancipatory, methodological if not political system into knowledge creation and knowledge sharing in the community. This is important to ensure the community does not stagnate in past cultures and traditions but is open to continuous creative and dynamic interaction between tradition and modernity, individual and community, the indigenous and the exogenous. Such *trans-* and *inter*disciplinary interaction is the unique strength of the communitalist process of knowledge creation, leading to a true Pax Scientia, communitalism in action.

Another characteristic of our communiversity (community university) within the context of Pax Africana and the Ewu local community is the embrace of the spiritual, which we call the 'sanctuary'. Efforts of our so-called modern intellectuals to remove the sanctuary from the university have not been successful. Separating the spiritual from the secular is as absurd as separating teaching from research. The spiritual, within the context of Pax Spiritus, is not about going to church or external religious rituals. It is more about cultivation of a spiritual outlook that sees the inherent beauty and goodness in nature and in others.

ACIRD is set up to research the relationship between nature, community and science, and their impact in the socio-economic development of the society. In this way, we overcome imbalanced worldviews (transcultural), alleviate disciplinary imbalances (transdisciplinary), unravel missing depths (transformational) and transcend individual overemphasis (transpersonal). ACIRD will continue to evolve, research and conceptualize the theory of communitalism, integral healing, integral research, integral education and integral enterprise, all emerging from Ewu in Edo State, Nigeria, and evolving to embrace other centres in Nigeria, Africa and other parts of the world.

A university, in our integral use of the term, is also a laboratory, a place of action research, philosophy-in-action, where theories and action, dream and reality are dynamically merged. It is a place where knowledge is translated into capabilities and capabilities are translated into knowledge. In this case, ACIRD, representing Pax Scientia, and Paxherbal, representing Pax Economia, are intrinsically linked. Education, then, is not something done in isolation from one's community. Rather, education takes place in full embeddedness in the real-world of one's community.

The dynamism of integral development is this blend of the indigenous and the exogenous, the local and the global, the new and the old. While it is essential that we reconnect with our origins and our roots in order to discover our identity and originality, it is equally important that we reach out to other people, other cultures, other worldviews and other ways of doing things, as expressed in an Igbo proverb: '*When something stands, another thing will stand beside it.*' There is not one but many ways of knowing, doing, seeing and being. An integral university helps to build an integral society where we all have a voice and share in the same wisdom embodied in humanity's cultural heritage and diversity.

Part I

Introduction to the integral journey

1 Overview of my research trajectory

Introduction

In 1996, as a young student interested in the ethnography of development, I travelled around the length and breadth of rural Nigeria, a country of 356,700 square miles, about 3.75 times larger than the UK, or three times the size of Germany, with a population of 120 million people, who speak over 250,000 dialects. I was amazed at the amount of knowledge, mostly tacit, available among the local communities. German pharmacist Martin Hirt and his African counterpart Bindanda M'pia (1995) rightly observed that the waste of knowledge is indeed the saddest feature of African life, especially in the rural communities. There is evidence of waste everywhere. For example, after eating oranges, the peels are thrown away, for the people are unaware that the peels of fruits are in fact more nourishing than the fruits themselves. High-quality cattle are taken to the city to be sold, and the money is used to buy poor-quality imported corned beef. A poor woman in the village sells her nutritious cassava flour to buy biscuits for her child attending secondary school. Precious beeswax is thrown away after honey is harvested, while imported shoe polish contains poor, artificial wax. To buy a bottle of coke, a mother sells oranges rich in vitamin C in order to quench her child's thirst. Africans export cheap but high-quality palm oil to Europe, where it is used to make an expensive soap and then exported back to Africa and sold at a price the people can hardly afford.

In many indigenous societies, when a knowledge bearer dies his knowledge dies with him. Indeed, a lot of knowledge is being lost, knowledge that appears to be worthless because it is not properly valued. Today we speak of protecting our environment from abuse and of protection for rare species of plants and animals. Equally important is the need to set up international efforts to protect and preserve indigenous knowledge. With each death of an old person in our villages, a whole library of books is lost.

My research work developed from my fascination with indigenous knowledge, and the need to develop it, document it and modernize it. My fascination led me on one hand to the world of African medical knowledge and the knowledge of herbs. On the other hand, it led me to a search for wholeness in a broader sense, to the realization that healing is a transformation of worldview, including a transformation of economy and enterprise in an African context. Healing is not just about an absence of pain. True healing is integral. Integral healing includes not only an absence of diseases but also self-knowledge; harmonious living within one's community; access to basic human needs, such as food, housing, clothing and social security; and indigenous–exogenous value creation (Larkin, 2011).

Background of the research work

In 1997 I started a small herbal garden. From the herbs that grew, I prepared some herbal mixtures for malaria, coughs and other common ailments. My office was a bamboo tent. Six months later and with a loan of $200, I was able to construct a three-room wooden shaft. A young man from the village, John Okoh, came to join me. We prepared herbal remedies based on local medical knowledge. The villagers who took the cough syrups and malaria medicine came back with very positive results. Before long, the news had spread round the village, which comprised Christians, Muslims and traditional religion practitioners in a balanced proportion. The three-room clinic was called PAX Herbal Centre.

By the year 2008, Pax Herbal Clinic and Research Laboratories, as the herbal centre came to be known, had become one of the biggest, best-equipped, best-organized and most modern herbal research centres in Africa, with fully computerized research and clinical laboratories, rated among the best in Africa. Within a record five years, over thirty-three of the herbal supplements produced were approved by the National Agency for Food and Drug Administration and Control (NAFDAC). This makes Paxherbal the best manufacturing practise in Nigeria, with the highest number of NAFDAC-approved products.

The research question

The research question that will guide the orientation of this research work is as follows:

> How could the issues of indigenous-exogenous knowledge and value creation addressed by Paxherbal in the Ewu Village of Edo State be focused on more widely in Nigeria, Africa and more generally in the wider world? How, specifically, could such a business, community health and social innovation be contextualized, evolved, conceptualized and thereafter more widely and universally applied?

Part of this research work describes how Paxherbal got to its present state and the challenges and philosophy (and spirituality) behind its business model. The other part explores how the business, community health and social innovation actualized by Paxherbal can be systematized, conceptualized and documented (from tacit to explicit knowledge) in such a way to lead to the development of a communiversity in Edo State, Nigeria, that recognizes and releases individual and communal potentials. In other words, how can Paxherbal be a model for a synergy between culture, spirituality, science, economy and enterprise in the context of the global world?

The next section gives a general overview of the paths and methods on which this research work is built.

Structure and flow of the research-to-innovation journey

This research work is based on a method or theory of research termed 'integral research', as propounded by Lessem and Schieffer (2010). The integral research-to-innovation model was designed to bridge the disconnect between academic research and pragmatic social innovation. In other words, integral research was conceived precisely because social research rarely leads to social innovation. We are used to thinking of innovation in connection with technology and inventions by the physical sciences. Inventions in engineering, medicine, agriculture, mobile technology, biotechnology and chemistry have transformed human life and quality of life. The achievements of the physical sciences are so pervasive that the words *technology* and *innovation* are often used solely in connection with the physical sciences. The idea of a social scientist being an 'innovator' might therefore sound strange to most people.

The burning issue for Lessem and Schieffer is that there is a disconnect between research as it is done in the social sciences and its 'social essence'. In other words, social research tends to remain a mere intellectual exercise with no measureable social impact. Why is it that most research in the social sciences only stops at information and hardly ever leads to transformation? The problem, as identified by Lessem and Schieffer (2010), is that social research is built on a faulty foundation, a one-sided methodology that is heavily biased towards the West and systematically neglects the South and East, if not also the North. Yet the foundation and origin of civilization lie in the South. The only way forward is for research to go backwards to reconnect with the foundation story of humanity, in order to chart a meaningful path towards the future. A truly integral research therefore will embrace the four worlds of South, East, North and West, each with its own distinctive strengths and weaknesses (Figure 1.1).

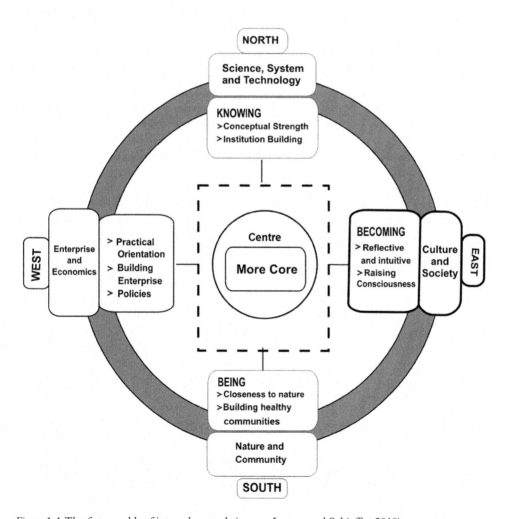

Figure 1.1 The four worlds of integral research (source: Lessem and Schieffer, 2010)

The integral worlds approach puts emphasis on a holistic way of research and social innovation built on the dynamics of the symbolic four worlds of South, East, North and West, as shown in Figure 1.1. It helps to understand the strengths and weaknesses of each world, and what lessons each can learn from the other. Each of the four worlds reflects a certain part of the world. Therefore, the South is linked with Africa, the East with Asia, the North with Europe and the West with America. In reality, the four worlds are metaphorically present in every society, in every organization and in each person. I use the term 'spirit' to describe these worlds. In each society, organization and person, there is a southern relational spirit of nature and community, an eastern holistic spirit of culture and spirituality, a northern spirit of reason and, finally, a western spirit of enterprise, structure and continuity. Each spirit embodies the worldview of its particular world. One of the four worlds usually predominates; in other words, it very rarely happens that the four worlds exist together in a dynamic equilibrium in any particular society, organization or individual.

The next subsection will explain the flow and structure of my research-to-innovation journey based on the integral worlds approach as explained earlier, and identify my particular research path.

The 4Cs of integral research

While the foundation of the integral research method lies in the theory of the four worlds, the research path itself follows a fourfold research trajectory called the four (4) Cs: Call, Context, Co-creation and Contribution. These correspond to four research paths called origination, foundation, emancipation and transformation. Finally, each research path follows a particular research method. My research work is based on a southern relational path of nature and community (see Figure 1.1). Following Table 1.1 and based on my southern relational path, my call corresponds to origination, the research level, and my research method follows the descriptive approach.

The integral research journey requires that the researcher reconnect with his or her inner call, discover his or her subjective burning desire concerning social innovation, and link them with the outer challenge or particular objective burning issue. The second C (Context) requires that the researcher critically examine the imbalances and excesses in his or her particular context. This includes the analysis of the transformational, transcultural, transdisciplinary and transpersonal imbalances in one's particular context with a view to correcting them. This is akin to making a diagnosis before commencing treatment. The objective burning issue the researcher seeks to address is directly related to the imbalances located in the researcher's context. Here also, I will form a dynamic and formidable ecosystem, a movement so to say, energized by the desire for real practical change and development in the Ewu community and Nigeria as a whole.

Table 1.1 The 4Cs

My 4Cs research trajectory	Research levels	Research methods
Call	Origination	Descriptive
Context	Foundation	Phenomenology
Co-creation	Emancipation	Feminism
Contribution	Transformation	Participatory action research and cooperative inquiry

The third C (Co-creation) means that one transcends the limitations of one's particular cultural context, and embarks on a transcultural journey through an exploration of research-to-innovation methods, existing theories and literatures. The guiding research question at this stage is, 'How can research and development be designed in such a way that they lead to social and technological innovation?' Such co-creation is significant in two ways. First, the relationship between academics and students is transformed into one of mutual co-creation, not to mention the relationship between fellow researchers as co-creators across Africa. Second, the division between research method (methodology) and research work content (literature) is co-creatively transcended.

The third C, covered in Chapters 6 and 7, draws on feminism as the emancipatory critique of my research work, which is consonant with my southern relational research path. Feminism gives voice to theories from the South, to the oft-neglected 60 per cent of the world's population. That the opinions of the so-called bottom billion do not count in shaping world events is a paradox. Thus, we find ourselves in a situation where some 20 per cent of the world own and control 80 per cent of the world's wealth and resources as well as the means of knowledge creation. Now we ask, 'What kind of concrete institution can we (my ecosystem) put in place to integrally develop and transform Africa educationally, economically, spiritually, socially, politically and health-wise?' Here, alongside the 4Cs research trajectory, I will introduce the four tenets of CARE – namely, Community activation (C), Awakening of consciousness (A), Research-to-innovation (R) and Embodiment via transformative education/transformative enterprise (E). CARE is the acronym employed by Lessem and Schieffer (2015) to describe this aspect of 'CARE-ing' for the society. The 4Cs and CARE form a dual-rhythm research dynamism of integral research-to-innovation (Figure 1.2). While the 4Cs focus on the individual researcher's innovation

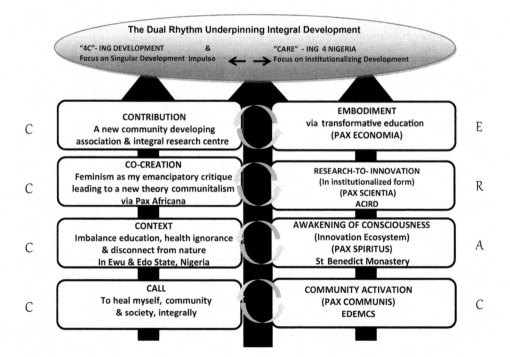

Figure 1.2 My dual-rhythm research-to-innovation storyline (adapted from Lessem and Schieffer, 2015)

in his or her particular context, the CARE aspect of the dual-rhythm research focuses on the institutionalization of the individual's integral process towards a self-sustaining, dynamic and ongoing development.

The fourth and final C (Contribution) is the final distillation of the research journey towards practical application of the knowledge generated to effect social change. The research question at this stage is, 'How can innovation-oriented research and development contribute to the creation of new types of universities (knowledge creation)?' Chapters 4 and 5 discuss the second C (Context), which pertains to my research methodology. Based on my southern relational research methodology, I will use the tenets of phenomenology to thoroughly analyse, discuss and explain my particular context, which forms the foundation of my research work.

My research odyssey along the southern relational path at this final stage will include the holistic eastern path of renewal, making use of John Heron's (1996) cooperative inquiry model alongside participatory action research (PAR). My final transformative practical contribution is geared towards a new model of business and enterprise based on nature, community and humanism, and finally, the foundation of a communiversity where authentic community-based participatory action research and knowledge creation, rather than mere accumulation of theoretical knowledge, are the focus.

Part II: call: origination of research

The next two chapters will be devoted to the first C (Call), which is divided into subjective calling and objective challenge. Here, the descriptive research method is employed to analyse the subjective and objective originations of my call as a social innovator, following the southern relational research path.

Chapter 2: my subjective inner call

My inner call is a desire to explore the field of knowledge – most specifically, knowledge and enterprise as a healing force and tool of liberation and empowerment, drawing on my own context at Paxherbal within Edo State. I describe this as searching for the truth. In other words, my inner burning desire is not just to explore the truth in all fields of knowledge but also to use such knowledge to develop my community, my society and myself. It is often said that knowledge is power. However, knowledge is power only when it makes a difference in the life of the people. My deep inner burning desire is to make a difference in the life of my people, my fellow human beings, my community, my society and the world at large, using the platform of Paxherbal, a healing enterprise based on authentic indigenous African culture and knowledge.

Chapter 3: my objective outer challenge

The third chapter will discuss the outer burning issues I seek to confront. The vital question is, 'What are those issues/problems in my society, community and organization that my research wants to solve, mirroring my inner calling?' Here, some level of objectivity will be required to examine the issues critically and systematically. The objective challenge is that traditional, indigenous knowledge and wisdom are systematically suppressed in favour of a diluted, artificial form of exogenous knowledge, leading to an identity crisis, a poverty of the mind and a poverty of economic if not also political institutions, among the rural population of Edo State. Rather than looking inwards to explore the abundant riches of their fertile imagination, inventive skill and natural intelligence, the rural population of Esanland is engaged in a futile pursuit of health, wealth and prosperity, which they have been brainwashed to believe are attainable when they neglect traditional indigenous knowledge and focus on western knowledge and institutions.

My research work aims to show that the journey to physical, mental, social and economic-and-enterprise health must in fact follow the reverse order – that is, must start from the village and grow outwards. In other words, healing, biologically and metaphorically, must start with nature and community.

Part III: context: phenomenology

The second of the 4Cs within the integral research model is Context. Context refers to the concrete, lived experience of the researcher and his or her community. No one is an island. We all originated from somewhere and grew up within a certain environment. In Chapter 4, I will describe in lucid terms the people who make up my particular context, and their geography, challenges, inclinations and imbalances. This chapter, then, is like a diagnostic laboratory where pathogens, viruses and bacteria are examined and various tests carried out to diagnose the exact disease. A wrong diagnosis will lead to a wrong solution; it is therefore important to examine my society critically and objectively with a view to proffer practical solutions. The basis of this research work is the fact that change is possible and that most diagnosed diseases can indeed be cured.

My methodology, within the integral research framework, is phenomenology. Phenomenology here refers to an existing school of thought, or philosophical path, a particular way of knowing, experiencing and analysing phenomenon, in order to arrive at a deeper knowledge of what we observe.

What really lies at the core of the African sense of community and enterprise? Could it be just tribal sentiments? Fear of the unknown? Is this sense of community a hindrance to individual freedom and sense of responsibility? In Chapter 4, we shall embark on an exciting intellectual odyssey to the traditional African philosophy of health, prosperity and well-being, through reconnecting with relevant literatures in the fields of history, economics, spirituality, anthropology, philosophy and political science. The goal is to show that every society has the capacity to grow and develop once the basic needs of food and shelter have been met.

Chapter 4: uncovering imbalances in my context (transcultural)

This chapter asserts that there is a problem in Esanland, which is the immediate focus of my research work. The young people are being indoctrinated by a colonized and one-sided form of education that distorts their view of nature, of the community and of themselves. The youths of Ewu village, like other Nigerian youths, are acquiring information about other places and lands while losing knowledge of their land, their environment, their culture and their people. No nation can truly develop until it develops, preserves and nurtures its deposit of local knowledge. True and lasting development is that which is home-grown and indigenous, albeit also informed (not dominated) by the exogenous, and not imported from other lands.

The major areas of imbalance in my immediate context are, first, the Paxherbal context; second, the Ewu local community context; third, Edo State and Nigeria nationally; and finally, Africa and the world at large. These all correspond to this research work's aim to alleviate the imbalances by evolving a dynamic knowledge-creating company (integral enterprise), evolving an authentic integral healing community, CARE-ing for Edo State and Nigeria through institutionalization of a self-sustaining ecosystem (integral society), and finally, evolving and reshaping medicine, community and enterprise in the world through education.

Alleviating disciplinary imbalances (transdisciplinary)

This subsection examines the harm a narrow-minded and one-sided focus on a western-ized form of knowledge acquisition is doing to the psyche of Nigerians and Africans. Many scholars in various fields of the social sciences (Stiglitz, 2003; Connell, 2007; Rod-ríguez, Boatcă and Costa, 2010; Breidlid, 2013) have argued for a decolonization of the social science space, which is heavily biased against the South. Eisenstein (2013) describes how popular theories in biology, such as Darwinism and evolutionism, are in fact coloured by cultural, epistemological and ontological bias of the North and West, and more often than not are a reflection of the North/West culture rather than a reflection of the science. Rodriguez et al. (2010) vehemently challenged the dominance of northern and western theories in the social sciences.

Theories in economics, psychology, sociology, anthropology and health care reform often take on a universal air of certainty, and these theories are applied to people of all races and cultures as if written on marble. For example, Easterly (2006) describes how the Washington-based economists, the neo-capitalists, the Washington consensus caucus and the free-market evangelists, whom he called the 'planners', formulate, prescribe and impose foreign-made solutions on developing countries based on the assumption that globalization and free-market economy are the cure for the poverty-disease in African countries. The integral approach offers a new approach to transdisciplinary cooperation, where the arts, social sciences, natural sciences and physical sciences acknowledge their rootedness in nature and culture.

An overemphasis on westernized education in the fields of medicine, for example, has created a perennial interdisciplinary conflict between traditional medicine and western medicine. The same goes for the fields of economics, business and management, where the West is in charge. This research work explores how this imbalance can be corrected against the backdrop of health set alongside economics and enterprise, and draws on Paxherbal and learnings in community development.

Transcending individual overemphasis (transpersonal)

This subsection will unveil my integral ecosystem, which consists of the people I will be working with to actualize my goal of community holistic development. Such people will be drawn from Paxherbal itself, from my local community and from our research com-munity in the rest of Africa. Holistic development refers to good and adequate health care, financial stability, spiritual maturity, social welfare and a healthy natural ecosystem. This will be achieved by making use of the existing well-established platform of Paxherbal, a centre for the scientific cultivation, identification, utilization and promotion of African medicine. Paxherbal has demonstrated that a lot can be achieved by making use of the oft-neglected indigenous knowledge of health, business and enterprise.

Beyond the Paxherbal team, my research-to-innovation process will work with a large team of village leaders, youth leaders, village chiefs, entrepreneurs and female leaders as well as the king of the community, as partners in community building and transformation. The big challenge for Paxherbal is how to convert the challenge of getting enough raw materials to an opportunity of job creation for the local youth. To this effect, several raw materials suppliers will provide a platform for the local women, men and youth to cultivate more crops, plants and medicinal herbs, which will then be purchased by Paxherbal. In this way, the rate of unemployment in the local community will be greatly reduced, if not totally eradicated.

Chapter 5: unravelling missing depths (transformational)

This chapter, which continues my context analysis, explores the transformational enterprise topography on which this research work is based. My topography will follow a twofold path of an indigenous-exogenous format. Thus, I will begin with the core images, the bedrock, where the Yoruba supreme God is described as *Olodumare*, one who sustains all things in being.

The next stage is the subsoil level, which refers to the institutions in place in every society usually built on societal ideology. For example, the African central ideology of 'I am because we are,' also called the Ubuntu ideology, gave rise to community cooperative institutions all over traditional societies in Africa, where the ideology is further cognified and developed. African communities do not have an unbroken history of such institutions due to the interruption brought about by colonialism. However, postcolonial Africa witnessed political systems combining African humanism, communism and capitalism to produce an Ubuntu system by African leaders, such as Nyerere, Senghor and others. In the contemporary world, Paxherbal represents a new system building a new theory of business and enterprise that is private yet has far-reaching effects on the local communities and the wider community. For the western exogenous tradition, the universities had served as a means of preserving traditions and worldviews and shaping ideas. Eventually the western exogenous institutions dominated the entire institutional landscape so much that thinking of an alternative became nearly impossible until very recently.

The final stage of my topography, called the topsoil, refers to the level of everyday behaviours and attitudes. To better understand the basis of people's behaviours and attitudes, an unravelling of their core images and subsoil ideologies is essential. For example, why do a majority of educated Africans in the urban areas still travel to the village to get treatment from traditional healers? A degree in medical science cannot provide an answer to this behaviour, but unravelling their core beliefs and ideologies will provide clear explanations.

Part IV: co-creation

Feminism is a research method that challenges the suppression of emotion in favour of reason. The dichotomy between reason and emotion is an expression of the societal dominance of the male species over the female. In other words, rationality is associated with men and emotions with women. One of the core tenets of feminism is the need for liberation of women and other disadvantaged people from the domination of men. One key feature of feminism is the effort to eliminate gender biases in research, leading to a more balanced and holistic knowledge creation for the transformation of individuals and society. All knowledge, even scientific knowledge, is subjective. Recognizing and acknowledging this will lead to a more genuinely objective and liberating knowledge (Shepherd, 2007).

Following the southern relational path, my critique will be based on feminism, which represents a qualitative approach to critical research. On this level of my integral research path, personal experiences, feelings, opinions and subjective experiences are part of the research process leading to knowledge generation. The focus of my critique is the need to open up the social science – most specifically economic and management/business studies – intellectual and cultural space, heavily dominated by theories from the North, to allow viewpoints from other parts of the world to be heard. The key question here is:

> How can the successful health and business enterprise model of Paxherbal be applied to other parts of Nigeria, Africa and indeed the rest of the world? Can the theory of communitalism be a genuine alternative to capitalism? In addition, how can this theory lead to the liberation of the oppressed, the poor and the marginalized economically, educationally, politically and health-wise?

My ecosystem includes human beings, animals, plants and spirit, and embraces nature itself, the soil, the people and the environment.

Chapter 6: emancipatory critique: introduction to feminism in an African context

Through the utilization of common plants and weeds, Paxherbal was able to develop science-based herbal recipes that have been of help to the local community and to millions of Nigerians. It also has a home-grown business model that puts the interest of the local community as its central focus point. Rather than practise capitalism, which encourages the individual to acquire as much for himself as possible, Paxherbal has developed a business model of communitalism. The term 'communitalism' is different from communalism. Communitalism is a business concept that makes up for the imbalance of capitalism. Communitalism affirms that some aspects of capitalism, such as individual inventiveness, are good, but such inventiveness must be used to serve the community so both the individual and the community prosper. The key philosophy of communitalism is 'We are either happy together as a prosperous community or unhappy together.' The health and prosperity of the individual cannot be separated from the health and prosperity of the local community. Global health must start from local health, not the other way round. In the process, the link between individual, community and enterprise health and whole-making, integrally so to speak, will be made.

Chapter 7: towards a true Pax Africana: communitalism as an approach to health, community and enterprise in Ewu, Edo State, Nigeria

This chapter describes Paxherbal as an authentic and fully indigenous-exogenous enterprise that focuses on the systematic cultivation, identification, promotion and development of African herbal medicine. Paxherbal, as a flourishing health and business enterprise within a particular local community, activates the local community, using the tenets of the integral CARE paradigm, to become an integral community.

A flourishing agribusiness that allows all families in the Ewu local community to engage in profitable cultivation of medicinal plants and other cash crops will transform the village into an economic hub. When there is an improvement in the material well-being of the community, the health of the members of the community will also improve. This is the essence of community medicine. Unlike biohealth, which tends to focus on disease and neglect the root cause of diseases, such as financial inequality, unjust wages, unfair work-ing conditions, dysfunctional literacy and so on, community medicine adopts an integral approach to health and well-being.

Part V: contribution and transformation

Chapter 8: participatory action research in Ewu village, Edo State, Nigeria

Moving from a fully activated Ewu community as discussed in the last chapter, we now focus on Edo State and Nigeria before we can finally conclude with 'CARE-ing' for Africa and the world at large. My inner burning call, as indicated in Chapter 2, is to con-tribute to the integral development of my community, society and the world at large. I am an advocate of a new way of looking at health and health policy reform in Nigeria. My interest in promoting traditional medicine is geared towards a rediscovery of our tradi-tional African culture of care and concern for one another and for our environment. As major stakeholders in the health sector, my co-creative partners, organization (Paxherbal) and I are calling for a new thinking about health care management, policy and reform in Africa. We call for a reawakening of the traditional African approach to health in which the health of an individual cannot be separated from the health of a community. Instead of pursuing a 'healthy lifestyle' characteristic of modern, individualistic culture, we preach a return to the older wisdom traditions of Nigeria that value community-based well-being and harmonious living.

Chapter 9: cooperative inquiry in an African context: the case of Paxherbal and ACIRD

In this final chapter of Part 5, my individual 4C process of integral research, which focuses on biological, physical healing and its business/enterprise aspects that deal with the man-ufacturing of herbal medicines, providing access to health care, employment and bet-ter living conditions, also evolves to a broader vision of healing beyond bodily care to CARE-ing for Nigeria and for Africa. This means rethinking and reshaping the concepts and practise of healing, enterprise and community development in a holistic, integral and life-sustaining way.

For over three decades, Africa was a recipient of billions of dollars in aid funds meant to catapult the continent from undeveloped to developed status. Yet the more the aids poured in, the poorer African countries became. Authors such as Stiglitz (2003), Collier (2008) and Moghalu (2013) have written extensively on the devastating effect of western economic models imposed on Africa. Now it is time to ask what alternative economic models Africa has. How could the issues of health, well-being, education and development be reshaped?

Biohealth is not interested in addressing the disparities in wealth, trade imbalance and rich/poor divisions in the world communities. Biohealth turns away from the fact that poverty, unfair trade imbalance, poor sanitation, poor nutrition and unbridled monetiza-tion of public health are the root causes of health inequality and poor health in the world, especially in Africa.

Biohealth not only treats diseases but also invents them only to turn round and provide the medication to cure the invention. This medicalization of human life, from infancy to adolescence, pregnancy, middle age and old age, partly explains the rapid expansion of the medical enterprise in the past twenty years. It is not a health for all but rather, in the language of modern medical capitalism, a health for the rich – health of the 1 per cent, for the 1 per cent and by the 1 per cent.

Part VI: distillation and conclusion of the integral journey

Chapter 10: CARE-ing for Nigeria: towards an integral university

Following my southern relational path, my research journey will culminate in participatory action research (PAR) as well as cooperative inquiry (CI). Cooperative inquiry is based on the four modes of knowledge creation as propounded by Heron (1996). Participatory action research seeks to understand the world by trying to change it, collaboratively and reflectively. The basic idea of PAR is that research and action must be done '*with*' people and not 'on' or 'for' people (Brock and Pettit, 2007).

The focus of my participatory action research (PAR) and cooperative inquiry (CI) will be to discuss how a new, independent and self-sustaining business enterprise can emerge and develop from the existing business model of Paxherbal to promote a rapid, all-embracing (integral) development within Ewu village and beyond.

This research work has been an exploration spanning my inner calling and my outer challenge. My inner calling was to find meaning in life through healing. I described my outer challenge as a lack of knowledge manifesting in illnesses, unemployment and disharmony in the community. Through the platform of Paxherbal, I, together with my co-creation team, was able to contribute to the alleviation of the physical ailments of the local community. Our medicinal products were popular beyond the local community to the whole state to such an extent that the name Paxherbal became a household name nationwide. My research became an effective tool for my dual-rhythm journey of the '4C-ing' and 'CARE-ing', beginning my Call to Context to Co-creation and Contribution on the one part. On the other part, it was fully involved in the process of CARE-ing for my community through community activation, community consciousness via innovation ecosystem, institutionalized research-to-innovation and transformative education. This culminated in the emergence of the *Africa Centre for Integral Research and Development* (ACIRD). ACIRD, together with the University of Ibadan Institute of African Studies, and the Trans4m Centre for Integral Development, designed a new master's programme in transformation studies to promote ongoing research-to-innovation in and for Nigeria and Africa.

References

Breidlid, A. (2013). *Education, indigenous knowledges, and development in the Global South: Contesting knowledges for a sustainable future.* New York: Routledge.

Brock, K. and Pettit, J. (2007). *Springs of participation: Creating and evolving methods for participatory development.* London: Practical Action.

Collier, P. (2008). *The bottom billion: Why the poorest countries are failing and what can be done about it.* London: Oxford University Press.

Connell, R. (2007). *Southern theory: The global dynamics of knowledge in social science.* Cambridge: Polity Press.

Easterly, W. (2006). *The white man's burden: Why the West's efforts to aid the rest have done so much ill and so little good.* London: Penguin Press.

Eisenstein, C. (2013). *The ascent of humanity: Civilization and the human sense of self.* Berkeley, CA: Evolver Editions.

Heron, J. (1996). *Cooperative inquiry: Research into the human condition.* London: SAGE.

Hirt, M. and M'pia, B. (1995). *Natural medicine in the Tropics: Tropical plants as a source of health care: Production of medicines and cosmetics.* Winnenden, Germany: Anamed.

Larkin, M. (2011). *Social aspects of health, illness and healthcare.* New York: Open University Press.

Lessem, R. and Schieffer, A. (2010). *Integral research and innovation: Transforming enterprise and society.* Farnham, UK: Gower.

Lessem, R. and Schieffer, A. (2015). *Integral renewal: A relational and renewal perspective.* Farnham, UK: Gower.

Moghalu, K. (2013). *Emerging Africa: How the global economy's 'last frontier' can prosper and matter.* Ibadan, Nigeria: Bookcraft.

Rodríguez, E. G., Boatcă, M. and Costa, S. (2010). *Decolonizing European sociology: Transdisciplinary approaches.* London: Ashgate.

Shepherd, L. (2007). *Lifting the veil: The feminine face of science.* Lincoln, NE: iUniverse.

Stiglitz, J. (2003). *Globalization and its discontents.* New York: Norton.

Part II

Origination of research

Research method

We shall not cease from exploration, and the end of all our exploring will be to arrive where we started and know the place for the first time.

—T. S. Eliot

2 My subjective inner call

The emotive researcher

Introduction: embarking on the journey

The foregoing quotation from T.S. Eliot aroused in me an emotional surge of memory. Now I could clearly remember. It was in November 1979 that I read those lines from a little, worn book in a corner of my father's bookshelf, *The Four Quartets* (1969) by T.S. Eliot. I did not know why those lines so powerfully struck a chord in my brain. It seemed to have given me a glimpse of what life is: *an exploration*. Looking back now, thirty-five years later, I can understand a little bit better. Life is indeed a journey, and the goal is to arrive at that place, where we gain knowledge, or put in another way, where we are transformed through knowledge. For me, life is indeed an exploration. I used to be curious to know how the end of the journey would look. My imagination was often awash with images of arriving at the end, anxious to see in order to experience the *eureka!* that follows the feat. After all, the goal of every athlete is to arrive at the end of the race as soon as possible, and the first to arrive at the goal wins the prize. That, in the language of modernity, is often called success. Now I have discovered that arriving at the end of our exploration is not even the goal of life. The goal is the exploration itself: the movement, the journey, the struggle. In the end, we shall perhaps discover we never left in the first place, but have only discovered a new way of looking at life, a transformation of worldview.

Once upon a time

I was born in a serene environment of a modern government hospital in Akure, the capital of Ondo State, Western Nigeria. No fuss. No complication. Just the normal birth of an ordinary child on a normal day. I read about the birth of a child named Jesus, who was born in Bethlehem of Judea. According to the biblical story, at his birth angels flew all around and the whole multitude of angelic hosts sang 'alleluia' at his birth. Well, nothing close to such happened at my birth. I asked my teacher in the nursery school why no angels were flying around when I was born. She said the angels were probably too busy preventing genocides and civil wars in many African countries, including Nigeria, and had no time to hover over a tiny little thing like me.

Indeed, a few hundred miles away, war was raging in Eastern Nigeria – the Nigerian civil war in which one million lives were lost. It was a war between the Nigerian government and the Igbo tribe, one of the largest ethnic groups in Nigeria, who had declared secession from the Nigerian nation state. Nigeria, a concoction of different ethnic tribes, is an artificial creation of the British colonial power. Forcing the whole tribes that made up this vast geographical space under one umbrella was a convenient way for the British government to exercise control and governance. In fact, the sole reason for the amalgamation was for the convenience of the colonial power, not the well-being of the colonized.

The Biafran War lasted from July 1967 to January 1970. The war ended three months after I was born. A few hundred miles away, in the eastern part of Nigeria, hundreds of thousands of newborn children like me died of starvation, their families displaced and hope shattered. This contrasted sharply with the serenity of the environment in which I was born. I later grew up to read about this war and its atrocities in the history books. Neither I nor my parents or anybody close to me was directly affected by the war. So even in wartime, I grew up in a peaceful household.

My father was a school principal and science lecturer. My mother was also a school-teacher. So it was that I grew up not surrounded by the mythical African thick bush, mysterious forests, wild animals or rich vegetation of the stereotypical African life. Life in Africa is in fact more complicated than that. I grew up among a forest of books, my father's library. My father was an avid reader and never missed the daily newspapers. The most frequent visitor to our house at that time was Tunji, the newspaper vendor who used to deliver fresh newspapers to our house every morning. By the age of fourteen, I had read *The Brothers Karamazov* by F.M. Dostoyevsky, *Animal Farm* by George Orwell, *Gulliver's Travels* by Jonathan Swift, *The Pilgrim's Progress* by John Bunyan, the works of William Shakespeare and many others.

I also immersed myself in the works of Yoruba authors and read Yoruba classics, such as Fagunwa's *Igbo Olodumare* (*The Forest of God*, 1949a), *Ireke Onibudo* (*The Sugarcane of the Guardian*, 1949b), *Irinkerindo ninu Igbo Elegbeje* (*Wanderings in the Forest of Elegbeje*, 1954), and *Adiitu Olodumare* (*The Secret of the Almighty*, 1961). Fagunwa's works portray the Yoruba worldview, a world in which spirits, human beings and animals relate, where the line between the visible world and the invisible world is very thin, and one can easily move from one realm to the other. In such a world, spirits take on human forms to carry out different assignments, while human beings, especially hunters, diviners and herbalists, borrow animal bodies to carry out different functions as well as search for information about nature, spirits and the supernatural. Fagunwa's works are rich in picturesque fairy tales containing many folklore elements: spirits, monsters, gods, magic and witchcraft.

A taste of death

When I was just five days old, two days before the customary naming ceremony, I suffered from convulsions and difficult breathing, which left doctors at the hospital confused and helpless. The verdict, based on *materia medica*, was, 'This child will die.' The diagnosis was that my lungs had collapsed. Having been condemned to death, my grandmother consulted with the family Ifa priest, who offered the necessary ablutions to *Orunmila*, the Yoruba god (*orisa*) of knowledge. It was a natural course of action to take, since my grandfather was an *Ifa* devotee, as indicated in the family generic name, *Ifalodun*, which means, 'Ifa's festival is *the* real feast.' The festival of *Ifa*, the Yoruba *orisa* of knowledge, was celebrated every September in my grandfather's household, and was usually the biggest feast of the year – forget about Christmas. After consultation with *Ifa*, the verdict, to my grandmother's bewilderment, was the same: 'The child will die!' But why? Because he is an *Abiku*.

Abiku, the spirit child

Abiku, according to a belief among the Yoruba of Western Nigeria, are spirit-possessed children who come into this world with the sole purpose of dying young so as to inflict pain on the unfortunate mother. Abiku literally means 'born to die' (*Abi*, 'born'; *ku*, 'die'). An Abiku is a spirit child that lurks around in lonely forest paths and riverbanks and, on sighting a pregnant woman, sneaks into her womb and drives away the natural child. When born, an Abiku child hardly lives beyond twelve years. Some may wait until after graduation or just before or after a wedding before dying, but the majority die between one week and ten years. It is believed that an Abiku usually enters into a contract with fellow spirits to stay for a particular period of time, after which he or she must return to the spirit world (Ilesanmi, 1989). It is important for the Abiku to keep to the terms of this contract and resist all allurement of the physical world. So when it comes to the appointed time to return (die), the Abiku begins to suffer frequent and intermittent bouts of illnesses that defy all medications. As expected, the parents of the Abiku spend all their earnings and savings in their bid to find a cure for the Abiku's sickness. Most parents of an Abiku often go bankrupt before the Abiku finally dies. Herbalists are known to decline to treat an Abiku because they know all their medications will have no results. A Yoruba proverb says, '*Abiku so Ologun d' eke*' ('The Abiku makes a genuine medicine man appear like a quack'). The belief is that an Abiku's condition is incurable by medicine.

An Abiku is usually not content with coming and going once, but usually completes some life cycles with the same mother (Kosemanii, 1987). Thus, an Abiku evokes intense fear in women, and the most frequent prayer uttered by every woman is that God should protect her from giving birth to an Abiku.

There are many ways of detecting whether a child is an Abiku. The first sign is frequent sickness. If a child suffers from frequent illness shortly after its birth, there is a suspicion that the child might be an Abiku. If a child is born with some marks in any part of the body, or some mild deformity in the hands, fingers or ears, he or she is suspected of being an Abiku. This is because one of the traditional ways of deterring an Abiku from returning to the same mother is by making some deep marks in the face, neck, back or stomach, or cutting off a segment of his or her finger. If the Abiku is reborn, the marks will still be visible. If a child is exceptionally beautiful and attractive, he or she may be suspected of being an Abiku. A child that manifests above-average intelligence in school could also be suspect. Such a child easily grasps ideas and passes well in examinations, even though he or she may appear not to be as studious as the other students (Ladele, Mustapha, Aworinde, Oyerinde and Oladapo, 1986). A child who prefers to be alone or shows unusual introversion is suspect. The mother, hoping special care and affection will make the child prefer the comfort of this earth to the uncertainty of the other world, often treats an Abiku suspect with great care and devotion. An Abiku is believed to have some spiritual powers, which can be used to harm those whom he or she loathes, or bring good luck to those whom he or she likes. The use of the word 'like' is deliberate, for an Abiku does not love. An Abiku's real love is for his or her mates in the spirit world.

An Abiku who refused to die

Since I fell sick even before the customary naming ceremony, which usually took place on the eighth day of birth, it was easy to conclude that I was an Abiku – a wicked one at that. I could not even allow my parents the joy of a naming ceremony, usually a crowd-pulling social activity. On my eighth day of birth, I hovered between this world and the next in a hospital bed. A renowned Ifa priest confirmed that I was indeed an Abiku child and that I would return to the spirit world within six months. There was no need for my mother and grandmother to waste scarce resources on me. Had I been born some thirty years earlier, I would certainly have been taken to the evil forest, dumped and abandoned to be eaten by wild animals. But this was in 1970, born in a modern hospital, to a father who was critical of 'unproven, old-fashioned' traditions. My mother was a devout Christian whose Christian faith called some traditional fetish practices into question. And my grandmother and grandfather were believers in tradition, but not to the point of fanaticism or foolishness.

Six months came and passed; one year came, two, three . . . six years, and the Abiku did not die. When I began my primary school education, my teachers were warned that I was a suspected Abiku and so should be given special treatment, devotion and respect by the big boys in the school – not a bad idea. The big boys in the school dared not make the mistake of offending an Abiku, so I was always treated with special attention.

Secondary school

My secondary school education was pleasant and enjoyable. My school was a Catholic boys' college, famed for discipline, high academic standards and excellence in sports. My father wanted me to become a scientist, and I showed flashes of becoming one. I excelled in mathematics, physics, chemistry, agriculture and the sciences. However, I had always lived in many worlds – the world of an exogenous, scientific, non-religious father; a holistic-minded, Christian mother; an indigenous grandmother who believed in traditional knowledge systems; and a grandfather who was an Ifa oracle devotee, a firm believer in traditional religions who later became a Christian convert without throwing away the traditional Yoruba values. It was within this multifaceted worldview of science, nature, tradition and culture that I grew up. I felt at home being alone in the gardens, the forest pathways and the forest of books that was my father's library. As I grew up, I learned a lot from my grandmother, who told me stories about the moon, the stars and the spirits. My grandmother used to tell me that the palm trees, the mango trees, the baobab trees, the Iroko trees and the forest could talk. And I asked, 'How can the palm trees, the mango trees and the Iroko trees talk? Are they human beings?' And she would smile and reply, 'There is more to hearing than what you hear; there is more to seeing than what you see; there is more to life than being awake.'

Searching for knowledge

The world of biology, chemistry, mathematics and physics fascinated me. I could not help but marvel at the intricate complexity of the single-celled amoeba, the sophistication of the human heart and its incessant rhythm, the intricate complexity of the human brain, and the laws of physics and chemistry. I also wondered at the audacity with which these laws were stated, as if they were infallible church dogmas. In later years, I came across this quotation from Robert L. Weber (1992), an American scientist: 'It is disconcerting to reflect on the number of students we have flunked in chemistry for not knowing what we later found out to be untrue.' Weber was expressing the reservation I had about the so-called unquestionable claims of science. So after all, those laws of physics and chemistry were not written in gold!

The invention of the microscope was a big step forward in the human search for knowledge, as hitherto unseen microbes, bacteria and viruses, invisible to the naked human eye, could now be seen, studied and examined. Is it possible that one day human beings could invent a machine that can penetrate the world of the spirits and expose the invisible world? The impact of the microscope was immediately felt in the field of medicine, as it led to the discovery of new drugs, especially antibiotics. Could this invisible world of bacteria, microbes and viruses be the invisible world that my grandmother was referring to when she said there is more to things than what the eyes can see? I was determined to know more about this invisible world. I devoured books on eastern religion and spirituality, such as the *Bhagavad Gita*, the Upanishads and series of Vedic literature. I read the complete works of Lobsang Rampa, the *Epic of Gilgamesh* and many others. From African literature, I read the works of Gabriel Okara, Wole Soyinka, Amos Tutuola, Ayi Kwei Armah, Chinua Achebe and a host of others.

Due to my preoccupation with books, I gradually metamorphosed from an Abiku suspect into a confirmed Abiku among my peers. They believed my preoccupation with books was just an excuse to be alone to communicate with my friends in the spirit world.

My childhood was a pleasant experience of growing up in a middle-class, educated family where I cultivated the habit of reading and studying early in life. My family context did not put me in a situation where I experienced the English language as a tool of oppression or suppression, nor did I feel I had been deprived of something by learning a second language, but rather was fascinated by the beauty and magic of words in both English and Yoruba languages. While communication in my father's household was done in my native Yoruba language, we also discussed in the English language, listened to news and music in both languages, watched movies in both languages and read literatures and newspapers in both languages. My grandmother used to tell me that there is more to language than the spoken words, and that wisdom consists in drilling beyond the surface of words to discover the deeper meaning of sound. The Yoruba worldview in which I was immersed as a child is a world of relationships between the living and the dead, between human beings, animals and spirits, between this world and the beyond, between the physical and the metaphysical, the indigenous and the exogenous. Growing up as a city boy in the 1970s also meant I did not experience the often-stereotyped village life of half-naked African children sitting in the open courtyard at moonlight, listening to folklores and stories at night, or begging for food to eat during the day. At night, I watched the television, listened to highlife music or, at other times, immersed myself in books. However, from time to time, when the situation permitted it, my grandmother did tell me stories of the spirits, of the ancestors and family traditions while Mother was away to the church and Father engaged with bacteria in his laboratories.

My 'revolt'

At the age of sixteen, I graduated from secondary school with a grade 'A' in all the subjects. No one was surprised, or even impressed, because what else could they expect from an Abiku? I had one year to prepare for university education. Being born into an educationist's household meant I would not have difficulty in gaining admission into a university. My father diligently worked out my admission to study biochemistry in a prestigious Nigerian university. Meanwhile, unknown to him, I had, along with four of my school friends, paid for an explorative visit to a Catholic monastery in Edo State, in mid-Western Nigeria, where a group of strange-looking monks live, work and pray. We interacted with the monks and spent four days with them. An African proverb says, 'The man who beats the drum for the mad man to dance is himself a madman.' By dining with these 'mad men', I too seemed to have become a 'mad man'. As a child, I had read about monks, and their austerity, discipline, solitude, contemplation and expertise in various fields of human endeavours. In November 1987, I abandoned my university admission and joined the monastery. When my grandmother heard of my decision, she responded with a proverb: 'When the saliva from the mouth of one whose head is not correct enters the mouth of one whose head is correct, the person's head will also become not correct.' For her, my decision to enter into the monastery was a clear sign that my head had become 'not correct'. My father was very angry and disappointed and vowed never to set his eyes on me again unless I came back to my senses and returned home. He had always hated everything that had to do with organized religion, and regarded the Christian missionaries as agents of colonialism. He was a heavy smoker, heavy drinker and an extrovert of the highest order. He had always been a man of his word, and so I shivered when he vowed never to set his eyes on me again. And he never did. In March 1988, he died of lung cancer associated with smoking.

Why I joined a monastery

It is noteworthy and praiseworthy that Catholic schools would never demand a Muslim or non-Catholic student, for example, be converted to Catholicism. My father shared this same view. He believed that true religion cannot be imposed but must be a conscious decision of the individual. Where religion is imposed, fanaticism abounds. He therefore did not have any reservation in sending me to the St Thomas Aquinas Catholic secondary school, the best school for boys in the town where I was born. However, my father did not support the idea of a boarding school, which my mother would have loved.

As it turned out, most of my friends and classmates were enrolled as boarding students, while I came as a day student. The white missionary priests certainly had a special skill in discovering potential candidates for the seminary from the hundreds of students in the school. The orientation was to recruit potential candidates for missionary work and as diocesan priests. Encouraging young people to join monasteries was not part of their brief. Eventually, eight of my secondary school classmates became missionary priests.

My decision to join a monastery was based on my preference for a more reflective, contemplative life. I was not particularly keen about being ordained a priest, but was drawn more towards the monastic ideal of discipline, study and civilization. As a teenager, I had been edified by the central role of monasticism in the evolution and development of European culture: education, literacy, art, music, manufacturing, industry, hospitality, economy, politics and health care. In addition, the Benedictines were right at the heart of these revolutions, some of which will be discussed in later chapters of this research work.

I did not join the monastery because of a sentimental fear of hell, or due to any puritan's tendency or childish piety. It was based on my belief that the monastery might just be a place where my spiritual and intellectual virtues could bloom. On my first explorative visit to the Benedictine monastery in Edo State, I knew I had come to the right place.

Monastic studies

Perched on a hill one thousand feet above sea level, St Benedict Monastery was founded by a group of Irish missionary monks, with the aim of spreading the monastic tradition to West Africa. They chose Edo State, geographically located right in the middle of Nigeria, linking the north, east, west and south. Today, the St Benedict Monastery is of one of the most culturally diverse monastic communities in Africa, representing fifteen different ethnic groups in Nigeria.

When I joined the Catholic Benedictine monastery as an eighteen-year-old boy, it was like an adventure, a fairy tale, an Alice-in-Wonderland journey into the unknown. I was searching for answers to questions about life. A monastery is a cultural unit with age-long traditions, practices and ways of life, a place where a group of people live together in community to devote time to prayer and meditation. The Catholic Church shares in a long history of monasticism dating back to the pre-Christian era. The monastic context is vital to the evolution of my objective challenge, spirituality and transformed worldview, and is the foundation of my work as a social innovator. As a young monk, I studied Church history, spirituality, meditation, patrology and scripture, and read many of the spiritual classics. In the novitiate (a place where a religious novice receives his initial one or two years initiation into a spiritual order), the norm was to read at least a book per month. I sometimes did three in a month. Such a daily immersion in the spiritual classics and spiritual thoughts of others had a transformational effect on my thinking about God, the world and others.

As a professed young monk (one who has taken temporal vows), I was assigned to various offices at different times: as gardener, farm manager, assistant liturgy director and assistant bursar. The bursar is the general coordinator of the monastery's economy. As an assistant liturgy director, I was fully involved in evolving a more African liturgical celebration based on enculturation. We initiated the process of replacing the monotone Gregorian chants with rhythmic African chants and traditional music, making use of drums, percussions and local instruments, among others.

In 1992 I took my final vows, a lifelong commitment to live in the monastery as a monk, at the age of twenty-one. For the next seven years, I was involved in intensive studies and undertook courses in philosophy, logic, scripture, Church history, religion and theology up to postgraduate levels. It was during this period that my thoughts and ideas on philosophy, politics and development and interest in action research were shaped. It was also when I saw the importance of making one's beliefs felt in the lives of the people. Theology, if it is to be relevant, must not end with knowledge accumulation. In my view, it must also bear fruit in action.

In 2004, after seventeen years of living in the monastery as a monk, I was privileged to be assigned the task of editing a book that tells the story of the St Benedict Monastery, as part of the celebration to mark the silver jubilee of the existence of the monastic community of Ewu. In the book, titled *The Story of Ewu Monastery: Silver Jubilee Reflections* (2004: 146), I wrote,

> Monastic life did not start in the desert lands of Egypt, or in the fertile green farms of Canaan, or in the Garden of Eden. Monastic life did not originate in the high mountains of the Himalayas, or on the holy mount of Horeb. Monastic life originated in the human heart. It started the moment God, the almighty and all-powerful said, 'I am one, let me be many'. God desired to express God's self in creation. Humanity exists because of this desire of God. God desired us into existence . . . There is in the human heart a desire for God, which manifests itself in search for meaning, love, acceptance and happiness. Anybody who seeks for meaning in life, then, is a monk. If everybody is a monk, why then do some people separate himself or herself from the society and live a secluded life of prayer and solitude, and are generally regarded as closer to God than others? Well, the question is an interesting one. It was in order to find an answer to such a question that I came to visit Ewu as a school-boy 17 years ago. I came with a bag-load of questions. I wanted to know what 'madness' could drive a group of people to live a silent and secluded life away from the 'normal' active life in the world. But alas, I made a very grievous mistake on my first visit to the monastery: I ate and dined with the monks, whom I used to regard as 'mad people'. According to

an African proverb, 'the man who beats the drum for the mad man to dance is himself a madman'. So it was that rather than find answer to my questions, I found myself in the garb of these strange men. Until today, 17 years after, I am still asking the question: who is a monk? Why do people become monks?

My intellectual odyssey

In my study of philosophy, I was fascinated by the unending search for truth by human beings from different traditions, culture, races and religions. The history of humanity is simply the history of the human search for truth. What is the truth? How is truth to be found? Is truth absolute or relative? What is reality? This has been the subject of many philosophies and formed the subjects of the writings of many philosophers down the centuries. They include Plato, Socrates, Francis Bacon, St Thomas Aquinas, Emmanuel Kant, Karl Marx and Teilhard de Chardin. These are just a few of the philosophers and theologians whose ideas influenced my way of thinking and understanding.

Aside from philosophy and theology, I made a foray outside the realms of religion into the social sciences, and studied anthropology, sociology and history of development. The study of philosophy provided me with an opportunity to explore the world of ideas and knowledge in my search for the truth.

Looking at the list of philosophers mentioned earlier, something is surely missing – there is an absence of African names. While African literature had already established itself as an important discipline as early as the 1960s, the same cannot be said of African philosophy. In the 1980s, a fierce debate was still raging among African intellectuals about whether there was ever anything called African philosophy in the first place. That is only one side of the story. The other side of the story is that I studied in a very conservative Catholic setting that is suspicious of new ideas. Because of their political and social contexts, African philosophers naturally appeared to be critical of the Church because of the perceived association of the Church with slavery and colonialism. Education for Africans means imbibing a new language, new thought forms, new core images and new logic. African philosophers usually began their philosophical training by studying western thought systems, logic and ideas, and had to express their ideas using the western lenses imbibed from western education.

Kenyan philosopher Henry Odera Oruka (1997) identified three categories of African philosophy. First is *ethnophilosophy*, which describes the worldview or thought system of particular African communities as philosophy. This type of philosophy sees the African way of thinking as 'communal thought' and describes its emotional appeal as one of its unique features. Notable philosophers in this category are Placide Tempels, Leopold Sedar Senghor, John S. Mbiti and Alexis Kagame. The second category is *nationalistic-ideological philosophy*. This consists of works of founding fathers and political leaders in Africa, whose social-political theories were based on traditional African socialism and family values. Among them were Kwame Nkrumah, Sekou Toure, Julius Nyerere and Kenneth Kaunda. The concept of *Ubuntu* (a bantu word meaning 'human kindness'), a philosophical concept based on distinctive African values of communitarianism, welfarism and brotherliness, emerged from this philosophical school of thought. The third category is *professional philosophy*. This is the position generally taken by the professionally trained, if not westernized, students or teachers of philosophy. They reject ethnophilosophy and instead adopt a universalistic point of view. In their opinion, African philosophy should be approached with the same forms of critical analysis, logic and intellectual rigour applied to mainstream western philosophy. They argue that a descriptive approach, by itself, is more appropriate to the field of anthropology and applies different standards to African thought. Notable among the professional philosophers are Kwasi Wiredu, Paulin Hountondji, Peter O. Bodunrin and Odera Oruka himself.

My call and inner desire

I used to think my calling was to change the world, do unusual and extraordinary things and compete with others. Now I know my business is none of these. My mission is to search for truth. Life is an adventure, a dream, a play and a dance. It is not competition. It is not even a struggle. This is the lesson one learns from Azaro, the spirit child (*Abiku*) in Ben Okri's prize-winning book, *The Famished Road* (1992). Life is *reli-gare*, a Latin word meaning reunion, reunification and reconnection with the Divine, from which the English word 'religion' is derived. Today, humanity is passing through pangs of pain and disillusionment caused by a sense of separation or disconnection from nature and from one another. Charles Eisenstein in *The Ascent of Humanity* (2013) has explored this theme recently. As humanity looks inwards to rediscover itself and practise *reli-gare* in its true, liberating form, the concept of the Abiku becomes more relevant and vital than ever. The reconnection (*reli-gare*) that we long for happens so naturally to the Abiku. What makes the Abiku so unique, special and 'mysterious' is their ability to live in both worlds without contradiction. For the Abiku, like the little prince in Antoine De Saint-Exupery's *The Little Prince* (1995), the sense of self embraces nature, community and the spirit world. The Abiku represents for us today the utter simplicity, openness, transparency and innocence of the child.

I believe humanity has lost touch with the child within and we are desperately making efforts to reconnect with this aspect of ourselves. We live in a world filled with tension, anxiety, fear and restlessness. Humankind seems to be engaged in an endless pursuit of nothing. We are fighting, struggling, rushing and pushing. But where are we running to? What are we fighting for? Who and why are we pushing? We live in an age of fast and effective technology, of quick communication, which has turned the world into a 'global village'. Thanks to computer technology, all we need do is log on to the right website and we will find answers to our questions. But what is *the* question? Our modern technological culture has been able to provide answers without knowing what the questions really are.

After all is said and done, modern men and women are still preoccupied with what we call the *questions of life*. What is the origin of life? What is the purpose of life? Where did we come from, and where are we going? Through myths, riddles and legends, every culture through the centuries has strived to provide answers to the deeper questions of life. There is in the human heart a desire for self-knowledge. Somewhere deep within us we know that, in spite of the claims of science to the contrary, life is more than we can observe, that there are many riddles about life that the human intellect cannot solve. The answers that every society provides to these questions are called myths (Dunne, 1972). Our modern, scientific mind is often tempted to condemn myth to the refuse-bin of unreality as products of primitive minds and uncivilized intellects. However, behind every myth is an enduring truth, and this truth is what really matters (Eliade, 1959). The Abikus, like the poets, the musicians and the artists, remind us of the power that lies within us. If we do not reconnect with this world, and befriend it, it will destroy us.

In Gabriel Okara's novel *The Voice* (1970), Okolo is 'the voice' who offends the village elders by his search for the truth. Okolo is told to stop searching for '*it*' (truth) because the very effort to search for 'it' makes the elders uncomfortable. They promise to make life easy for him and leave him to live his life in peace if only he will stop his search. The elders eventually exile him, but he returns to make a final gesture of defiance. For Okolo, life consists of searching for the truth, and loses all meaning if he stops searching. In 2000, I published my second book, titled *Nature Power*, a book about holistic health, harmonious living and integral development of the whole person. In the introduction, I stated my inner calling thus:

> Are you asleep? Why not wake up today? The cock crows, the snake hisses, the lion roars, the birds sing. Singing the song of liberation, the song of freedom. Can you hear it? Wake up o sleeper and come back to your senses. This book is an invitation, a clarion call from a human being like you, to wake up and become the person you are meant to be. This is a message of hope from your fellow human being in search of knowledge, happiness, wholeness and peace. From one who believes in life and the sacredness of the Cosmos and everything in it. I am your fellow seeker after truth. I am not one who has more knowledge than you have, or more superior in the things of the spirit. I am only a storyteller; is anybody ready to listen? I am only a singer, but is anybody willing to sing? I am only a drummer, but is anyone ready to dance?
>
> (Adodo, 2000, p. 14)

Today, after twenty-nine years of living in the monastery, I have discovered that my search has only just begun.

The 'angel' in the bush

What was I searching for the morning of November 2, 1995, on a lonely pathway in the monastery's farmland? Was I searching for the truth? What was the 'truth' doing in the bush at 7:30 in the morning? I was strolling quietly on the lonely farmland, fully alert, listening to the rhythm of the swaying trees, the chirping of the hundred-plus colourful birds and the beatings of my heart. There, on an open plot of farming land, was a little girl, dressed gorgeously in a bright golden gown, truly angelic, playing all alone. It was usual for mothers to bring their children to the farm. However, it was very unusual, and forbidden, to leave one's child out of sight, and very unusual to dress a child so gorgeously when going to the farm.

I moved closer and asked the child, who looked like a four-year-old, 'Where is your mother?' Silence. I walked around and raised my voice, saying 'Hello' many times in the hope someone else was around. No answer. Suddenly, it appeared as if the swaying trees stood still and all the birds quieted and listened in rapt attention to the unfolding drama. I went back to the child and asked, 'Who are you, and why are you here alone? Where is your mum?' The little girl smiled and held out a hand, beautiful innocent hands, in which she held a freshly uprooted weed. Of course I was not going to accept a piece of familiar fresh weed from a strangely beautiful four-year-old in a strange location. Then she spoke: 'This plant will eradicate viral infections in any sufferer who uses it.' I do not know if that was exactly what she said, or exactly how she said it. Nevertheless, it was what I heard. And my hearing, at least at the time, was in excellent condition. A few minutes later, the little girl was nowhere to be found. Did she disappear? Was she an angel? Or an *Abiku?*

I walked back to the monastery, my pace faster than before. The trees were now swaying vigorously as if dancing to music. The birds were singing louder than ever, and the thick forest looking brighter than ever as it stared at me with a million eyes. I arrived at the monastery's open entrance, where another drama awaited me.

It was an emergency. A dying man was lying on the back seat of a car, accompanied by his wife, uncle and two children. He had just been discharged from the nearby city's specialist hospital some one and a half hour's drive away. His case was terminal, and he had been brought home to the village to die. In Nigeria, the terminally ill prefer to die in the village, their ancestral home. The family wanted the dying man to be anointed with the *viaticum*, the Catholic Church's sacrament for the sick, formally known as 'the last sacrament'. That was their purpose for coming to the monastery.

The man had AIDS and, according to the medical prognosis, was not expected to live longer than two weeks. Under the car and all around were the weeds the little 'angel' had shown me in the farmland. I told the family about my encounter on the farm and asked if they would like to collect the weed and administer it to the dying man. The man's wife said no! – not that they were not going to make use of the weed, but that they were not going to harvest the weed in the monastery grounds because the weed already grew all over their family compound. Later that day, I came across this popular quotation from a nineteenth-century priest and healer, Sebastian Kneipp: '*Many people die, while herbs that could cure them grow on their graves.*'

Ten days later the sick man with his family returned to the monastery. The sick man actually drove the car! His health improved once he started taking the decoction of the herbal weed based on the protocol I taught them, and had kept improving daily. By the fifth day, he was already on his feet, and now, ten days later, he felt like a new man. Without the weeds, he would probably have died and the medicinal weeds that eventually cured him would certainly have grown on his grave!

The following morning, I ran to the scene of my encounter with the little girl, with a pen and notebook in one hand and a tape recorder in another. I needed to see the little 'angel' and learn more, take notes, chat with her, take photographs and ask her to teach me more lessons about herbs. This time another monk, the witty Br John Mary, with whom I had shared my experience, accompanied me. Br John Mary armed himself with a catapult. When I asked him why a catapult, he said it was just a precaution, in case my little 'angel' turned out to be a monkey! Alas, the little 'angel' was nowhere in sight. I searched and searched to no avail. I am still searching. I wish I had paid more attention on that memorable morning. I remember the story of the baby fish. The baby fish asked the mother, 'What is this thing called water? I hear about it all the time. Where and how can I find it?' The mother fish replied, 'My child, you are *in* the water.' 'Me in the water? I don't get it,' replied the baby fish. How often do we miss the divinity around us in our pursuit of something else we think is more relevant! On that fateful morning, I, like the baby fish, did not get it.

The truth shall heal you

It was not long before news of the miraculous recovery of the dying man went round the local communities. My abstract search for truth led me to a concrete experience of the truth and power of herbal medicine. After the encounter with the little 'angel', I had a new understanding of some of the familiar passages in the Christian Bible.

> Jesus said to the Jews who believed in him, 'If you remain in my word, you will truly be my disciples, and you will know the truth, and the truth will set you free.'
>
> (John 8:31)

> My people perish for want of knowledge.
>
> (Hosea 8:31)

My search for truth means self-discovery in nature and through nature. This, for me, is the key to happiness, health and wholeness. Every day I watch as people die from common diseases that can be remedied by herbs growing around them. People, *my people*, perish for want of knowledge. My people need to embrace knowledge so they can experience freedom. This is how I interpret the quotation from the Gospel of St John: *You will know the truth, and the truth will set you free.* My desire, my inner calling, is to explore knowledge, not just for the sake of exploration but also as a tool for innovation, inner freedom, healing, transformation and self-discovery. Truth heals. Science, according to Jacob Bronowski (2011), is only a Latin word for knowledge. Knowledge, integral knowledge, is our destiny.

Conclusion

This chapter is not an autobiography but only a rough sketch of my life as it relates to my subjective inner desire. It is so readers can have a glimpse of my family life and educational background against which they can situate my objective outer challenge, which will be the subject of the next chapter. The following poem was written by me and published in my book *Nature Power* (2000), which has been a West African bestseller since 2008. It seems to be a good summary of my inner burning desire, and an apt conclusion to this chapter.

Identity

Go to the Ancestral Shrine
The Sacred groove in your chest
And hear again the silent echoes
Of the Ancestors' voices
Calling you to Awake, to arise.
Shake off the shackles of inferiority
O sons and daughters of Africa
Face the void
Love the darkness.
Go the Ancestral Shrine
The Sacred groove in your chest
And hear again the silent echoes
Of the Ancestor's Voices
Calling you to Awake, to arise

For you can transform the earth
Only when you discover
Who you are.

References

Adodo, A. (2000). *Nature power: A Christian approach to herbal medicine.* Akure: Don Bosco Printers.

Adodo, A. (ed.). (2004). *The story of Ewu Monastery: Silver jubilee reflections.* Irrua, Edo State: Omon-Law Printers.

Bronowski, J. (2011). *The ascent of man.* London: BBC Books.

De Saint-Exupery, A. (1995). *The little prince.* Trans. Testot-Ferry, I. London: Wordsworth.

Dunne, J. S. (1972). *The way of all the earth: Experiments in truth and religion.* New York: Macmillan.

Eisenstein, C. (2013). *The ascent of humanity: Civilization and the human sense of self.* Berkeley, CA: Evolver Editions.

Eliade, M. (1959). *Cosmos and history: The myth of the eternal return.* New York: Harper & Row.

Eliot, T. S. (1863). *Four Quartets.* Ed. B. Bergonzi. London: Palgrave Macmillan.

Fagunwa, D. O. (1949a). *Igbo Olodumare.* Ibadan, Nigeria: Printmarks Ventures.

Fagunwa, D. O. (1949b). *Ireke Onibudo.* Ibadan, Nigeria: Printmarks Ventures.

Fagunwa, D. O. (1954). *Irinkerindo ninu Igbo Elegbeje.* Ibadan, Nigeria: Printmarks Ventures.

Fagunwa, D. O. (1961). *Adiitu Olodumare.* Ibadan, Nigeria: Printmarks Ventures.

Ilesanmi, T. M. (1989). *Ise Isenbaye.* Ibadan, Nigeria: Claverianum Press.

Kosemanii, S. (1987). *Owe ati Asayan oro Yoruba.* Ibadan, Nigeria: Vantage.

Ladele, T. A., Mustapha, O., Aworinde, I. A., Oyerinde, O. and Oladapo, O. (1986). *Akojopo Iwadii Ijinle Asa Yoruba.* Ibadan, Nigeria: Macmillan.

Okara, G. (1970). *The voice.* New York: Africana.

Okri, B. (1992). *The famished road.* New York: Vintage.

Oruka, H. O. (1997). *Practical philosophy.* Nairobi: East African Educational.

Weber, R. (1992). *Science with a smile.* Bristol, UK: Institute of Publishing.

3 My objective outer challenge

How I expressed my inner desire in confronting concrete challenges in my society

If you want to go FAST, travel alone. If you want to go FAR, travel along with others.

—African proverb

Introduction

The previous chapter described my childhood experiences, my family background and my subjective inner desire, which is to search for the truth. I explained that for me, searching for the truth is not just an abstract desire. Rather, it is understanding myself, my world and my community, and the concrete realities of this world. I stated that my inner desire is to be a healer, not in the sense of a miracle worker or magician but in the sense of the Sanskrit term '*guru*', which means to dispel darkness. I concluded that knowledge is our way into a better future. Continuing along the origination of my southern relational path, which follows the tenets of descriptive research method, I will outline in this chapter the outer challenges in the local community of Ewu, Edo State and Nigeria that this research work seeks to address. In order to change my situation, I need to understand and accept the reality of what it is, and only then can I confront it. This chapter seeks to make explicit my implicit inner desire of being a change agent in a fast-changing world.

Monk, priest, scholar, herbalist: what sort of a man?

Over the years, people have wondered what sort of man I am: a Christian, priest, scholar, herbalist? In several write-ups in the national dailies, references were made to 'a monk in herbal medicine' (*The Nation*, 2007), 'the healing monks of Ewu' (All Africa, 2006) or 'Reverend Father herbalist' (Latest Nigerian News, 2012), all hinting at the contradictions of Anselm Adodo, a Catholic priest, herbalist, philosopher, theologian and a social scientist. These articles were positive, a tribute to the uniqueness of what I was doing: promoting African traditional medicine and preserving indigenous knowledge. They also hinted at the paradox of a Catholic priest belonging to a highly conservative order who dedicates himself to the promotion of traditional medicine. It was the paradox of a man engaged in fusing indigenous knowledge with exogenous knowledge to create a truly integral future, and the writers of these articles must have wondered, like many other observers, what sort of a man this is, as combining both the indigenous and the exogenous is certainly a challenging and intriguing task.

The personal challenge of preserving African medical knowledge

Considering my plural family background that I described in Chapter 2, it should come as no surprise that I found myself engaged in many activities at the same time. When I returned from theology study in 1996 armed with a bachelor's degree in religious studies from University of Nigeria, Nsukka, and a master's degree in systematic theology from Duquesne University of the Holy Ghost, Pittsburgh, USA, I was recruited to teach phenomenology of religion. I also taught theology and sociology of religion as well as comparative religions in the same nearby Catholic seminary where priests are trained. At the same time, I was made the monastery's bursar. This time I was fully in charge of the monastery's finances, and the issue of financial independence was becoming more urgent. The burning issue for the monastery then was how to become economically self-sufficient rather than totally dependent on aid from the parent house in Ireland for survival. My duty was to change the orientation of work in the monastery's farms, palm plantations, bakery and poultry from work done just to keep busy or pass the time to profitable business ventures.

In 1997, I was ordained a priest. That, however, did not change my normal course of work. Ordination in the monastic setting is different from the diocesan set-up in the Catholic Church. The abbot or superior of the monastery decides who among his monks he wants ordained as a priest, whose main clerical function will be to carry out sacramental duties within the monastery. A priest in the monastery can also work in the kitchen, farms and gardens as well as in the classrooms as a professor.

Aside from the duties that go with the priestly office, I also became very busy with research in the fields of ethnobotany, as I was fascinated by the world of plants, energized by the practical experience of its effectiveness because of my experience with the 'little angel' and the extraordinary cure of the sick man described in the last chapter.

The village of Ewu has a rich tradition of medical healing. There were traditional healers everywhere, and traditional shrines can be spotted in many corners of the village. There was a mission hospital and a government hospital in the village, but the majority of the people patronized traditional healers. Herbal medicine was identified with witchcraft, sorcery, ritualism and all sorts of fetish practices. Because of this, African Christians went to traditional healers in secret, and the educated elite and religious figures did not want to be associated in any way with traditional African medicine. At that time (1996), for a religious figure, especially a Catholic priest, to openly propagate traditional medicine was seen as a taboo of the highest order. I conceived the idea of Paxherbal as a tool for changing the concept of traditional medicine from an esoteric practise by mysterious, fearsome old medicine men to that of a useful, profitable, rational and explicable venture in this context. The goal of Paxherbal is to change the face of African traditional medicine.

In my interactions with local healers, I observed how they applied local music and rhythms to treat depression and madness. I sat down with elderly local healers, traditional midwives, local bonesetters (orthopaedic specialists), local psychiatrists and psychotherapists in different parts of Nigeria to observe different methods of traditional medical treatment. There were also professional counsellors and diviners who applied divination systems to proffer solutions to personal problems, success in business, protection against witchcraft and so forth.

Other scholars have devoted time and energy to the study of some aspects of the traditional African healing systems, especially the *Ifa* divination system of the Yoruba (Bascom,

1991; Fatunmbi, 2013; Olaleye, 2013), and the traditional psychiatrist healing homes in Yoruba communities (Awolalu, 1979; Sadowsky, 1999). However, I was more interested in looking at the healing system in itself as a field of discipline, to study the underlining theory, cosmology and science behind the practise. One of the burning issues for me is how to preserve this vast body of indigenous knowledge in writing, thereby making it explicit, so that it can be passed on to others.

Meanwhile, the traditional healers had become an endangered species, as many of them died because of old age without passing on their knowledge and expertise to their children. The children have all migrated to the cities to attend modern universities and acquire degrees in modern medicine, or business administration, banking, architecture, geography, criminology, engineering and a host of other fields. Some became fire-spitting evangelists, pastors and Christian crusaders who declared 'war' on traditional medical practices and branded their patrons as idol worshippers and pagans. Modern Christian education and western education managed to brainwash children to turn against their traditions, against their families and against their culture.

In 1999, I witnessed a moving display of misdirected evangelical piety as a young man who had just graduated from a Pentecostal college in a nearby city returned to the village and discovered that his father, a renowned traditional healer, had died at age ninety two days earlier. The young pastor brought out all the religious paraphernalia in his father's 'laboratory', the cooking pots and concoction jars, and, with the King James version of the Bible in one hand and a made-in-England firelighter in another hand, set the whole collection ablaze. Thus, a whole library of medical knowledge was destroyed. In some other parts of the world, if a library were set ablaze, it would be seen as arson, an offence punishable by law. In Africa, with every old person who dies, a library of books is lost. And we did nothing to stop this. Shortly after this incident, I participated in a workshop on natural medicine directed by Dr Hans-Martin Hirt, a German pharmacist and herbalist. The workshop took place in the remote village of Ikposogye in the Obi local government area of Nassarawa State, Northern Nigeria. In attendance were nurses, midwives, pharmacists, physicians, chemists, botanists, farmers and housewives from different parts of the world: Germany, France, Senegal, Britain, Ireland, India and Nigeria.

For one full week, this group of forty men and women lived together, ate together, danced together, discussed together, tilled the soil together and cleared the bush together. We lamented the spread of diseases all over Africa, diseases that can be cured by the plants growing around us. We concluded that the truth about natural medicine should not be allowed to die. A year later, in the year 2000, my book titled *Nature Power: A Christian Approach to Herbal Medicine* was published. The choice of the title was deliberate: to show that traditional herbal medicine is not all fetish and that Christians can make use of traditional medicine in such a way that it does not involve fetishism, voodoo or occultism. I discovered that my status as a religious figure, a Catholic priest belonging to a highly conservative and orthodox order, puts me in a unique position to change people's understanding of traditional medicine. And I did. As I would later discover, the issue is far deeper than just medicine, physical well-being or alleviation of pain. Medicine is about culture, identity, politics, behaviour, worldview and education. Medicine is conditioned by how people perceive their bodies in the context of society. Medicine is as much a culture as it is a science, if not more so. In fact, for Lupton (1994), medicine *is* culture.

The societal challenge of addressing Nigeria's health debacle by restoring traditional African health systems

On paper, Nigeria's 'orthodox' health care plan looks impressive and appealing. However, in practise, it has not made much difference in improving the health of the nation. Nigeria's performance in the area of health calls for serious concern. According to the World Health Organization (WHO), in 2005, Nigeria was ranked 197th out of two hundred nations. Life expectancy was put at forty-eight years for males and fifty years for females. It is therefore obvious that unless there is a quick intervention, Nigeria will get to 2020 without a change in her health status (WHO, 2005). From the 1950s, the nascent political parties and their successors to date have invariably included health along with education in their development programmes. The goal of the current national health policy is to bring about a comprehensive health care system, based on primary health care that is protective, preventive, restorative and rehabilitative to every citizen. However, the reality is another matter. Like several other countries of the South, Nigeria has a medical set-up dominated by the western allopathic or biomedical system, dependent on high-tech equipment, and serviced and controlled by multinational drug corporations. Imported during colonial rule, this practise was initially used exclusively for the ruling class. Today most biomedical doctors prefer to practise in the urban areas and avoid rural areas altogether (Viterbo and Ngalamulume, 2011).

In general, despite the efforts of the government, working closely with volunteer agencies, private practitioners and non-governmental organizations, provision of health care in Nigeria is poor, and official data indicate a worsening in recent years (Sikosana, 2009). There has been an alarming resurgence and spread of 'old' communicable diseases once thought to be well controlled – such as cholera, tuberculosis, malaria and yellow fever – while 'new' epidemics, notably HIV/AIDS, threaten the last century's health gains (World Bank, 2014). Among the major causes of morbidity in Nigeria are malaria, dysentery, pneumonia, typhoid and food poisoning, all of which are closely related to the level of economic development, including the poor conditions and standards of living (Viterbo and Ngalamulume, 2011).

In the *World Development Report, 2014*, the World Bank claims that health outcomes improved in the second half of the twentieth century. But it also recognizes that hopes for an ever-improving trend are fading since progress slowed down in the 1990s. High-income countries and low-income ones do not share the same situation. The former have many good hospitals and health specialists, while the latter can hardly satisfy the essential health needs of their citizens, and often act as pools of medical staff for high-income countries (Bartley, 2004).

The health situation of poor nations began to deteriorate greatly when the World Bank and the IMF imposed economic adjustment policies on the governments of these countries. In Africa, the implementation of the structural adjustment programmes led to resource shortages in government health systems with detrimental welfare effects (Kawachi and Kennedy, 2002). In general, governments were asked to cut their spending on public services, including health, and poor patients have remained without any secure access to essential drugs.

Despite this failure, the World Bank, the IMF and other international financial institutions have changed very little in their policy on health. They now encourage public and private partnerships (PPPs). But their goal remains quite the same: a push towards the privatization of services essential to health. No matter how humane-sounding the rhetoric of the leaders of those institutions, privatization of health services means health only for those who can pay (Turshen, 1999).

Two health systems exist in Nigeria today: the orthodox and the traditional. The orthodox system is exogenous and is often referred to as 'scientific medicine' as opposed to traditional medicine, which is termed 'unscientific' or 'folk' medicine. This dichotomy, based on a narrow definition of science, points to an intrinsic interdisciplinary tension between these two systems. The orthodox, exogenous medical system is the official and legally recognized health care system of Nigeria. While traditional medicine is not legally recognized, and therefore is 'unorthodox', its existence is widely acknowledged, its impact pervasive and its effectiveness noticeable. The World Health Organization (2011) reported that over 80 per cent of Africans use traditional medicine in one form or the other.

As mentioned earlier, the rich patronize medical doctors in the cities, but in the urban slums and rural areas, traditional medicine remains dominant. The medical elite often operate as if oblivious that a health system already existed centuries earlier, and make very little effort in applying their western analytical methods to study the existing traditional health systems in order to see if there are points of convergence. The situation is described by Green (1999: 12) as follows:

> Secure in their minds that they have done the right thing by rejecting African medicine, health officials promote western allopathic medicine as if there were no medical system already in place, as if Africa were a tabula rasa. When Africans do not quickly embrace whatever is offered them from the alien system, they are criticized for being stubborn or backward.

This 'scientific attitude' of the medical elite has its origin not in science but in religion. Since the Christian missionaries operated under the auspices of colonial masters, Africans came to identify colonialism with Christianity. Western medicine was called Christian medicine and western doctors called Christian or 'white' doctors. The doctor's white garment was said to symbolize purity and cleanliness. African traditional medicine, as I mentioned earlier, was referred to as 'pagan medicine' and traditional healers referred to as pagan doctors. What this meant for converts was to 'renounce the devil and all its establishments', which included traditional, 'pagan' medicine. In an intriguing turnaround, the term 'native doctor', which was originally used by western physicians to describe their African colleagues until independence, was now used to describe traditional healers from the mid-1960s to date (Patton, 1996). It is ironic that African medical doctors who complained bitterly about the arrogant attitudes of their white colleagues exhibited the same arrogant and superior attitudes towards traditional healers.

There have always been many discussions on how to improve health care services in Nigeria and Africa as a whole. Hundreds of conferences and health workshops take place almost daily in different parts of the country to discuss ways and means of improving the health of Nigerians. Proposals and recommendations from these conferences and workshops litter the offices of the state and federal ministries of health in Nigeria. It is therefore clear that the Nigerian government is not in short supply of ideas and proposals on how to improve the health of its people. An analysis of most of these proposals and recommendations reveals the following:

- Over 95 per cent of the recommendations come from medical practitioners who are very much part of the current health care bureaucratic system and therefore are linked either directly or indirectly with the politics and problems of health care in Nigeria.

- Most of those who make the proposals and recommendations on health reform in Nigeria are government-paid officials who benefit from the status quo and are likely to resist any reform that threatens their monopolistic power and influence.

- Almost all the proposals use worn-out phrases and sentences that indicate unwillingness to think outside the box, but simply repeat proposals straight from the textbook – for example, that the government should inject more funds into the health care system. Of course, the proponents of this idea are also the people who will eventually decide how the funds are spent. Such funds eventually end up in private pockets.

Nigerian leaders need to develop a health system built on indigenous as well as exogenous health belief systems, culture and spirituality, a worldview-based health system, so to speak; otherwise, health ideals will continue to fail. The neglect of indigenous knowledge is reflected in all facets of public life: economics, politics, education and health care. Later in this research work I will demonstrate that this neglect is symptomatic of a deeper disease, a disconnect between nature, community and culture. The way forward, I will argue, is to embrace healing holistically. This is what the concept of integral healing, which is the overriding theme of this research work, is about.

The institutional challenge to harmonize clinic- and community-based approaches to African medical knowledge: the idea of Paxherbal

There are two approaches to herbal medical practise: the clinic-oriented approach and community-oriented approach (Le Grand and Wondergem, 1990). In the clinic-oriented approach, emphasis is placed on scientific identification, conservation and use of medicinal plants. Laboratory research and screening are done to determine the chemical composition and biological activities of plants. Great interest is shown in quality control of raw materials and finished products, and the development of methods for large-scale production of labelled herbal drugs. The herbal drugs are labelled and packaged in the same way as modern drugs. They are distributed through similar channels as modern drugs – that is, through recognized health officials in hospitals, health centres or pharmaceutical supply chains. The government, private companies and non-governmental organizations invest relatively huge sums of money in promoting further research in herbal medicine. In the clinic-oriented approach, minimal interest is shown in the sociocultural use of the plants.

In the community-oriented approach, the emphasis is on the crude and local production of herbs to apply simple but effective herbal remedies to common illnesses in the local community. Knowledge of the medicinal uses of herbs is spread to promote self-reliance. Information is freely given on disease prevention and origin of diseases. No interest is shown in mass production of drugs for transportation to other parts of the country or exportation to other countries. The cultural context of the plants used is taken into account, and local perception of health and healing often takes precedence over modern diagnostic technology. Simple herbal recipes are used for the treatment of such illnesses as cough, cold, catarrh, malaria, typhoid and ulcers.

The approaches analysed earlier are two extremes of the same reality. There is a need to harmonize these two extremes to complement each other, as there seems to be little cooperation between people working on either side. Scientists, pharmacists and medical doctors who follow the clinic-oriented, exogenous approach sneer at traditional health practitioners and look down on them. And traditional healers guard their indigenous knowledge and refuse to reveal their formulae and production system to the so-called professionals. This inevitably leads to herbal medicine practitioners being labelled as 'secretive', 'esoteric' or 'unscientific'.

Paxherbal emerged as a bridge between these two approaches to traditional medicine, and aims at correcting the imbalances in the two approaches. Paxherbal is the registered business trademark of Pax Herbal Clinic and Research Laboratories. Though Paxherbal was established in 1996, it was not registered as a private liability company until 2002. The company is officially described as *a Catholic research centre for scientific identification, conservation, utilization and development of African medicinal plants.* Some of its objectives, as stated on its website (Paxherbals.net), are as follows:

- To serve as a centre for genuine African holistic healing that blends the physical and the spiritual aspects of the human person.
- To become a model comprehensive health care centre where the western (North, West) and traditional (South, East) systems of healing are creatively blended.
- To be an example of how proper utilization of traditional medicine can promote grassroots primary health care systems that is culturally acceptable, affordable and relevant.
- To disseminate knowledge of the health benefits of African medicinal plants through documentation, publications, seminars and workshops.
- To carry out researches into ancient African healing systems with a view to modernizing them and making them available to the wider world through education.
- To demystify African traditional medicine and purge it of elements of occultism, fetishism and superstition and promote its rational use so as to make it a globally acceptable enterprise.
- To be a truly indigenous herbal phyto-medicine centre that combines respect for nature and community with wealth creation.

In this vein, Paxherbal has become a model profit-making enterprise that strives to put nature, community and people at the heart of its existence.

Conclusion

In this chapter, I described the challenges I seek to address in my local community and country. I argued that the neglect of traditional African medicine is part of a general trend to suppress traditional, indigenous knowledge and wisdom in favour of western exogenous knowledge, leading to an identity crisis and a poverty of the mind, as well as a poverty of economic and political institutions among the rural population of Edo State. Rather than looking inwards to explore the abundant riches of their fertile imagination, their inventive skill and natural intelligence, the rural population of Ewu and Edo State is engaged in a futile pursuit of health, wealth and prosperity, which they have been brainwashed to believe are attainable when they neglect their traditional indigenous knowledge and turn to western knowledge and institutions.

The world is heading back to the South, to its roots. The planet and its people are living in times of major change. Our very survival is dependent on raising the collective consciousness of humanity, on shifting from conflict and war to love and compassion. In order to do this, we need to unite the old with the new, North with South, indigenous with exogenous, 'Christian' with 'pagan'. We look at the past to learn lessons that will help us to face the future with stronger hope, not to be stuck in the past. The richness of the ages must be drawn together to create a synergy that utilizes the accumulated knowledge of ancient tradition, religion and science, while also embracing modern exogenous knowledge. As we evolve, rather than dismiss that which went before, a respect must be cultivated for traditions that have stood the test of time (Krishnapada, 1997). I chose to confront the divide between indigenous and exogenous knowledge and do what I can to heal this divide. My conviction is that an integral approach to health, politics, economics and education is essential for the sustainable growth of Africa.

References

All Africa. (2006). *Nigeria: Healing monks of Ewu.* [online] Available at: http://allafrica.com/stories/200606230676.html [Accessed 27 Sep. 2016].

Awolalu, J. O. (1979). *Yoruba beliefs and sacrificial rites.* London: Longman.

Bartley, M. (2004). *Health inequality: An introduction to concepts, theories and methods.* Cambridge, UK: Polity Press.

Bascom, W. (1991). *Ifa divination: Communication between gods and men in West Africa.* Bloomington, IN: Indiana University Press.

Fatunmbi, A. (2013). *Iwa-Pele: Ifa quest: The search for the source of Santeria and Lucumi.* Charleston, SC: CreateSpace.

Green, E. C. (1999). *Indigenous theories of contagious disease.* London: AltaMira Press.

Kawachi, I. and Kennedy, B. (2002). *The health of nations: Why inequality is harmful to your health.* New York: The New Press.

Krishnapada, S. (1997). *Leadership for an age of higher consciousness: Administration from a metaphysical perspective.* Chicago, IL: Hari-Nama Press.

Latest Nigerian News. (2012). *Reverend Father herbalist.* [online] Available at: http://www.latestnigeriannews.com/news/176275/reverend-father-herbalist.html [Accessed 27 Sep. 2016].

Le Grand, A. and Wondergem, P. (1990). *Herbal medicine and health promotion.* Amsterdam: Royal Tropical Institute.

Lupton, D. (1994). *Medicine as culture.* London: SAGE.

The Nation. (2007). *A monk in herbal medicine.* [online] Available at: http://www.thenationonlineng.net/archive2/tblnews_Detail.php?id=21441 [Accessed 27 Sep. 2016].

Olaleye, S. K. (2013). *Ebo as a healing technique in Ifa divination system: An investigation of a potent therapeutic mechanism for today's health problems.* Saarbrucken, Germany: Lap Lambert Academic.

Patton, A. (1996). *Physicians, colonial racism, and diaspora in West Africa.* Gainesville: University Press of Florida.

Sadowsky, J. (1999). *Imperial Bedlam: Institutions of madness in colonial Southwest Nigeria.* Berkeley: University of California Press.

Sikosana, P. (2009). *Challenges in reforming the health sector in Africa.* Bloomington, IN: Trafford.

Turshen, M. (1999). *Privatizing Health Services in Africa.* New Brunswick, NJ: Rutgers University Press.

Viterbo, P. and Ngalamulume, K. (2011). *Medicine and health in Africa: Multidisciplinary perspectives.* East Lansing: Michigan State University Press.

World Bank. (2014). *World development report 2014: Risk and opportunity: Managing risk for development.* Washington, DC: World Bank.

World Health Organization. (2005). 'Evaluation of certain food additives: Sixty-third report of the joint fao/who expert committee on food additives'. Technical Report Series. Geneva.

World Health Organization. (2011). *World health statistics 2011.* Geneva: World Health Organization Catalogue Series.

Part III

Context

Phenomenology

4 Uncovering imbalances in my context

A description of Ewu Community, Paxherbal and St Benedict Monastery

Knowledge is better than wealth: you have to look after wealth, but knowledge looks after you.
—Zambian proverb

Introduction

The two previous chapters dealt with my *call*, or inner desire, which is the first of the 4Cs of my research trajectory. I explained that my inner call was to search for knowledge as a tool for healing others, my society and myself. I identified my outer call as the desire to be an agent of healing and change in a practical way in my immediate community of Ewu and Nigeria at large. This desire is expressed through Paxherbal, an herbal medical centre I founded in 1996. I applied the descriptive research method to make the origination of my research journey clear, moving from my subjective call to my outer objective call.

In the next two chapters, I move on to *Context*, which is the second of the 4Cs trajectory. At this foundational level, my research method is phenomenology. As indicated in the first chapter, phenomenology here refers to an immersion in the life-world of my immediate community, to experience, understand, express and interpret in a rational way the imbalances in my organization, my local community, my society and myself.

Lessem, Schieffer, Tong and Rima (2013) argue that a neglect of foundational phenomenology, of the subjectivity of knowledge, contributed immensely to the crisis brought about by a dichotomy between science and the natural environment. This crisis had its root in Descartes's theory of 'I think; therefore, I am.' For Lessem et al. (2013), building on the works of Husserl (1970) and Abram (1997), the individual cannot separate from his or her immediate locality in order to gain knowledge, for knowledge gained in such a way is not only shallow and artificial but also divorced from the authentic experience of being human.

The key tenets of phenomenology according to Lessem et al. (2013) are as follows:

- To concentrate on illuminating the 'inner world' of one's origins.
- To immerse oneself in the context of one's immediately perceived essences.
- To go beyond surface traits and empirical 'facts' to underlying moral values.
- To locate what is unique in the local context to what one authentically is.

Scientific inquiry cannot be devoid of the subjectivity of the subject and the immediate environment. The properties of a papaya leaf, for example, should not just be tested in a laboratory. One need also understand how a community thinks about and uses it. This approach should be an integral part of the scientific research. It provides a line of inquiry for the scientist to explore, and without this inquiry, the scientist cannot claim to have tested the properties of the papaya leaf fully.

Chapter 3 described the challenges I seek to address in my society, community and country. Also highlighted was the neglect of indigenous knowledge as foundation for a sustainable knowledge and innovation-driven development. In this chapter I will describe and analyse the context in which my research work is based, and chart a pathway to alleviating the imbalances. Nigeria is a complex country, with a complex mixture of cultures, traditions and customs. It also has a complex political history and structure. It is simply not possible to discuss all aspects of the Nigerian reality at once. My attempt in this chapter is to present the current socio-economic situation in Nigeria in general, and in Esanland, my immediate context. I will describe three major imbalances – transcultural, transdisciplinary and transpersonal – with a view to alleviating them. Particular attention will be paid to the tension between indigenous and exogenous knowledge in the politics, economics and health management of Nigeria in general and Esanland in particular. I will conclude by introducing my transformational ecosystem, which will be further developed in subsequent chapters.

Overcoming imbalanced worldviews

This section describes Ewu and its surrounding communities as land rich with natural resources, occupied by a hard-working, fun-loving and good-hearted people. However, an overemphasis on foreign education, foreign goods and city life has led to a massive migration of youths to the cities. Rather than serving as a tool for holistic development, a one-sided western educational system is causing the young people to lose interest in their traditional culture and values. The youth are surrounded by wealth in the forms of fertile soil, rich vegetation and medicinal plants, but the interest lies somewhere else: in western lifestyles and movement to the cities. How this imbalance can be corrected is the subject of this section.

Describing the context

The Esan people (pronounced /aysan/) are a small ethnic group of about half a million people who make up a tiny fraction of Nigeria's two hundred–plus ethnic groups, each with distinct dialects. They occupy the central part of Edo State in the midwest of Southern Nigeria.

Esanland is made up of small towns and villages on the periphery of Benin City, the Edo state capital, which is some 200 kilometres away. A mostly rural and semi-urban territory, it has no large city. The Binis form the largest ethnic group in the present Edo State, and tend to regard the Esans as their historical subordinates (Omokhodion, 1998).

There are thirty-five clans in present-day Esanland, each of which is headed by a king called an *Onojie*. The clans are: Ekpoma, Uromi, Ekpon, Emu, Ewohimi, Ewatto, Irrua, Ubiaja, Egoro, Wossa, Ukhun, Ugbegun, Igueben, Idoa, Ohordua, Okhuesan, Oria, Ogwa, Okalo, Ebelle, Uzea, Onogholo, Orowa, Urohi, Ugun, Udo, Ujiogba, Iyenlen, Ifeku, Iliushi, Amahor, Opoji, Ugboha, Uroh and Ewu. The Nigerian government divided these clans into five local government areas (LGA):

- Esan West LGA, with headquarters at Ekpoma
- Esan Central LGA, with headquarters at Irrua

- Esan North East LGA, with headquarters at Uromi
- Esan South East LGA, with headquarters at Ubiaja
- Igueben LGA, with headquarters at Igueben.

Esanland's landscape is flat, one lacking in rocks and mountains, and it is well suited for agricultural purposes (Figure 4.2). Rubber trees and palm trees rank highest among Esan's trees. The land's variety of fruits range from mango, orange, grape, pineapple, guava, cashew, banana, plantain, black pear, avocado pear, lime to walnut and even more. Cassava, yam, cocoa yam, sweet potato, pepper, okra and rice are some of its farm produce. It has numerous streams, many of which serve as sources of water and centres of ritual for traditional religion, but are not suitable for fishing. It is common to see shrines located near streams in Esanland, such as the one shown in Figure 4.1.

The Esan people are fun-loving, as evidenced in their various festivities and ritualistic traditions, many of which are centred on water rituals and farm festivals, like the New Yam festivals. Their folktales and folklores serve as forms of learning and entertainment, and a way of maintaining order and obedience to established traditions (Omokhodion, 1998). As in many traditional settings in Africa, adherents of Esan traditional religion, rituals and festivities have reduced under the onslaught of Christianity, and some combine the traditional religion with Christianity.

Esan people are proud of their ancestry and heritage. They are positive in outlook, very hospitable and intelligent. The men tend to have a tendency towards polygamy, and family commitment is often weak. They value children and want to have as many as possible. It is commonplace to see families of ten where the children have the same mother but different fathers or the same father but different mothers (Otaigbe-Ikuenobe, 2012).

Figure 4.1 A shrine beside a stream in Ewu village

Figure 4.2 Esanland's landscape is well suited for agricultural purposes

There are various, often conflicting histories of the Esan people. One popular version is that they hailed from ancient Bini, the dominant tribe of present Edo State, and their language is a Kwa subdivision of the Niger-Congo language family. The Esan dialect has different variations and accents, which makes it difficult even for the native speakers to understand. For example, the Esan word for person (or somebody) in the dialects is variously ọria (Uromi dialect), ọhia (Uzea dialect), ọyia (Unea dialect) and ọhan (Ugbọha dialect). This obvious difficulty associated with speaking dialects other than one's mother dialect has given rise to the widespread use of Pidgin English, which is a concoction of British English, Nigerian English and Nigerian local languages (Omokhodion, 1998).

The population of Esan Central in Edo State is said to be 105,310, comprising 53,834 males and 58,912 females. Out of this number, Ewu has a population of twenty thousand (Nigerian Population Census, 2006).

Ewu village is unique among the other clans in Esanland. Unlike the other clans, Ewu is made up of Christians, traditional religion adherents and Muslims in equal proportion. This is probably because of its proximity to Agbede, a bordering, predominantly Muslim village. The population of Ewu consists of mainly juniors (children aged seventeen and below), elders (middle-aged men and women of forty and above) and a large population of the aged (sixty- to eighty-year-olds). The youth have migrated to cities such as Benin, Lagos and Abuja to seek 'greener pastures'. After secondary school, young boys and girls who want a bright future for themselves are expected to move to the cities. This is seen as a sign of progress, even though it is clear that the prospects of getting jobs in the cities are very poor. It is common to hear some elders ask the younger ones questions such as, 'What are you still doing in the village?' The village is seen as a place of little or no economic potential. Even though the land is excellent for farming and the environment suitable for agriculture (see Figure 4.2), only the old folks engage in farming. Omokodion (1998) admits that the Esan people have participated less fully in recent social change and economic development than most others of Southern Nigeria's population, while their mortality rate is also said to be above the average level of Southern Nigerian standards.

A distorted worldview

Even though the soil in Ewu village is very fertile and rich in resources, the youth prefer to travel to the cities to look for jobs. This phenomenon is the same in most rural communities of Nigeria. In the village of Ewu, the youth do not have enough incentives to make them stay in the village. Their attention is fixed on the glaring expensive cars in the city, night parties, electronic gadgets and all sorts of modern technological allurements. While the young people go to school, the curriculum does not teach them about the beauty of the land, or the importance of ideas such as the capital needed for innovation.

The young men and women of Ewu village know the latest news about soccer in the English premier league. They can tell you when Manchester United is playing Chelsea. They can even predict who will win and at what margin. They know, thanks to the CNN or DSTV, how many soldiers are killed in Iraq daily, and how many suicide bombings occur and how many people are kidnapped by militants. They know the countries with the most relaxed immigration rules. But ask them what the health benefits of banana are, or how bush burning affects the productivity of the soil, or what a balanced diet is, and you will be surprised at their level of ignorance.

The youths are acquiring information about other places and lands while losing knowledge of their land, their environment, their culture and their people. No nation can truly develop until it develops its deposit of local knowledge, preserves it and nurtures it. True and lasting development is that which is home-grown and not imported from other lands. Sustainable and affordable technology must be based on indigenous knowledge. The best solution to a nation's problem is that which comes from within, not from without.

In many indigenous societies, when a knowledge bearer dies his knowledge dies with him. Indeed, a lot of knowledge is being lost, knowledge that appears to be worthless mainly because it is not properly valued. There is a need, therefore, to protect endangered knowledge as a world heritage. Today, we speak of protecting our environment from abuse, and about protection for rare species of plants and animals. Equally important is the need to set up international efforts to protect and preserve indigenous knowledge.

Looking at Nigeria as a whole, and Esanland in particular, one does not see any growth of basic and mature engineering, automation, post-harvest preservation, food processing and packaging technologies, infrastructural developments, social amenities, oil management technology and water technology, all of which are vital for poverty eradication. Rather, in its place is the spread of dogmatic/religious knowledge, the extraordinary sprouting of churches, Pentecostalism and piety, which demand dogmatic and unquestioning submission to revealed 'truths', and discouragement of reason, dissidence and logic. The only visible activities seem to be in the religious sphere, where new, gigantic churches are being constructed and millions of new small churches are mushrooming, along with huge billboards and media advertisements of miracle crusades, prosperity vigils and 'spiritual war'.

Twenty years ago, there were just a handful of churches in the village of Ewu. Today there are close to one hundred churches, an increase of over 400 per cent. In the same period, the number of schools has increased by a mere 5 per cent and no new factories have sprung up, except the Paxherbal herbal manufacturing company. There is no denying the fact that there are many potentials for development in the local community. What is lacking is the right education and training to enable the local community to initiate their own development.

Excessive religionism and spiritualism may be one of the greatest obstacles to the progress of African nations. In addition, the greatest challenge facing Africa today is her ability to cultivate a mindset steeped in chemistry, mathematics and physics while still maintaining a reasonable and balanced approach to religion. This requires creative syncretism or the ability to hold different realities together in a positive way. Later in this research work, I will explore this creative syncretism further in a new theory of community, natural and socio-economic development, which I call *communitalism*.

Moving beyond the monocultural

In some local communities, the knowledge of healing is a family inheritance, shared by immediate members of the family. For example, a clan in a village called Ogwa in Esanland is renowned for its specialization in bone setting. In February 2013, along with Yinka Olayioye and Tunde Owolabi, both research scientists at Paxherbal, I took time to interview the fifteen traditional healers in this village in order to understand their concept of healing, as well as how their knowledge can be modernized and translated into a profitable community enterprise.

The oldest man in the community narrated the origin of their healing knowledge:

> Centuries back, two men, Enahoro and his brother, were captured by Ezesa and were taken into captivity for many years. One fateful night, some elders were discussing when they saw a man approaching them. The man had the appearance of a gorilla because his hair was bushy and his body covered with hair. The elders withdrew out of fear. When the strange-looking man moved near the house, he shouted the name of some of the elders and introduced himself as Enahoro. Thereafter he was warmly welcomed, his hair shaved, and given a warm water bathe and new clothes to wear. The following day there was rejoicing in the village of Ogwa for the return of their lost-but-found son. Enahoro was happy with the warn reception given him and told the community that he had been given a special gift of healing – namely, the ability to mend broken bones. The people actually doubted his power until a man fell off a palm tree while tapping wine and he had his wrist broken. Enahoro was able to cure this man and so he gained acceptance and prominence in the community as a healer. The family of Enahoro has carried on this healing work until today. It is a gift from above to Enahoro and his family, and the family alone.

During an interactive session with the healers, the following conversations took place:

Question: Apart from this family, is there any other bonesetter around this community?
Answer: *No, we have this association existing for long, and the healing technique remains a family affair.*
Question: Does it mean that an outsider cannot learn this healing skill?
Answer: *An outsider cannot learn the skill because the secret of this healing lies in the palms of the family members, who inherit the skill naturally from birth.*
Question: What are the things you will request if government is willing to assist you?

Answer: *We will accept help from government after proper dialogue between the members of the family.*

Question: How do you think you can modernize your patterns of healing?

Answer: *If there will be any change at all, it can only come from the elders' resolution.*

There is a lot of verifiable evidence to show the efficacy of the treatment given by the local healers. However, there is a deep-rooted distrust of government and other organizations, which causes the local healers to guard their healing knowledge carefully. This has in turn led to the popular stereotype of traditional healers as secretive. The traditional healers rely excessively on the authority of the elders, and will not accept any change in their treatment patterns since it is seen as a divine system.

This underlies the problem of indigenous and exogenous integration in local communities in Nigeria and Africa as a whole. One key step towards the alleviation of this imbalance is for government to set up an appropriate intellectual protection policy to ensure that traditional healers are well remunerated for disclosing their knowledge. Until this is done, traditional healers have every right to hide their cherished knowledge, which is often the source of their livelihood and prestige. Keeping industrial secrets is part of the northern exogenous manufacturing tradition. Manufacturing giants such as Coca-Cola, Guinness and McDonalds will never reveal their manufacturing formulae to outsiders.

A lack of openness on the part of traditional healers means they will not be able to upgrade and renew their knowledge bases. Education is vital to helping them see the need to open up to new ideas and innovations. Such education, holistically and integrally, which is one of the objectives of this research work, will promote functional development, as well as transformational knowledge, in the communities.

Transformational knowledge refers to knowledge as an asset, skill, advantage or tool. It is not an end but a means. It embraces economic knowledge or expertise which can be transformed into goods and services. Transformational knowledge creates, adapts and uses knowledge effectively for its economic and social development. It moves beyond segmented knowledge and sees knowledge as unity.

Transformational knowledge is a process, a continuum: always evolving, becoming, flowing. It cannot be monopolized, blocked, tied down or controlled. It upgrades and renews cultures open to it and eliminates those closed to it. It has its own inner dynamic, flow and logic, its own way of spreading, and is unpredictable. Transformational knowledge, as this research work will demonstrate, is the force behind historical and social changes. As knowledge evolves, society changes, institutions change and people are transformed. Inferior, fetish, superstitious and manipulative knowledge gives way to superior knowledge. Knowledge for development has a universal character even as it creates local identities. The most important thing for a nation is not its natural resources but its ability to create knowledge to transform its society and make the necessities of life available. Knowledge in this context is grossly neglected and unused in Africa, in Nigeria and in Esanland. Most often, it is wasted.

The way forward

The way forward is the way home. Appropriate measures need to be put in place to promote a dynamic and creative interaction of indigenous and exogenous knowledge in agriculture, economics, medicine and politics. The situation in which knowledge flows only in one direction – that is, from the exogenous North (Europe and America), to the indigenous South (Africa) – will do no good except create unending tension, inferiority complexes and sustain distrust between the North and the South and the East and West.

In Esanland and Nigeria, and Africa as a whole, what urgently needs to be taught is not just knowledge in itself but also the love of knowledge and knowledge acquisition as a lasting concern. In other words, theory building is the foundation of sustainable integral education, a gap this research work seeks to fill by evolving an institutionalized research centre in and for Nigeria, Africa, and developing a new theory of community enterprise and integral development grounded in nature, community and culture.

If the Nigerian government is truly serious about improving health care services, it must give the required support and recognition to traditional/alternative medicine and set appropriate regulatory policies in place to ensure standards. The current, imported biomedical system of health is inadequate to cater to the health needs of Nigerians. One hopes the Nigerian government will have enough foresight and wisdom to collaborate with reputable alternative medicine research institutions so as to improve the health of the nation.

Alleviating disciplinary imbalances

This subsection deals with the imbalances that arise because of the neglect of the local culture, philosophy, worldview and tradition in government policies, educational curricula, health care and medicine. The way forward for sustainable development is to pursue a creative integration of both indigenous and exogenous knowledge.

Disciplinary imbalances

The origin of organized medical services in Nigeria is exogenous (Schram, 1971). When British, French and Portuguese explorers came to sub-Saharan Africa, they found already established empires, such as the Songhai, Mali, Hausa and Oyo empires, with well-organized political and social systems, artwork and sculptures (most of which now adorn the British Museum). When Count Volney, friend of Benjamin Franklin, visited Egypt from 1783 to 1785, he saw age-old monuments and temples half buried in the sand, which gave evidence of an advanced civilization, arts and sciences. However, the gradual transition of Africa into a more scientific community and its emergence as a unique, independent cultural identity were abruptly interrupted by colonialism (Finch, 1990).

As the British conquered land after land, it also brought its physicians along to treat its administrators and troops. British administrators and troops died in the thousands due to diseases common in the tropics. Since Africans had immunities to some of the tropical diseases, it was decided to train Africans as doctors to assist British doctors in the imperial system. Imperial needs, rather than concern for the health of the local population, led to the training of African physicians in the eighteenth and nineteenth centuries under the colonial regime (Patton, 1996).

The route to medical professionalism for those early Africans started at Edinburgh or Dublin. The Anglican Christian Missionary Society selected three young adult Africans for training in Scottish Universities in 1854. In 1855, these three students were summoned to King's College, University of London. The oldest, Samuel Campbell, was a Wolof. The second, William Broughton Davies, was a Yoruba. The third, James Beale Horton, was an Igbo. They were well educated in music, mathematics, the Greek and Roman classics and geography. Their manners and intellectual habits were moulded in accordance with those of the English middle class. However, Samuel Campbell could not cope with the sudden change in weather, suffered severe cold and pneumonia and had to return home. Within a short time of his arrival back in Freetown, he died of bronchitis in 1855. Davies fell ill but survived and completed his course. Horton coped remarkably well with the weather, won top honours in his class and was soon made a member of King's College Medical Society. Both Horton and Davies passed the qualifying exams, earning membership in the Royal College of Surgeons (MRCS) in 1858, and were given licenses in medicine. Horton and David proceeded to Scotland for their MD in medicine (equivalent to a PhD). While a student, Horton took the name Africanus as a sign of pride in his African ancestry. They both returned to Sierra Leone in 1859 (Adeloye, 1985; Patton, 1996).

The sole purpose of sending these Africans to study medicine was essentially to help the colonial army and administrators. There was no interest in their local identity; they had none anyway, since they were former slaves. They rather would have considered themselves extremely privileged to be selected to study the 'white man's medicine'.

Despite the fact that they attended the same medical school and passed through the same training, the medical officers of the British middle class generally refused to regard the Africans as their peers and resented their presence. These attitudes were a big barrier to progress for the African doctors.

British physicians referred to their African colleagues as 'native doctors' distinct from 'European doctors'. In fact, the term 'native doctor' was the official colonial term for African doctors from the 1800s until independence. This term was greatly resented by the African doctors who went to the same school as their European colleagues and often scored distinctions but were not allowed the same prestige as European doctors. The 'native doctors' treated only blacks, while Europeans doctors treated both whites and blacks. On no account was an African doctor allowed to examine or treat a white woman (Patton, 1996).

In the 1950s, one main developmental concern was the establishment of extensive modern health care systems among the poorest countries. These newly independent countries built modern hospitals in the cities, while the majority of people lived in scattered villages without access to modern curative institutions. The traditional healers remained the health care providers for the majority of the people, not only for the rural communities but also for many of the city dwellers, who still preferred the services of traditional healers to that of allopathic doctors, or a combination of both. The newly created health system had little impact on the health of many people because all health services were located in urban cities where the armies and expatriates were stationed. Rural areas continued to play host to the majority of the population despite lack of organized health services (Airhihenbuwa, 1995).

As mentioned in the previous chapter, by independence in 1960, two health systems prevailed in Nigeria: orthodox and traditional. The emerging African elite patronized medical doctors in the cities, but in the urban slums and rural peripheries, traditional medicine remained dominant (Patton, 1996). The medical doctors in the cities made very little effort in applying their western analytical methods to study the existing traditional health systems in order to see if there were similarities. This led to an inter-professional conflict, which persists into the present time.

Theory of disease in traditional African medicine as distinct from western theory

Africans believe sickness is a result of disharmony between the physical and the spiritual. The aim of the priest-physician is to restore this harmony. To do this, he has to find out what causes the disharmony. He uses different diagnostic tools to find this out – the oracle, for example, like the Ifa Oracle of the Yoruba, or counselling with the sick. Having then diagnosed the problem, the next thing is the treatment. Treatment could involve rituals, prayers and confession of one's guilt if one has offended the gods. It could also involve the preparation of herbs and animal parts as medicine. When the cause of the sickness is confirmed to be a result of poor hygiene or sanitation, the sick person is referred to the medicine man, called *onisegun* ('producer of medicine', the equivalent of a modern pharmacist), who will prescribe the appropriate medication and advice about hygiene.

As one fully involved in the move to find a point of convergence between western allopathic medicine and traditional African medicine, I have attended hundreds of conferences in the past twenty years where I often hear western-trained allopathic doctors speak in denigrating manners about traditional African medicine, which they describe as incompatible with 'their own'. Of special interest to me is the fact that these men, who most probably were delivered in local maternities through the competence of traditional birth attendants, did not back up their assumptions-turned-facts with any academic reference or authority. The mere fact that they are medical doctors seems to give them a cloak of orthodoxy, similar to the orthodoxy of a priest at the pulpit.

The popular stereotype of African indigenous medicine is of magic, witchcraft, voodoo, sorcery and spirit possession. Some assume that there is no concept of germs, bacteria and infections in traditional medical knowledge systems. I have observed and interviewed many traditional healers, and their analysis of the various illnesses shows that they have their own theories of contagion and pollution, and not all illnesses are interpreted as a spiritual attack. Anthropologist Edward Green (1999, p. 12) also confirmed this:

> I have found that Africa's most serious diseases tend to be interpreted within a framework that is essentially naturalistic and impersonal. Diseases like malaria, tuberculosis, schistosomiasis, cholera, amoebic dysentery, AIDS and other sexually transmitted diseases, typhoid, and acute respiratory infections including pneumonia, yellow fever, leprosy, and dengue are usually understood within a framework or a body of health knowledge that I call indigenous contagion theory (ICT). ICT is un-supernatural in character: One becomes ill because of impersonal exposure. One comes into contact with something that anyone could come into contact with – not because an avenging spirit or an ill-intended person singles one out for misfortune in the form of sickness.

Modern medicine and the profit motive

Biomedicine, or 'scientific' or clinical medicine, took shape in nineteenth-century Europe under the emerging biomedical conception of the body (Brunton, 2004). By the early part of the twentieth century, safer surgical techniques, vaccines and drugs helped people to avoid, escape or recover from otherwise fatal diseases (Downing, 2011). The aim of biomedicine was to defeat disease and death, and it succeeded largely (Le Fanu, 2011). Biomedicine sought to discover the true cause of disease, identify it, label it, isolate it, fight it and, ultimately, kill it. Given its fixation on disease and death, biomedicine was not particularly concerned with other details of its patients' lives. According to Downing (2011), the patient was often viewed by biomedicine as not a person in need of care and human concern but rather a vehicle for bringing diseases to the clinic, where problems could be fixed. The clinic was similar to a mechanic workshop where faulty cars are fixed, damaged parts replaced and the engine serviced. Like the mechanic, whose scope of work is defined by faulty cars, the doctor was bound to the field described by disease and limited to periods of illness (Le Fanu, 2011). American physician Mendelsohn (1979) argued that doctors were, quite erroneously, trained to identify disease, not to identify health. The doctor was a warrior, and the enemies were infection-causing germs: bacteria, viruses, protozoans.

The germ theory, which had dominated medical theory for over two hundred years, came to its climax in the twentieth century, when new antibiotics were discovered. The years 1900 to 1950 marked the golden age of drug discovery: penicillin (1929–1940), streptomycin (1944), chloramphenicol (1947), chlortetracycline, cephalosporin (1948), neomycin (1949) and oxytetracycline (1950) (Le Fanu, 2011). By 1950, biomedicine had discovered potent antibiotics to fight and defeat most of the viral infections that had plagued humanity for decades. The last, and the most stubborn, of the infectious diseases, tuberculosis, eventually fell to the firepower of biomedicine in 1950 with the successful application of streptomycin as the cure (Le Fanu, 2011).

The idea of the patient as a person (rather than a machine) began to feature in medical textbooks in 1950. Thus began the growth of biohealth, described by Downing (2011) as a corrupted form of biomedicine. Biohealth is a form of medical practise with an exaggerated and overwhelming dependence on computers and high-tech gadgets to diagnose diseases. Unlike biomedicine, biohealth thinks of patients as people, subject to natural human growth, decay and mortality. By 1980, the good of biomedicine had been overshadowed by biohealth (Downing, 2011). Under biohealth, medicine moves away from defeating disease and death towards the management of living (Turshen, 1999), as if being alive in itself is a disease. Increased longevity, especially in the advanced economies of the global north, means more people are subject to diseases of advanced age, such as arthritis, hypertension and cancer. These chronic diseases bring many people under lifelong medical surveillance. The emphasis on screening is based on the argument that non-sick people need to visit the clinic to check for signs of diseases that are possible but not yet diagnosed (Cassels, 2012).

Whereas in the past people went to the hospital when they felt ill, biohealth advised everybody to head for the hospital for sicknesses they may suffer from in five or ten years' time. As a result, modern medicine appeared to have abandoned its role as a health care provider to become *a health scare promoter.* Fear is a very effective weapon in the armoury of modern medicine. The sick go to the hospital because they are afraid of death, and the healthy go to the hospital because they are afraid of falling sick. Herein lies one of the extraordinary powers of organized medicine: the ability to control people through fear.

From its activities, it is obvious that biohealth is not interested in addressing the disparities in wealth, trade imbalances and the rich/poor divide in the world communities. Biohealth turns away from the fact that poverty, unfair trade imbalances, poor sanitation, poor nutrition and unbridled monetization of public health are the root causes of health inequality and poor health in the world, especially in the weaker economies (Turshen, 1999; Larkin, 2011). How does this apply to Nigeria and Africa, one may ask, against the background of the fact that most African countries have rudimentary and basic health facilities? To answer this question, one has to keep in mind that the world is highly globalized, and health policies are often shaped by the politics and neo-liberal health theories of the global north. Just as Africa has been a testing ground for various economic, social and political theories from the global north, so is Africa also an attractive market for medical equipment manufactured in the advanced economies. In other words, it does appear that there is a connection between neo-liberal capitalism and biohealth (Chomsky, 1998). Biohealth is not about health for all, but health for the rich, the elite and the powerful. It is all about money!

Does medical science have an African background?

For African–American historian Charles Finch (1990), the origin and evolution of healing as a special skill long antedate other important human inventions, such as agriculture and animal domestication and might as well deserve consideration as 'the oldest profession'. In 1930, J. H. Breasted translated the Edwin Smith papyrus, which antedates Hippocrates by over 2,500 years, and it became clear that Imhotep, an African, not Hippocrates, a Greek, is the real 'father of medicine' (Finch, 1990).

The excavated Ebers papyri and the Edwin Smith papyrus are the most important medical textbooks of ancient Egypt. They date back to pre-pyramid times, over four thousand years ago. Imhotep was adviser to the pharaoh Djoser, a political leader, designer and builder of the world's first great edifice in stone, the step-pyramid of Saggara. Hippocrates was said to have descended from a long line of 'Asclepiads' – that is, devotees of the Greek healing god Asclepios, often identified with Imhotep. Imhotep's father was Kanofer, a distinguished architect in the service of the pharaoh. His mother was Khreduankh, from Mende. Although he served and excelled as prime minister, chief scribe, ritualist and architect under the pharaoh Djoser of the third dynasty, Imhotep's gifts as a physician overshadowed all the others.

Hippocratic medicine, according to Finch, had direct antecedents in Egyptian medicine. The Egyptians were writing medical textbooks as early as five thousand years ago. Out of the hundreds and thousands of papyri that may have been written, we are lucky to have at least ten, which give us a window into medical practise among those ancient Africans. The city-state of Athens used to import Egyptian physicians, as did most of the kingdoms of the Near East. The magico-spiritual and rational elements intermingle in Egyptian medicine (Hancock, 2015). Healing has a psychic base. Today, modern medicine concedes that as much as 60 per cent of illness has a psychic base, and the 'placebo' effect of modern medicine arises from this (Peters, 2001; Moerman, 2002).

The dissemination of medical knowledge was often limited to a few families, though others who showed enough talent could be allowed to practise. The physician was highly respected, and was referred to as *Hakim* (a wise man or philosopher). Doctors had their own boats and travelled the Nile to treat patients (Patton, 1996). Rulers surrounded themselves with physicians to ensure they were well taken care of in case of illness. Medical cures ranged from the use of potent speech (incantation or magico-spiritual element) to the more preventive and rational diagnosis based on Egyptian medical practices at the time. Egyptian medical enterprise flowed across Rome and the rest of Europe, where it was modified over many centuries.

There were three routes to becoming a skilled physician in the medieval period. The first was through tutorship by one's parents. Sons and daughters of learned physicians often learned the profession from their parents, and medicine became a family's major profession for generations (Patton, 1996). The second method was through self-teaching, whereby serious-minded students taught themselves by compiling a list of medical texts, which were then read until the students were satisfied that their contents had been learned. The major pitfall of this method was that the student might misinterpret certain scientific terms in a way different from the intended meaning. Notwithstanding, successful doctors did emerge from this tradition. The third method, according to Patton, was that a student entered the medical profession through classes in hospitals or medical schools. Long before hospitals emerged in the Christian world, Egyptian medicine already was highly regarded in the Islamic world, where it reached a high degree of sophistication and was opened to practitioners of all faiths.

The tradition of medical specialization is said to have originated with the Egyptian ancient medical system. There were specialists who treated the different parts of the body: eyes, head, teeth, intestines and so forth. Skulls found from ancient Egyptian graves indicated that they practised trephination. This operation was a forerunner of neurosurgery, and involved boring a hole through the skull to the outer covering of the brain to remove fragments from a skull fracture compressing the brain in order to treat epilepsy and headaches (Finch, 1990). The tradition of specializations seemed to have disappeared for some centuries until it came back again in the fourth century BC. Once again, this tradition disappeared around 30 BC and did not resurface until the twentieth century (Finch, 1990).

The nature of medicine as practised in Nigeria and sub-Saharan Africa

Why, one would ask, did the Egyptian medical expertise and sophistication not spread to sub-Saharan Africa? The reason, according to Finch (1990), is that external invasions after 661 BC caused the Egyptian officials to look northward towards Europe rather than towards the south. Thus trade in material goods and culture and medical knowledge was only trans-Mediterranean. Added to this is the factor of the famine and dry phase of ca. 2500 BC that created the Sahara Desert and caused the Negroid cultures of middle Africa to move southwards. This effectively isolated sub-Saharan Africa from the scientific changes occurring in the Mediterranean basin (Davidson, 1998).

Sub-Saharan Africa, with the exemption of Ethiopia, was predominantly non-literate until the eleventh century AD when Islam introduced Arabic literacy into western Sudan. That literacy came late into sub-Saharan Africa does not mean that it has no history. In fact, some of the best ideas in the history of human thought were the earliest, yet most histories of ideas ignore them. This is due to the wrong assumption that history started with the invention of writing, thereby leaving out the ideas of our earliest ancestors. However, most societies, for most of history, have esteemed oral tradition more highly than writing. Their ideas are inscribed in other ways – left in the fragments of material culture for archaeologists to unearth, or buried deep in modern minds for psychologists to excavate, or preserved in later ages by traditional societies, where anthropologists are sometimes able to elicit them.

Secondly, some people's prejudice makes them suppose that there are no ideas worth the name in the minds of the ancients, whom they called 'primitive' or 'savage', mired in 'pre-logical' thought, or retarded by magic or myth. However, there has not been any evidence of any change in human brain capacity or in human intelligence since over thirty thousand years ago.

Medical practise in sub-Saharan Africa is a combination of the magical, the mythical, the spiritual and the scientific. In Africa, a human being is a person, not just an individual. An individual is one who is on his own, who does his own thing, goes his own way and separates himself from others. He has a 'soul', a 'mind' and a 'body', all of which are distinct and at times opposed. A person, on the other hand, is a being who exists with and for others. A person is a person with and because of others. A person cannot define himself except in relation to others.

African medicine does not just involve herbs. The use of animal parts, music, sacred chants, potent speech, dance and touch is also prominent. In many parts of Africa, animal parts, such as the liver, kidney, gall bladder and gizzard, are burnt to ashes and used as part of herbal ingredients for various illnesses. For example, cow tail and liver burnt to ashes are said to be a good remedy for diabetes. An energetic analysis of these animal parts shows that these organs are high vibratory organs with high electromagnetic fields, and taking them as medicine is a good way of transmitting these energy waves to the diseased organs.

Legend has it that the earliest form of healing in Africa is vibrational healing. As an example among many others, the Yoruba of Western Nigeria have a highly developed system of vibratory healing. The founding father of African-Yoruba medical practise is a man called *Orunmila*, who, like many other African heroes, was deified, or, to use a more technical term, immortalized. Just as European scientists, such as Galileo, Faraday, Newton, Descartes and Einstein, have been immortalized in our memories, so also do African heroes deserve to be remembered and appreciated, not just by Africans but also by the world.

Even though *Orunmila* is regarded as the founding father of African-Yoruba medicine, the title of 'father of Yoruba medicine' is accorded to a man called *Osanyin*. *Osanyin* had the gift of communicating with plants. He could so attune himself to the energy field of plants that through his perception of the vibration of these plants, he gained knowledge of their uses. As a young man, whenever he was sent to the farm, he would refuse to cut any grass because he was psychically sensitive to nature and was aware of the usefulness of each plant (Apata, 1979).

Osanyin did not just have knowledge of herbs. He also knew how to use the energy of plants to effect changes in human bodily conditions. This he did through the chanting of sacred chants or potent speech. Osanyin taught that one way to attune oneself to the energy waves of plants is to learn their names and pronounce them audibly. African tradition is an oral tradition, and so pride of place is given to memory work and careful use of words. As a child grows up, he or she is taught how to use words and to avoid saying certain words that may attract a negative spirit. Rhythm governs words, discussions and daily life as a whole. By rhythmic combination of words, Africans attune themselves to universal cosmic vibrations and so are able to maintain balance in their lives. This explains why music permeates and defines every aspect of the daily lives of Africans. When going to the stream to fetch water, children chant. When working in the farm, farmers sing. When eating, the eaters follow a rhythmic pattern of washing hands, putting the food in their mouths, chewing and drinking. When nursing, mothers never cease to sing lullabies. In times of danger, Africans sing or recite sacred mantras to ward off danger.

Various methods are used to detect the medicinal values of herbs. In traditional African societies, and indeed in other parts of the world, people look at the colour and shape as well as the location of a plant to get an insight into its use and importance. This is called the theory of signatures. They believe that plants grow in any specific area because there is a need for them. Herbs that grow on mountains are believed to be good for the respiratory system – lungs, bronchi, nostrils – and the nervous system. They cure high blood pressure as well as pneumonia. Herbs that grow in water are regarded as medicinal. They are usually edible since poisonous herbs very rarely grow in water. They are also good for the circulatory system and help in repairing the liver and the kidney, two vital organs in the body. Herbs that grow in water are also believed to be good for treating all forms of infertility in both men and women. At this junction, the words of Sebastian Kneipp once again come to mind: '*Many die while the herbs that could cure them grow on their graves.*'

Herbs that grow close to the soil are believed to be good for digestive and circulatory problems. Since they are close to the ground, the mineral content is high, and so they are good for the bones and blood. Those who suffer from anaemia would find these herbs useful. Granted that the theory of signatures is not always true, it is amazing to see how much of the insights of the ancients has been confirmed by modern science as true.

From time to time, traditional healers have prescribed that certain herbs should be harvested only at a certain time of the day. Sometimes they insist that certain plants should be harvested before sunrise, some after sunset. At times, they go out themselves in the middle of the night to collect some herbs. This practise in itself is scientifically correct. In the night, when the sun has already traversed the earth and has set for the day, the chemical compounds in many plants, especially trees, settle down to the roots of the trees. In order to get the best out of these roots, then, it is advisable to harvest them at sunset, which in tropical countries begins from five in the evening. When the sun begins to rise, plants, especially trees, draw up their chemical compounds and distribute them to the leaves and barks. By the middle of the day, these compounds are fully concentrated in the leaves of the plants. For this reason, the best time to harvest the leaves of medicinal plants is at midday, when the sun is about to reach its peak. By late afternoon, the chemical compounds in trees begin their downward journey back to the roots through the stems and barks. For this reason, the best time to collect the bark of a tree is late in the afternoon or in the evening, before sunset. Science has validated this practise of the ancients, which may at first appear to us as superstitious and mythical.

It is one of the sad aspects of the history of sub-Saharan Africa that we have no written records of the medical system of our ancestors. However, from the excavated surgical knives, the concoction jars and the carved statues of the various deities, we have a good idea of African medical practise in the ancient world, and we can now rewrite our history.

Transcending individual overemphasis

The previous subsections have served to define my particular context, examining the different imbalances and looking at possible ways to overcome them. However, it is not enough to merely unravel problems and imbalances. The integral research model requires that the researcher go beyond description to taking concrete steps to alleviate some of the problems described. This final subsection aims to activate my ecosystem by introducing other participants in my research-to-innovation system. At this stage, I am no longer a lone researcher carrying out his particular research. I am an activator of a transpersonal ecosystem working towards a sustainable transformation of my community and my society. At this stage, it helps to again revisit the objectives of this research work, which are as follows:

- To reinvent, through the platform of Paxherbal, indigenous knowledge as a tool of health and wealth creation in Nigeria, with focus on the Ewu village community of Edo State.
- Develop a new theory of business, economy and enterprise based on Christian monastic ideals and traditional African values.
- Apply the concept of CARE as a metaphor for reshaping medicine, community and enterprise towards integral healing in Africa.
- Use education and research as a tool of social innovation and social transformation through the establishment of a centre for integral research in Nigeria.

Paxherbal clinic and research laboratories: reshaping medicine in Nigeria

In 1995, on a virgin piece of land in the monastery garden, populated by seemingly useless common weeds, there sprouted life-giving herbs. On a piece of land in an African bush in Ewu village, there came an inspiration that a new way of life, a new source of livelihood, can sprout from the earth. After all, the earth is our home. We were made from the earth, and the secret of our health and well-being lies in the earth. It is not a surprise that the more we are alienated from the earth, the sicker we become. High rates of depression, suicide, violence and conflicts between nations all point to a lack of inner harmony and connection to the earth. Sickness here is not just biological but also mental, psychological and moral (Krishnapada, 1997).

From the virgin soil in the St Benedict Monastery sprouted the Paxherbal tree, which has grown into a giant tree in Ewu village, with roots spreading out beyond Esanland to the whole of Nigeria (Figure 4.3). The concept of Paxherbal, among others, is first to locate health, medicine and health care within the social context of the local community, and second, to correct the distorted educational curricula in the local schools in Ewu, Edo State and Nigeria, which do not allow young people to understand the language of the earth, the trees, the soil and the streams.

In the 1990s, the practise of herbal medicine in Nigeria and in most parts of Africa was identified with witchcraft, sorcery, ritualism and all sorts of fetish practices. Paxherbal, like a lonely voice in a wilderness, has been able to correct this misconception. It has contributed immensely in changing the attitudes of both the government and the generality of Nigerians towards the practise of herbal medicine. It has also helped to show that health is more than an absence of disease. Health is wholeness of mind, soul and body.

Innovation ecosystem in my local context of Ewu, Edo State

The focus of my innovation ecosystem is to build on the successes of Paxherbal as a health care provider and enterprise-in-community in order to actualize the other three objectives, which have to do specifically with developing a new theory of business, economy and enterprise based on community, spirituality, knowledge and social technology. These are carefully structured on the alternating, dual-rhythm research trajectory of the 4Cs and CARE, leading to new sustainable institutions. In other words, I will proceed from an activated innovation ecosystem to an actualized integral ecosystem.

Figure 4.3 The virgin land from which sprouted the Paxherbal tree

An integral transpersonal ecosystem, according to Lessem et al. (2013), involves four key participants, all working in unison to the rhythm of integral dynamics. An Igbo proverb from Eastern Nigeria says that '*When something stands, another thing will stand beside it.*' This proverb gives an insight into the concept of integral dynamics. Nothing in nature stands alone. Interconnectivity, interrelationship and intercommunication are the very nature of life, and are a model for an integral community.

My integral ecosystem

One important characteristic of integral research is that the researcher carries out his or her research with the people and not just for the people. The researcher does not separate him- or herself from the people but is instead a part of the people. Thus, in my particular case, though born into a Yoruba lineage and having grown up in a Yoruba cultural background, as described in Chapter 2, I identify spiritually and culturally with the local Ewu community in which I have lived as a member of a Catholic religious order for over twenty-eight years. I know them and they know me. I share their joys and sorrows, their challenges and aspirations for development, better living conditions, better health care. I share their desire for societal transformation. Every human community values development, peace and progress. A truly integral research is participative in nature. It is research with people and not just on people. My ecosystem comprises the major actors in my research process, interacting with each other, with the physical environment and with the community in order to achieve social innovation. Such an ecosystem also includes the *Ewu Development and Educational Multipurpose Cooperative Society* (EDEMCS), a community initiative by the local community, Paxherbal (Figure 4.4), the St Benedict Monastery, a community of monks in Ewu village and, finally, the *Africa Centre for Integral Research and Development* (ACIRD).

Figure 4.4 Some staff and management of Paxherbal

The St Benedict Monastery and the king of Ewu Kingdom are the chief stewards of the project. The king is the patron of the EDEMCS, which already has more than four thousand registered members, comprising male and female farmers, youth and entrepreneurs.

There is an association of more than one hundred accredited cultivators and suppliers of medicinal plants among EDEMCS (see Figures 4.5 and 4.6). They undergo frequent seminars on cultivation and harvesting of herbs, and have become significant employers of labour in the local community. This group will continue to cultivate medicinal plants and cash crops, and to meet the demand for raw materials, each member will employ more workers, thereby becoming employers of labour. The king of Ewu village often acts as a referee for most of these suppliers of raw materials, to ensure they keep to the code of conduct. These suppliers are beneficiaries of regular training on farming techniques, plant identification and food preservation.

Some members have already expanded their business beyond cultivation of medicinal plants to full-scale farmers, and their produce is being sold beyond the local community. Many of these suppliers will continue to be beneficiaries of microfinance schemes in partnership with Nigerian banks.

There is also an association of health care providers, comprising over one thousand independent distributors of Paxherbal products nationwide (Figure 4.7). The national president is Mrs Clara Oyibo, a graduate of business administration from Imo State University in Eastern Nigeria. Clara is married to a banker, and they both live in Lagos. The association is the official body through which Paxherbal products are distributed nationwide. It is important to note that these distributors are independent and each one controls

Figure 4.5 King Abdul Rassag Ojeifo of Ewu with EDEMCS executives

Figure 4.6 The researcher, Anselm Adodo, during a training session on innovation with the Youth wing of EDEMCS in 2015

Figure 4.7 Some members of the Association of Pax Health Care Providers at their national congress in 2012

how to expand their market. In a manual titled *Guidebook for PAX Health Care Providers (PHCP)* published in 2005, the aim and objectives of the association are clearly set out:

> A Pax distributor is one who shares the vision of Paxherbal, dispensing the herbal medicines in a spirit of love, care, sincerity and concern. A Pax distributor is always ready to defend the cause of Pax. They are ready to offer constructive criticism and resist anything that may injure the Pax apostolate. A Pax distributor should know when to refer a case to the hospital or to a health care professional. They should not attempt to handle all cases. In emergencies, please refer the patient to the hospital. If a patient's blood pressure is so high that a stroke is imminent, please refer the patient to a nearby hospital for emergency help. Herbal medicines are effective but they work more slowly and steadily. A Pax distributor must be educated, enlightened and must learn to study, study, study, read health books, and magazines. Please note that the official designation for a certified Pax distributor is 'Pax Health Care Provider' (PHCP), and this appellation can be added at the end of their names. A Pax distributor should have an identity card as proof that they are genuine.

The following are listed as terms and conditions for becoming a member of the association:

- Distributors shall undergo a minimum of two weeks' training, jointly organized by the zonal coordinators of the association and Paxherbal.
- Distributors must undergo a written examination before receiving the relevant documents (product brochure, price list, prescription manual, identity cards, etc.).
- Distributors shall attend zonal quarterly meetings /trainings scheduled by the zonal coordinators.
- Distributors shall participate in all trainings organized by the Centre.
- Distributors shall attend the yearly Paxherbal national convention.
- Distributors shall not inflate the price of the products above recommended prices by Paxherbal.
- Distributors shall respect clients' privacy and confidentiality.
- Distributors shall respect and promote the cause of Paxherbal.
- Distributors shall give objective feedback about the products to Paxherbal through their zonal coordinators. Membership of distributors is renewable every two years.

Educational ecosystem: linking research to innovation

My educational ecosystem plays a key role in the final contribution of this research work towards the establishment of a centre for integral research in Edo State, Nigeria. Such a centre, while fully locally grounded, will also have a Pan-African focus as well as a global outreach. The idea of local-global research and communiversity resonates with the dynamics of indigenous-exogenous synergy, which is the foundation of the theory of *communitalism*, discussed in full detail in the next part of this research work.

Already Paxherbal's commitment to education has allowed it to be part of a federal government industrial-training scheme that allows university students to spend between six and twelve months at the Paxherbal clinic and research laboratories for practical experience. This research work will carry this positive trend forward by collaborating with the social science departments of various Nigerian universities to establish centres of action research, leading to integral research institutes in Edo State and beyond.

The relevance of a centre for integral research-to-innovation in Nigeria and Africa is huge. There are brilliant individuals in Africa and other parts of the world who have done marvellous research work in various fields of social research. Most of these individual researchers often die unknown; some are frustrated due to lack of a platform to give flesh to their theories, while some simply lose interest in academic work and focus on 'more important things'. For African philosopher Paulin Hountondji (1983), this is one of the saddest features of knowledge creation in Africa. African intellectuals in diverse fields do research for the sake of research: research that contributes little or nothing to societal development. The result is that their research work ends in beautifully written dissertations and publications that gather dust in libraries. Integral research aims to reverse this trend by emphasizing a research-to-innovation process that leads to social innovation and development, in theory and in practise.

Conclusion

To conclude this chapter, it is appropriate to revisit the research question guiding this research work and see how close one is to its actualization:

> How could the issues of indigenous-exogenous knowledge and value creation addressed by Paxherbal in the Ewu Village of Edo State be focused on more widely in Nigeria, Africa and more generally in the wider world? How, specifically, could such a business, community health and social innovation be contextualized (grounding, being), evolved (emergence, becoming), conceptualized (navigation, knowing) and thereafter more widely and universally applied (effecting, doing)?

This chapter employed, at the foundational level, the tenets of phenomenology as the research method based on my southern relational research path. It aimed at surfacing the imbalances in my immediate community of Ewu and Edo State and in Nigeria as a whole. The imbalances were systematically categorized as transcultural, transdisciplinary and transpersonal.

The objective is to use the existing Paxherbal enterprise as a stepping stone towards the development of an enterprise-in-community model that is truly integral, African and sustainable. If Paxherbal could within a period of ten years turn the virgin land of Ewu into a land flowing with milk and honey through the rational use of medicinal plants, weeds and crops, which represent just 2 per cent of the available vegetation, then one can imagine the impact of making use of just 20 per cent of the available plants. Therefore, there are enough resources available in nature to sustain the community, the state and the nation. What is needed is to set up an appropriate educational system to promote systematic application of indigenous and exogenous knowledge. In this chapter, I have explored the obstacles to these ideals and possible remedies. In the next chapter, I will discuss the transcultural imbalances in my local context. That a separate chapter has been devoted to this topic underscores the key role of culture in the socio-economic life of any community. Failure to pay sufficient attention to the culture and tradition of local communities is one of the main reasons why most development projects and initiatives in Africa fail.

References

Abram, D. (1997). *The spell of the sensuous.* New York: Vintage Books.

Adeloye, A. (1985). *African pioneers of modern medicine.* Lagos, Nigeria: Ibadan University Press.

Airhihenbuwa, C. (1995). *Health and culture: Beyond the western paradigm.* Thousand Oaks, CA: SAGE.

Apata, L. (1979). The practice of herbalism in Nigeria. In: A. Sofowora, ed., *African Medicinal Plants*, 55–67. Ile-Ife, Nigeria: University of Ife Press.

Brunton, D. (2004). *Medicine transformed: Health, diseases and society in Europe 1800–1930.* Manchester, UK: Manchester University Press.

Cassels, A. (2012). *Seeking sickness: Medical screening and the misguided hunt for disease.* Vancouver: Greystone Books.

Chomsky, N. (1998). *Profit over people: Neoliberalism and global order.* New York: Seven Stories Press.

Davidson, B. (1998). *West Africa before the colonial era.* London: Pearson.

Downing, R. (2011). *Biohealth: Beyond medicalization: Imposing health.* Eugene, OR: Wipf and Stock.

Finch, C. S. (1990). *The African background to medical science: Essays on African history, services and civilizations.* London: Karnak House.

Green, E. C. (1999). *Indigenous theories of contagious disease.* London: AltaMira press.

Hancock, G. (2015). *Magicians of the gods: The forgotten wisdom of earth's lost civilisation.* London: Coronet.

Hountondji, P. (1983). *African philosophy: Myth and reality.* London: Hutchinson.

Husserl, E. (1970). *The crisis of the European sciences.* Chicago: Northwestern University Press.

Krishnapada, S. (1997). *Leadership for an age of higher consciousness: Administration from a metaphysical perspective.* Chicago: Hari-Nama Press.

Larkin, M. (2011). *Social aspects of health, illness and healthcare.* New York: Open University Press.

Le Fanu, J. (2011). *The rise and fall of modern medicine.* Preston, UK: Abacus.

Lessem, R., Schieffer, A., Tong, J. and Rima S. (2013). *Integral dynamics: Political economy, cultural dynamics and the future of the university.* Farnham, UK: Gower.

Mendelsohn, R. (1979). *Confessions of a medical heretic.* New York: McGraw Hill.

Moerman, D. (2002). *Meaning, medicine and the 'placebo effect'.* Cambridge, UK: Cambridge University Press.

Nigerian Population Census. (2006). Legal notice and publication of details of the breakdown of the national and state provisional totals of 2006 census. Gazetted on 15 May 2007. Gazette 94: 24, B184.

Omokhodion, J. (1998). *The sociology of the Esans.* Lagos, Nigeria: Obembe Press.

Otaigbe-Ikuenobe, E. (2012). *The Esan people of Nigeria, West Africa.* Bloomington, IN: Xlibris.

Patton, A. (1996). *Physicians, colonial racism, and diaspora in West Africa.* Gainesville: University Press of Florida.

Peters, D. (ed.). (2001). *Understanding the placebo effect in complementary medicine: Theory, practice and research.* London: Churchill Livingstone.

Schram, R. (1971). *A history of the Nigerian health services.* Lagos, Nigeria: Ibadan University Press.

Turshen, M. (1999). *Privatizing health services in Africa.* New Brunswick, NJ: Rutgers University Press.

5 Unravelling missing depths

My contextual transformational topography

Introduction

The last chapter discussed three of the four imbalances in the context of Ewu local community and Edo State. I focused on imbalances on the transcultural, transdisciplinary and transpersonal levels. I also made suggestions about alleviating some of these imbalances.

This chapter focuses on the fourth aspect of imbalances identified in my context. Unravelling the missing depths is central to the issues this research work seeks to address and so deserves a separate chapter. As the title suggests, there is something missing in my local community, organization and society. On the surface, one may see nothing wrong. The aim of this research work is to probe beyond the surface in order to unravel the missing depths and provide possible solutions. Too often, social science in the past has tended to be merely theoretical, with no move towards innovation. It analyses societal systems, societal structural decay and societal challenges with no move towards concrete action (Lessem et al., 2013). The action plan is often seen as belonging to the realm of the natural, medical and technical sciences. However, a truly integral research, such as propounded by Lessem and Schieffer (2010) and which is the model on which this research work is based, must always be geared towards both theory and practise.

The four-layered topography of integral research (shown in Figure 5.1) helps to go beyond everyday surface to a deeper analysis of one's society. Every society has its own story, its core images and its religion and spirituality, which bind all the members together as a people. What defines me is not just the people but also my natural environment. The soil, the trees, the rivers, the mountains, the air and the animals who inhabit the environment with me also define who I am. For us in the local community where I live, and indeed for us in Africa, a community is not just a place where human beings live. A community comprises the plants, animals, the ancestors and the spirit. In times of crisis of identity, each society needs to go back to its core values to rediscover its identity. In other words, nature and community are the home of humankind and are the foundation of all science, innovation and development. Above all, we find our identity by reconnecting with nature.

My contextual topography

My topographical and transformational focus will be both indigenous (southern traditional Yoruba) and exogenous (northern Christian), in each case focusing on their respective societal perspectives, generally, and health and enterprise-in-community perspectives, specifically. See Tables 5.1 through 5.4.

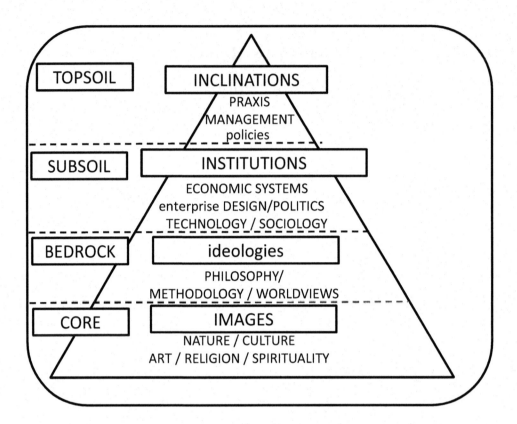

Figure 5.1 Integral topography (source: Lessem and Schieffer, 2010)

Table 5.1 My contextual topography: topsoil

Indigenous: Southern	Exogenous: Northern
Topsoil	↕
Topsoil: inclinations	**Inclinations**
• Yoruba concept of the human person as good	• Work and play not opposed
• Life as celebration	• A balanced spirituality of body, mind and soul
Imbalances	**Imbalances**
• Loss of interest in learning	• Excessive introversion
• Seeking job rather than creating job	• Holier than thou attitude
• Users of technology rather creators of technology	• Disconnect between larger society and the monastic community
• Dependency syndrome	• Dependency syndrome
Health care	**Health care**
• Youths migrating to the cities	• Neo-Christian Pentecostalism waging 'war' against traditional medicine
• Lack of interest of younger generation in traditional medicine practice	• Misconception of traditional medicine as synonymous with witchcraft and voodoo
• Herbal medicine not seen as a source of wealth	• Tendency to look down on anything traditional
Enterprise-in-community	**Enterprise-in-community**
• Inability to appreciate nature as source of intelligence	• Coloniality of knowledge and identity
• Loss of interest in agriculture	• Capitalism disguised as charity
	• Communitalism: a worldview-based economic theory

Table 5.2 My contextual topography: subsoil

Subsoil: institutions
- Paxherbalxe "Paxherbal:indigenous knowledge" as model of indigenous knowledge-creating enterprise
- Community elders as a social institute
- Market women's cooperatives as alternative financial institute

Health care
- Traditional healing homes
- Skilled traditional bonesetting system
- Culturally acceptable traditional birth attendants.

Enterprise-in-community
- An indigenous enterprise based on science
- Ewu village farmers: from agriculture to agribusiness

Imbalances
- Ineffective cultural organizations
- Inadequate integration of indigenous and exogenous
- Educational curriculum not geared towards development and entrepreneurship
- Lack of agribusiness hampering development

Health care
- Poor intellectual property protection for traditional healers
- Fetish practices
- Lack of openness to new ideas and new methods
- Lack of openness to new ideas and new methods.

Enterprise-in-community
- Overly westernized education producing graduates with no innovation zeal
- Food insecurity breeds social insecurity
- Political passivism in the communities

Institutions
- Religious orders of men and women
- St Benedict Monastery, Ewu
- Life in rhythm with the cosmos
- Exogenous learning centres

Health care
- Colonial medicine as organized health system
- Hospitals as treatment centres for infection control

Enterprise-in-community
- Communiversity of Life: a locally grounded community university
- Need for Africa centres of knowledge creation

Imbalances
- Christianity coated in western culture
- False sense of security
- Disparity in lifestyles
- Westernized education
- Ivory-tower universities

Health care
- Failure of government to regulate traditional medicine
- Privatized medicine interested only in profit
- Lack of health insurance: pay as you go medical care
- General dissatisfaction with western medicine
- Inability of western medicine to cure 'village malady'

Enterprise-in-community
- A consumer economy portends doom
- From food self-sufficiency to food security
- From agri-business to 'agri-politics'

Core images and imbalance

At the very core of every society is a sense of the sacred, a sense of a powerful 'other', which goes beyond what the human reason can grasp (Otto, 1959). This 'other' is what Otto, the German philosopher and theologian, referred to as the 'numinous'. Whatever name is given to this 'other' by each culture and religion, the image of the mysterious, almighty, divine power outside the self is common to all cultures and religions, and forms the basis of how people approach life.

Table 5.3 My contextual topography: bedrock

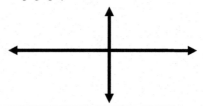

Bedrock: ideologies
- I am because we are
- Ubuntu: brotherliness as a way of life
- Community as harmony between human beings, Orisa, plants and animals
- Abiku: Yoruba concept of the spirit world
- Fagunwa: Yoruba world of the living and the dead

Health care
- Sickness as a communal experience
- Community as determinant of who is healthy or not
- The earth as healer
- Dance, music and poetry as medicine
- Power of traditional medicine
- The body as a living entity

Enterprise
- We are either rich together or poor together
- Individual wealth versus communal wealth

Imbalances
- Clash of cultures
- Distorted worldview
- Individualism
- Losing touch with nature
- Globalization
- Neo-liberal market philosophy

Health care
- Neglect of traditional concept of health
- Education curriculum not appreciative of traditional health care system
- Rampant practice of magic and witchcraft

Enterprise-in-community
- Neglect of worldview-based economic practices
- Weakened theoretical foundation

Ideologies
- I think, therefore I am
- Catholic philosophy: reason, epistemology, empiricism
- Catholic theology: between reason and faith
- Catholic dogma: papal infallibility and human error
- Mysticism: monasticism and western civilization

Health care
- Functionalist theory of health
- Social theories of health
- Biomedicine as a worldview

Enterprise
- The challenge of individualism
- Between nature and science

Imbalances
- Psychopassive education as opposed to psychomotor education
- Lack of proper enculturation
- Discouragement of reason in favour of dogma
- Colonial education geared towards dependency

Health care
- Eurocentric concept of health suppressing traditional view of health
- The body as an object like any other machine

Enterprise-in-community
- Excessive privatization of medicine
- Monetization of health care

The orisa in Yoruba cosmology

For the Yoruba, the core image goes back to the concept of *orisa*. The Yoruba culture into which I grew is shaped by the belief in the supreme God called Olodumare. Olodumare means one who sustains all things in being. Olodumare is one who is utterly reliable and has the fullness of power, of life, of greatness. Because Olodumare is the power behind the sky, the Yoruba call him Olorun ('owner of the sky'). Olorun knows everything, sees everything, for 'his eyes spread all over the earth.'

Because Olodumare is so mysterious and distant, the easiest way to reach him is through the orisa. The orisa owe their existence to Olodumare. Indeed, the orisa do not have an

Table 5.4 My contextual topography: core

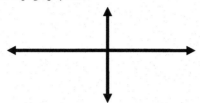

Core: images	Core: images
• Olodumare as Supreme God	• God as Creator of the Universe
• Yoruba Orisa as link to Olodumare	• Jesus as God not just a Son of God
• Connect with the Orisa through natural objects and the environment	• Love as centre of Jesus's message
	• Heaven as our final home
Imbalances	**Imbalances**
• Conflicting images of God	• Stereotype of God as a Father, headmaster and
• Pantheistic idea of God	foreigner
• Excessive veneration of objects	• Individualistic image of God

independent, objective existence. They represent the various dimensions of life as experienced by the Yoruba. According to Yoruba mythology, Olodumare sent 401 orisa from heaven to the earth. He gave each of them a particular function to perform. By creating an orisa for a particular phenomenon, such as birth, sickness, death, success in business and so forth, the Yoruba is able to cope with such phenomena and try to control them. In this way, he or she does not feel helpless and powerless in the presence of such phenomena, but rather is able to respond in a way that is wholesome and liberating.

Through sacrifices and rituals, the Yoruba harnesses the positive energies of nature and uses them to his advantage. All the sacrifices and prayers directed to the orisa are ultimately made to Olodumare. Thus, when the Yoruba is attacked by smallpox, he or she appeals to Sonpona, the orisa of smallpox. When the hunter is in trouble, he appeals to orisa-Oko, the orisa of the forest and patron of hunters. When knowledge is needed, the Yoruba appeals to Orunmila, the orisa of knowledge and wisdom. Any orisa that does not act when called upon can lose his or her dignity and be rejected. While the Yoruba need the orisa, the orisa also need the Yoruba, for the orisa feed and live only on the sacrifice and homage of its devotees. The Yoruba can dispose with any orisa that does not act and help its devotees.

The major orisa of the Yoruba are: Ogun, Sango, Obatala, Orunmila and Esu. These five orisa are believed to be the most widely worshipped and are central to Yoruba cosmology (Awolalu, 1979). Ogun was put in charge of all things related to iron and warfare. Sango was the orisa of thunder and rainstorms. Obatala was the orisa of creation. Orunmila was the orisa of knowledge and wisdom. Esu was made the police officer who sees to the general order of things.

Ogun, Obatala and Orunmila were the orisa that created human beings. According to the Yoruba myth of creation, there were two stages in the creation of the human body. The first stage was the creation of the head and chest and internal organs by Obatala. The second stage was the cutting and shaping of the hands and legs by Ogun (Awolalu, 1979).

When Obatala and Ogun had completed their job, they struggled to make the body move. But the body remained lifeless. Ogun went to consult Olodumare, and Olodumare told Ogun to consult Orunmila. Ogun went to Orunmila, who made sacrifice to Olodumare. Olodumare then allowed emi, spirit, soul, life, to flow into the body. The once lifeless bodies, which had now become living beings, proceeded to the throne of Olodu-mare. Each one knelt down and chose his or her ori. Ori is the third element that makes a human person. Ori means the physical human head. It also refers, as here, to the inner head or the spiritual head. To have a body (ara) or soul (emi) is not peculiar to human beings because other animals also have ara and emi. So it is ori that really makes one a person; ori is one's destiny, what one chooses to become.

The idea of ori is an expression of the Yoruba belief that life has a purpose and that no person is here on earth by chance. It is not by chance to be born a man or woman, tall or short. Riches and wealth are not just accidents but closely bound to one's ori. Even though one's ori is chosen and sealed in heaven before one's birth, the Yoruba believe ori can be altered here on earth, for better or for worse. Hence, ori is an object of cult. One sacrifices to one's ori so that it can achieve its purpose, if the purpose is good, or be altered if it is bad. The eldest woman in the family or the household normally plays the role of the priestess of ori. Ori has no special feast-day or temple; it is worshipped whenever one feels threatened or when things seem not to be going well.

In the cosmology of the Yoruba, Ogun, the orisa of iron and warfare, is referred to as the king of the other orisa. In the beginning, as the myth goes, all the orisa felt an irresistible urge to come to the earth. The orisa needed somebody to lead the way, but none was willing to play the leader. Ogun reluctantly volunteered. With sheer creativity and willpower, Ogun cut his way through the thick, impenetrable forest (from chaos to order) and led the others to the Earth. Ogun is the archetype of the creative, no-nonsense father, fierce and straightforward. He is often referred to as the protector of the weak and orphaned. He detests falsehood and punishes anyone who breaks an oath. The association of Ogun with blood is positive. Ogun drinks blood, swims in blood, sleeps in blood. Whenever there is blood shedding, there is Ogun; this is why Ogun is the patron of hunters and the orisa of iron and warfare.

Ogun destroys in a creative way. He is the embodiment of challenge, the promethean instinct in man, constantly at the service of society for its full self-realization. The aggression, violence and resourcefulness of Ogun represent the knowledge-seeking instinct and show him as the master craftsman and artist, farmer and warrior, essence of destruction and creativity.

Unlike the solitary Ogun, Sango, the orisa of thunder, is a king with three wives: Oya, Osun and Oba. Oya and Osun are popular female orisa. Oya is the orisa of the sea and of strong winds, while Osun is the orisa of the stream or river. Oba, the third wife, is the orisa of turbulent seas. Sango's three wives stand in sharp contrast to his firm and hot temper. Sango is admired for his sexual potency. Sexual licentiousness is condemned in society, but in Sango this has become something positive and good. This insatiable sexual passion is often mentioned in the oriki (oral praise song) of Sango: 'Wherever he (Sango) goes, he leaves behind crumbling walls and black ashes, and the blood of virgins raped by his greedy men, mingles with the blood of the slain.'
The Yoruba does not regard sex as dirty or sinful. Sexual desire is part of the human make-up, and it colours all human attitudes and behaviours, for we are sexual beings. The sexual motif also colours Sango worship. In his lifetime, Sango used to plait his hair like a woman's, and today, all Sango priests plait their hair like women's in imitation of Sango. Even the bata drum has some resemblance, no matter how vague, to the penis. When it rains heavily, the earth is said to be 'pregnant with the sperm of heaven' (Ladele, Mustapha, Aworinde, Oyerinde and Oladapo, 1986).

The third major orisa is Obatala, also called orisa-nla ('the big orisa'). Obatala is the orisa of creation, moral purity and beauty. As the name suggests, he is also known as the 'king of whiteness' or 'Lord of the white cloth'. Whiteness in Yoruba aesthetics is a symbol of purity and innocence. Because he is always associated with whiteness, Obatala is often referred to as orisa-funfun (the white orisa). Everything associated with orisa-nla is usually white: his temple is white-washed, his emblems are white chalk and white containers, his priests and priestesses are usually clad in white ornaments, his sacrifice consists of blood-less snail and shea-butter, and the water in his shrine must be changed every day to retain a degree of absolute cleanliness. The life of his worshippers should be pure, clean and clear as water drawn early in the morning from an undisturbed, unpolluted spring (Awolalu and Dopamu, 1979).

There is a direct link between knowledge and creation. To know is to create. Thus the Yoruba orisa of knowledge, Orunmila or Ifa, is associated with creation. Orunmila was present at the beginning when human beings were being created. It was he who made the sacrifice to Olodumare so Olodumare could put emi into the moulded human body. Orunmila was also present when human beings were choosing their ori. Hence, he is called Eleri-ipin ('the witness or advocate of human destiny'). Orunmila can change bad ori into good. He knows the past, the present and the future and so is often consulted before any project is undertaken or any decision made, or whenever there is a problem.

Ifa is an expression of the need for a deeper and holistic knowledge that transcends human intelligence. Ifa expresses the need to enter into the dark bosom of life's mysteries and symbolizes knowledge by intuition. When a troubled Yoruba consults the Ifa oracle, he or she normally accepts Ifa's verdict or solutions unquestionably. This easily exposes him or her to be exploited or manipulated by the diviner. Nevertheless, the fact remains that for the Yoruba, the Ifa oracle is higher than logic or solutions based on human reason.

Obatala personifies that part of human nature that is naturally compassionate and pure, always longing for beauty, for goodness, for holiness. Every human person is created to be good and holy (Soyinka, 2003). Wickedness is a perversion of this intrinsic goodness. To be good, to have *iwa*, is to be beautiful in the real sense of the term. The attribute Eleda (which means 'creator') used for Olodumare is also used for Obatala. Obatala is a creator not only because he moulded the human body, but also because he allowed himself to be what he was meant to be, because he put order into the chaos of his life.

Esu: towards a hermeneutics of life and death

The fifth orisa, Esu, is an enigma. Esu is not identified with any particular festival or shrine. Esu is neither male nor female, black nor white, and has no wife or husband. In Yoruba cosmological hierarchy, Esu is directly next to Oldumare, the supreme being; hence he is more powerful than the other orisa. Esu is said to be the supervisor of human relationships and communal living.

Yorubas delight in living physically close to one another. The well-known expression 'I am because we are' is an apt description of the social psychology of the Yoruba and Africans as a whole. The individual exists as part of a community. This is what makes him or her a person. A person is not an abstraction. For the Yoruba, a person is a particular human being born into a particular community on a particular day (Fadipe, 1979). The human person is defined by his or her relationship with others. For better or for worse, what one is, how one thinks and reacts, is largely conditioned by one's community. Of course, overdependence on the community is unhealthy because it can stifle one's sense of responsibility, freedom and creativity. However, the fact remains that true freedom and maturity are achieved only when one recognizes and accepts one's human dependence on others and relates to them creatively. Living in a community can be highly demanding. It is natural that problems, misunderstandings and quarrels arise where people live close together and often cross paths. In families, which are mostly polygamous, there are problems of envy, jealousy, suspicion and personality clashes. In the larger communities, the village or town, there are problems of quarrel over land ownership, theft, sexual immorality and so forth. There exists in the society and in the families then an elaborate code of manners and etiquette aimed at fostering peaceful coexistence (Awolalu, 1979).

Living together requires physical interactions. Yorubas are not afraid of touching each other's bodies. To touch the other is to affirm the other and say to him or her, 'I recognize you as a person. I affirm you as a fellow human being. We belong together.' It is this sense of belonging that is affirmed in Yoruba and African dance. Dance always has a communal character, even when done alone. When one dances with another, there is established a link, a bond between the two people, for dance unites. Two people dancing together reflects the paradox of life and death, joy and sorrow, pleasure and pain, creation and destruction (Ajayi, 1998).

Esu is associated with this twinness of reality, with the duality of day and night, white and black, good and bad, pleasure and pain, desire and separation, life and death (Figure 5.2). Esu personifies reality as perceived by the Yoruba. Life, for the Yoruba, is primarily a mystery, a paradox. Esu is the orisa of paradox or destiny or fate or contradiction or deceit – there is no one fixed word for what Esu represents (Awolalu, 1979).

Esu is believed to be the deputy of Olodumare and the most powerful orisa (Ogunbowale, 1978). He is said to be the keeper of the ase, the gourd that contains the divine potent creative sound with which Olodumare created the universe and preserves it in being (Abimbola, 1977). Before any attention is paid to the other orisa, Esu must first be worshipped, and before any sacrifice is made to any orisa, Esu must first be offered a sacrifice. According to Fadipe (1979, pp. 285–286),

> Eru, alias Elegbera, is undoubtedly the most ubiquitous of all orisa and also one of the most universally worshipped. A Yoruba proverb says that every head of a compound must have an Esu outside his compound and the baale who does not have one will have to give account to Esu. In addition to every baale having an Esu outside his compound (generally in the form of a block of Iron-stone upon which palm-oil is poured by worshippers, and beside which other sacrifices are placed), nearly every orisal to which a priest or priestess is attached has an Esu or Elegbera linked with it.

The early Christian missionaries, anxious to put a label on everything, wrongly pronounced Esu to be the devil and equated him with Satan in the book of Job (Frobenius, 1980). According to Ijimere (1966), Esu is the confuser of men. When he is angry, he hits a stone until it bleeds. When he is angry he sits on the skin of an ant. When he is angry he weeps tears of blood. While Esu delights in causing mischief and havoc in society, he is also a great benefactor who helps those who give him his due.

Esu is not just a religious experience but also reality as experienced, the personification of the duality of the self and the other, and the self and itself (Awolalu, 1979). Esu is often associated with dance because dance is regarded as one of the most creative ways of

Figure 5.2 Esu is depicted as always naked, having only one leg and almost always either licking a staff or licking the thumb (source: Frobenius, 1980)

responding to and coping with the complexities and ambiguities of life, which Esu symbolizes (Yvonne, 2005). What, then, is dance?

Dance as coping with contradictions in Yoruba cosmology

The Yoruba word for dance is *ijo*. *Ijo* is from the verb *jo*, which means to burn. *Ijo*, then, means burning. The notion of burning brings up the image of fire, for when we say that a thing is burning we are saying that it is being consumed by fire. The Yoruba word for fire is *ina*. The noun *ina* and the verb *jo* often go together in Yoruba usage: *Ina n jo* ('Fire is burning') *or O n jo ninu ina* ('It is burning in the fire'). *Ijo* can also be used figuratively to refer to a person's quality or manners. A child who constantly scratches his or her body in an unusual way is asked, *Ki lo n jo e?* ('What is burning you?'). If a person appears restless, we say, *Kini kan n jo o lara-* ('Something is burning him or her'). When we say that somebody is being burnt by fire, the image that comes to mind is not that of someone who is calm and relaxed. Rather, we have the image of someone crying, running helter-skelter, wriggling in pain. These gestures of pain are a response to the heat of the fire.

The Yoruba notion of *ijo* (dance) seems to be derived from these gestures or responses. Dance, then, is a response. This is a very important point to keep in mind. The person who dances is burning (*o n jo*), is on fire. For us to fully appreciate the notion of dance as response, we have to understand the words 'response' and 'fire' in the general context of life. Desire is a form of fire. Fire, *ina*, embraces whatever motivates, moves and calls for response. The responses could be fear, hatred, love, awe, adoration, fascination or dread. To dance is to react, to respond. To cease to dance is to die *(ku)*, become passive, having no fire (Ajayi, 1998).

The next life: indigenous foundation cosmology and exogenous Christian eschatology

For the Yoruba, death is a stark reality of life. From the way funeral rites are performed and the elaborate way death is celebrated, the Yoruba child has come to see death as a passage to another plane or mode of existence. The child can talk freely and openly about death. Death is not an evil which should not be remembered.

The Yoruba word for death is *iku*, which means to be immobile, to quench, to become unresponsive. *Iku* is a negation of *ijo*, dance, which, as we have said, is a response, movement. There are many stories about the origin of Iku, but the general belief of the Yoruba is that Iku is a messenger of Olodumare. Iku recalls anyone whose time is ripe back to Olodumare. Iku is believed to be meant for those in ripe old age, and so the Yoruba rejoices when such an elderly person is taken away. Such a person is said to have gone home to the ancestors. When a young person dies there is great mourning, for it is believed that something has gone wrong somewhere.

Iku is so powerful that he cannot be controlled, not even by the most powerful of the orisa, for Iku is subject only to Olodumare. Iku is not an orisa and so is not an object of cult. However, there is a very close link between Esu and Iku. In fact, Iku is a dimension of Esu in Yoruba cosmology. Esu, as we have said, is the deputy of Olodumare and the keeper of the ase, the sacred sound by which the world is sustained. Anybody who offends Esu may be visited by Iku. Any orisa that fails to pay due homage to Esu will fall victim to Iku. Thus, prayers to Esu are always in the negative. For example, instead of saying, 'Esu, give me long life,' one says, 'Esu, do not cut my life short.' Instead of saying, 'Esu, give me children,' one says, 'Esu, do not make me barren or infertile.'

When a person is sick, sacrifices can be offered to an orisa so the sick person may recover. However, when it is time for Iku to strike, no amount of sacrifices can stop him, as is expressed in an *odu-Ifa* (Abimbola, 1977):

> Aide Iku I'a nb osun
> Aide Iku I'a nb' osa'
> B' iku ba de Iku o gb ebo

> It is when *Iku* is not yet ready that it works to propitiate *osun*.

> It is when *Iku* is not yet ready that it works to propitiate *orisa*.
> When *Iku* is ready to strike, *Iku* does not yield to sacrifices.

What happens after death? The Yoruba believes there is a place where one goes after death. If the person lived a long, good or holy life, he or she goes to the world of the ancestors and is reunited with his or her friends and relatives. But if the person led a bad, ugly life, he or she will not be able to meet with the ancestors and his or her friends and relatives. Such a person will remain unfulfilled and unsatisfied because of this alienation. If this alienation from one's ancestors, friends, relatives and family, both dead and alive, is termed hell, then hell indeed it is.

Like the Old Testament Hebrews, the Yoruba has a concrete, down-to-earth view of heaven. Heaven is supposed to be a place of perfection, more perfect than the Earth. It is impossible, therefore, for the human mind to imagine it adequately, for the human mind cannot imagine something more perfect than itself. The Yoruba heaven is very similar to the Earth. Everything here is an imperfect, less orderly copy of everything in the Yoruba heaven. There are better foods, palm wines, cloths and houses in heaven.

In every religion, there is the temptation to use images to explain reality. We see this clearly in the history of the Christian use of images of hell, purgatory and paradise. Down the centuries the biblical images of loss and damnation, such as outer darkness, where there is wailing and gnashing of teeth (Matthew 22:13) and the fires of gehenna, or hell (Matthew 5:22–29, Luke 16:19–31), came to be taken literally, and thus Christian eschatology was interpreted solely in terms of hell, purgatory and heaven. The result was a neglect of present realities and a focus only on heavenly realities, as if the two have no connection.

Since the Second Vatican Council of the Catholic Church, there has been a shift from this inadequate view of eschatology. The incarnation of Christ sharply contradicts a cataclysmic view of the end time, where there is a complete discontinuity between human history and the kingdom of God. A return to scripture and to the understanding expressed in patristic writings and the early liturgy of the church has encouraged a renewed Christian reflection on the experiences of being human and a renewed focus on communal and this-worldly redemption. Today eschatology is no longer treated as a mere appendix to Christian theology. Eschatology stands at the very heart of Christianity and is the standpoint from which theology must proceed (Moltmann, 1967).

Bedrock: a look at the exogenous concept of the Christian God

Having examined the indigenous concept of God or Supreme Deity, we now look at the exogenous concept of the Christian God. We begin with the Israelites, the so-called people of God. For the Israelites, God is above all, before anything else, a god of justice. Before the Israelites began to speak of God as Creator or Father or even love, they experienced God as 'just'. Evidence of this is in Deuteronomy 26:5–9, which probably contains one of the oldest creeds of Israel: 'Then we cried out to the Lord, the God of our ancestors, and the Lord heard our voice and saw our misery.' The God of Israel is a just god, who hates oppression and wickedness: 'There is no god but me, a God of Justice, a saviour. There is none but me' (Isaiah 45:19–22). Wherever there is justice and love for the weak and the poor, there is Yahweh. Religious practices, worship and piety are in vain if they do not bear fruit in love and concern for the poor and oppressed. To be holy and pleasing before God, one must 'Cease to do evil. Learn to do good, search for justice, help the oppressed, be just to the orphan, and plead for the widow' (Isaiah 1:16–17). In Chapter 6, I will argue that modern feminism has its roots in this concept of God.

The prophet Isaiah, like all the other prophets, insisted on justice and equity. He made it clear to the powerful and rich people of his time that God is interested in and concerned for the well-being of the poor and will always protect them and provide for them: 'I, Yahweh, will answer them. I, the God of Israel, will not abandon them' (Isaiah 41:17). To the poor and oppressed Yahweh says, 'I, Yahweh, your God, I am holding you by the right hand; I tell you, do not be afraid. I will help you!' (Isaiah 41:13). The prophet Amos denounced the exploitation of the poor and the weak through various devices like price rigging, weight cheating, shortcoming and misinformation. The rich and powerful pretend to love the poor and fight for their rights while in fact they are exploiting them.

Yahweh's anger blazes against them: 'Trouble for those who turn Justice into wormwood, throwing Integrity to the ground; who hate the man dispensing Justice at the city gate and detest those who speak with honesty' (Amos 5:7, 10). The rich may keep on piling up riches upon riches and building houses upon houses, but 'those houses you have built of dressed stone; you will never lie in them' (Amos 5:11).

While the Old Testament presents Yahweh as just, the New Testament reveals 'Him' as Trinity. In the New Testament Christ becomes the revelation of God, the fulfilment of the Old Testament. God the father created the world out of love, a love so deep that at a certain time he became a creature in the humanity of Jesus to unite all things to himself in the Holy Spirit. The symbol of the kingdom of God is central to the teaching of Jesus. Jesus's use of the phrase 'kingdom of God' does not yield a precise, conceptual formula. He often speaks of the kingdom of God in figures of speech: 'The kingdom of heaven may be compared to a man who sowed good seed in his field' (Matthew 13:24). 'The kingdom of heaven is like a mustard seed.' (Matthew 13:31). 'The kingdom of heaven is like the yeast' (Matthew 13:33).

In parables and sermons, Jesus spoke about the kingdom of God: 'The time has come', he said, 'and the kingdom of God is close at hand' (Mark 1:15). 'What can we say the kingdom of God is like? What parable can we find for it?' (Mark 4:30). What, then, is the kingdom of God? In light of modern exegesis and based on contemporary experience, one can say that the kingdom of God means the reign of God in justice and peace (Schatzman, 1965). The kingdom of God is a religious symbol not only about something transcendent or eschatological but also about human existence as lived here on earth. The kingdom of God, then, as God's will, God's values, God's intentions for historical existence, also applies to history.

When we say that human beings are made in the image of God, what do we mean? Are we not simply saying that they are relational beings? That they have the capacity to go beyond themselves, to transcend themselves and reach out to others in love, openness and trust (Tillich, 2014)? When we transcend ourselves, we experience healing integrally.

According to theologian Hans Kung (1990), the world came to be because of the relationship, the communion between God the father, God the son and God the Holy Spirit. This communion between the three is a movement, a dance of love. To say that God is a Trinity, or self-offering, or self-giving, is to say that God is a dancing God. God danced, and the world came into being. God danced human beings into being. Whenever we reach out to our neighbours in love, whenever we resist oppression and fight for justice, whenever we uphold the dignity and sacredness of all life, whenever we genuinely love our fellow men and women, we are dancing them into being (Keen, 1970).

Establishing a balance between the indigenous and the exogenous images of God

Africans very often use the expression 'the white man's God'. By such expression, they are referring to the God the missionaries preached to them, the God the missionaries claimed to be the Christian God. While the Africans accepted Christianity with its attendant western culture and education with zeal, and practise it outwardly, in times of trouble they run back to the traditional religion, which they outwardly rejected for a solution to their problems. This is dramatically well described by Mongo Beti in his novel *The Poor Christ of Bomba* (2005: 29). The expatriate missionary priest asks his catechist, 'Why is it, do you think, that so many backslide from the true religion? Why did they come to Mass in the first place?' The missionary priest finds it difficult to understand why after so many years of 'evangelization' the Africans still remain 'pagan' and show nothing but an external interest in Christianity. The real answer does not come from the catechist but from the priest's cook, who says bluntly to him,

> I'll tell you just how it is, father. The first of us who ran to religion, your religion, came to it as a sort of . . . revelation. Yes, that's it, a revelation, a school where they could learn your secret, the secret of your power, of your aeroplanes and railways . . . in a word, the secret of your mystery. Instead of that, you began talking to them of God, of the soul, of external life, and so forth. Do you really suppose they didn't know these things already, long before you came? So of course, they decided that you were hiding something.
>
> (Beti, 2005, p. 29)

This shows the dichotomy Africans often experience with the images of God, and their struggle to find a balance between these different, if not conflicting, images. Mazrui (1986) described this as Africa's triple heritage. In reality, it is not so much a heritage as a persistent experience of identity crisis. While Africans may have discovered some balance in the vertical relationship with the Divine, their horizontal relationships show a lack of harmony. The effect of this imbalance is evidently catastrophic on the African continent – from religious fanaticism to extremism, from disharmony in family relationships to religious manipulations, religious materialism and fatalism.

Subsoil: indigenous health systems and exogenous health institutions: hope for synergy

Alleviation of disease and preservation of health, both conditioned by culture, have been a human pursuit since antiquity. Using drugs and diet as remedies for the disruptive episodes in the life process is as old as human existence. The prehistoric humans derived therapeutic agents from nature, without maligning the environment. The plant kingdom, since the very beginning of human civilization, served as the reservoir of medicine. Over time, because of the need to cover a wider variety of disease patterns and to augment the therapeutic potential of these agents, mineral and animal constituents began to be incorporated into these plant-based medicines. This use of natural resources as therapeutic agents was predicated on a unique belief system encompassing the concepts of health, physical or mental illness, diagnosis, treatment and prevention (Green, 1999).

The accumulated knowledge of such health practices and products is a rich cultural heritage common to all human societies, sometimes ignored or unrecognized in a formal or institutional sense. What separates this body of knowledge referred to as traditional medicine from modern medicine is the fact that the latter is anchored in science, while the former in practical experience. As long as science continued to be narrowly defined, traditional medicine remained largely unnoticed. It took sort of a scientific revolution, a paradigm shift, to draw renewed interest in traditional medicine.

Increasingly, the validity of the traditional-modern dichotomy is being questioned. Traditional medicine differs from the modern or western medicine not in terms of goals or effects but in terms of its underlying cultures and historical contexts. Viewed from this perspective, the World Health Organization (1977) noted, 'All medicine is modern in so far as it is satisfactorily directed towards the common goal of providing health care, despite the setting in time, place and culture.' This traditional/modern dichotomy is also a cultural construct that relates to certain sociopolitical dynamics.

It is important to note that western medicine in the nineteenth century was closer to traditional medicine than it is today. Western medicine laid emphasis on mixtures mainly from herbal extracts. The Europeans mixed their own drugs and measured them into brown bottles to preserve their potency. Huge extracts from the root of the Brazilian plant *ipecacuanha*, for example, were ordered to cure cough, a drug that remains one of the strongest cough ingredients today (Patton, 1996). Opium was also used to treat sick people. Yet the European pharmacists and physicians had no intention of working with traditional healers.

Following this tradition, African doctors sought to superimpose medical practices and experiences learned outside of Africa on communities that had little or no respect for western values. In order to survive, they had to 'fight' the traditional healers and win over their patients by exposing their ignorance of physiology and anatomy. It was clear that unless the status of the traditional healers was diminished, the people would continue to patronize them, thereby making the financial survival of doctors in private practise difficult.

On the other hand, African healers would direct their patients to the hospitals when their treatment failed, and it did not take long before the effectiveness of western medicine became recognized among the communities. The people's confidence in western medicine grew following the development of sulfa drugs in the mid-1930s and antibiotics in World War II, when physicians were able to attack most pathogenic bacteria effectively. One example was river blindness, which decimated many populations in West Africa. By the 1950s, drugs for this sickness had been found. This and other inventions humiliated traditional healers, who suffered diminished status in the eyes of African patients while African medical doctors enjoyed increased status (Patton, 1996).

Today, Africa is faced with the challenge of re-understanding, reinventing and re-expressing ancient (indigenous) knowledge in the light of modern scientific (exogenous) knowledge. This requires a synergy of both systems. In order to become global, one must first be local. While the indigenous needs the exogenous to rise to global integrity, the exogenous loses its substance and transformative power without the indigenous. When there is no proper synergy between the two, education becomes artificial and insubstantial. This is why we fail to see how absurd it is that a Nigerian lawyer, or a laboratory scientist, or a bank manager or medical practitioner is expected to observe a certain dress code (suited to European climate) without reference to the climatic condition where they live.

For African medicine, the future lies in the ability to be open to the challenges of globalization through proper documentation, analysis and research. While countries like China and India have already invaded the global herbal market like a colossus, Nigeria is still busy discussing whether herbal medicine is a good source of health care. While the global market for herbal medicine is estimated to be $60 billion, African western exogenous-trained professionals are busy attending seminars to convince them of the efficacy of herbal medicine. And while Chinese medical doctors, botanists, pharmacists and other scientists are all united in the development of their traditional medicine into a global transformative venture, Nigerian scientists are standing by the ringside, complaining about the attitude of charlatans and quacks. A better approach is to join hands in correcting the perceived weaknesses and mistakes of our traditional medicine, and help transform it into a globally acceptable enterprise.

Saying this is easy; putting it into practise is more difficult and requires determination. Paxherbal was founded in 1996 to confront this challenge and change the perceptions of herbal medicine as something outdated to that of dynamic and innovative enterprise. To do this, it is essential to operate as an institution rather than an individual. Over the past twenty years, Paxherbal, as an organized institution well grounded in the local community, has been able to alleviate many of the institutional imbalances of traditional medicine through collaboration with conventional exogenous medical institutions. That is only the beginning. The next chapter will unveil the theoretical and philosophical foundations on which Paxherbal's model of community development and integral health is based. In other words, can we transcend dichotomies of South and North, East and West, poor and rich, exogenous and indigenous, and maintain a creative balance? The theoretical basis of such a perspective, which I describe as Pax Africana later, is one of the key features of this research work. We now look at the final dimension of the transcultural topography, called topsoil, and its inclinations.

Topsoil: inclinations: towards a transformation of worldview

There is a tendency in our time to draw a sharp line between the 'developed' and 'under-developed' peoples of the earth. The 'developed' people are the workers, the revolutionar-ies, the 'world-changers'. The 'underdeveloped' people are the 'life-celebrators', known for their dances, folklore, music and 'archaic' mentality. The 'life-celebrators' are backward and lack inventiveness and intellectual rigour (Cox, 1970). They are passive receivers of western technology and civilization, with no capacity for originality of thought. (Is that not what often comes to mind when we use the word 'indigenous'?) Behind this divi-sion lies a false conception of work, indeed, of all reality, and an arrogant conception of western civilization as the ideal model of civilization. (Is that not what we call the exog-enous?) Work has come to be seen solely in terms of material utility – that is, being useful. The ideology is that human beings live to work. In addition, to be a worker means to be engaged in the production of consumer goods. The worker does not smile or play. His or her chief characteristics are: (1) an extreme tension of the powers of action, (2) a readiness to suffer just for the sake of suffering, in vain, and (3) a complete, total absorption in the social organism which is geared towards utility (Pieper, 2009). The worker is expected to be busy or at least to appear to be busy. Not to be busy is to cease to *be*.

For Kant, knowledge is work as opposed to intuition. Intuition, for the fact that it is effortless, is base and cannot lead to knowledge. But knowing, because it is discursive and therefore demanding, is superior. Knowing requires comparing, examining, relat-ing, distinguishing, demonstrating. It is work. Kant concluded that knowing, especially philosophizing, is, and must be regarded as, work. Any form of philosophy that does not involve toil and sweat is no philosophy. The philosophy of the romantics, or that of Plato, which is based on both intuition and enthusiasm, is not real philosophy. They are too easy, and nothing easy is worthwhile. However, the philosophy of Aristotle is 'real' because it is work. One can see echoes of this in the writings of exogenous African philosophers, such as Kwasi Wiredu (1980), Paulin Hountondji (1983) and Henry Odera Oruka (1990), to name a few. Unbeknown to them, they are proudly propagating 'Kantian' ideology, which makes them appear more sophisticated than their colleagues. Following Kant's argument, then, African philosophy and Asian philosophy, if they can even be called philosophy at all, are not real. They are for the lazy.

According to Pieper (2009), the tendency to overvalue work and the effort of doing something difficult is so deep-rooted that it affects even our notion of love. We want to earn and acquire love as we acquire other properties. From the African (indigenous) point of view, the human person is not just a working being, nor a thinking being. The human person is *homo festivus* (one who celebrates), *homo fantasia* (one who intuits) and *homo ludens* (one who plays) (Pieper, 2009).

To regard the human person as merely a trained functionary in a consumer society is an insult to human dignity. In societies where human beings have lost the capacity to celebrate and fantasize, and have jettisoned play in favour of work, cases of disillusionment, suicide, violence, depression and meaninglessness abound. The biblical saying 'What does it profit a man if he gains the whole world and loses his own soul?' has become a maxim for modern western culture. In the words of Cox (1970, p. 38),

> While gaining the whole world he (modern man) has been losing his own soul. He has purchased prosperity at the cost of a staggering impoverishment of the vital elements of his life. These elements are festivity – the capacity for genuine revelry and joyous celebration – and fantasy – the faculty for envisioning radically alternative life situations.

The word 'school' (*skole* in Greek and *scola* in Latin) originally means leisure. School is a place where one relaxes and lets go. Work in ancient times and indeed up until the Middle Ages in the exogenous North was closely linked with play and leisure (Pieper, 2009). The lazy man or woman was one who occupied him or herself with so many activities that he or she had no time to play, to be still, to simply be. It is precisely the fear of facing the truth, of facing reality, that drives the so-called hard worker to fanatical and restless activity. This is what laziness means – refusal to be oneself. The Latin word for this is *acedia*. Acedia is the incapacity to celebrate, to be leisurely. In monastic tradition, acedia is one of the major temptations of the monk. Within this context, it refers to boredom, a lack of interest in anything. For German philosopher and theologian Søren Kierkegaard (1980), it is the 'sickness unto death'. Even the charitable works of the social worker can be motivated by acedia. The social worker may be serving him- or herself under the pretence of serving God or the poor. This may be one reason why many poor people would prefer to die of hunger and preserve their personal human dignity than allow themselves to be exploited by the compulsive social worker. The compulsive worker is lazy. He or she cannot bear the pain of silence and gazing and letting go.

According to Cox (1970), a celebration or festival has three essential ingredients: (1) excess, (2) affirmation and (3) juxtaposition. Excess is a deliberate, conscious attempt to 'overdo' the celebration. During a festival in most places, conventional laws about food, modesty and moderation are relaxed. In some cases, drunkenness and overeating are allowed. In his novel *The River Between*, Ngugi wa Thiong'o (1965, p. 41) described an African festival's 'excess':

> The dance was being held at an open-air place in Kameno. Whistles, horns, broken tins and anything else that was handy were taken and beaten to the rhythm of the song and dance. Everybody went into a frenzy of excitement. Old and young, women and children, all were there losing themselves in the magic motion of the dance ...

They were free. Age and youth had become reconciled for this one night. And you could sing about anything and talk of the hidden parts of men and women without feeling that you had violated the otherwise strong social code that governed people's relationships, especially the relationship between young and old, man and woman.

Affirmation means that one says 'yes' to life, despite all the odds. Affirmation refers to the joy and peace that comes from letting go of the desire to possess, to dominate. It is an acceptance of one's mortality and human state. In Africa, every event is an occasion for festivity. In Yoruba society, when a hunter or devotee of *Ogun* dies, it is mandatory that the living celebrate with great, all-night dancing, for it is believed that unless this is done, the spirit of the deceased will not find rest. For the African there is no occasion that does not call for dance, for celebration, for festivity. There are dances that accompany storytelling. There are dances for birth and death. There are dances to welcome a visitor. There are dances for war and for peace. We dance the harvest of the crops and the cultivation of the land. To hold a celebration means to affirm the basic meaningfulness of the universe and a sense of oneness with it. Juxtaposition is linked to the element of excess. It means that the celebration must be markedly different from ordinary everyday life. The celebrators live in a different world from the everyday world.

Dialogue and understanding will help to bridge the gap between so-called world-changers (northern exogenous mindset) and 'life-celebrators' (southern indigenous mindset). This research work argues that such a dichotomy is extremely artificial, and sets about to propose an alternative viewpoint. There is no reason why those who celebrate life cannot also be committed to fundamental social change, and world-changers need not be joyless ascetics (Cox, 1970). Africans need to embrace and further develop their indigenous intellectual tradition and cultural heritage in order to be genuine contributors to modern civilization. African dance, music, vivacity and *joie de vivre* are relevant to a balanced and creative world.

Finding the missing link

The missing link in all the layers of existence is the inability to navigate creatively through the different dimensions of being. The religion of the Yoruba people, characterized by a multiplicity of deities, allowed people in the olden days to live healthily within the complexities and paradoxes of life. The Cartesian concept of reality, which conditioned western education, introduced a crisis of identity in modern Africans. The Yoruba Ifa religion served the people well and helped them to live a balanced life. The Cartesian worldview held that all reality could be broken into bits and pieces, like the atoms, with a view to mastering each component. The repercussion of such a dualism is evident in our modern globalized world, and in the persistent threat to the planet, on which our existence depends (Eisenstein, 2013). It is precisely because too much emphasis is placed on logic and reason that the erotic and sensuous are feared. Scientific knowledge is good and works for the material betterment of the world. This research work argues that there are other equally valid modes of knowledge creation and knowledge acquisition in the world. The Yoruba Ifa religion, for example, views logic and intuition, the rational and the non-rational, the linear and the non-linear as part of the same reality, and both are useful (Neimark, 1993). Thus, the dichotomy between good and bad, moral and immoral is alien to the religion of the Yoruba.

Alleviating the imbalance: a new hermeneutics of the Abiku phenomenon

George Worgul (1980) argues that from the Renaissance to today the epistemological attitude of Western Europe is that man/woman is a 'being for himself'. The institutions and patterns of behaviour in European culture during the Renaissance aimed at human fulfilment from within. Culture no longer relies on God or on the supernatural. It turns to human reason and science. This attitude lends itself to individualistic tendencies. The individual, because he or she is a 'being for himself', seeks to make him- or herself as comfortable as possible. What matters most is 'me', not 'us'.

The African epistemological attitude is essentially 'holistic'. Unlike the European, the African does not have to separate him- or herself from the object in order to know it. Objective knowledge is not a function of the rational faculties alone. There are two ways of knowing an object. One can know the object by its physical features and appearances. On the other hand, one can go beyond the physical qualities and know the object in its essence. To know the object in this latter way is to allow oneself to be affected by the object. One knows the object as part of oneself and not as something separated from oneself. Contrary to the classical European, the African makes no distinction between himself and the object: he does not hold it away from himself to be examined or analysed, or rather, after having examined it, he takes it in his hands, alive as it is, careful not to kill it. He touches it, he feels it, he is conscious of it. It is through his subjectivity that he discovers the other. It is not possible to analyse this unified experience into 'subjective' and 'objective' (Abram, 2011).

In Chapter 2, I described the Yoruba belief in Abiku and how I was associated with being an Abiku. While science and modern knowledge have helped to dispel some of the superstitious beliefs about the Abiku, the concept of the Abiku provides a powerful symbol of integral and holistic living in today's fragmented world. For Nigerian novelist Ben Okri (1992), the Abiku concept invites us to reconnect with the rational and the irrational, the known and the unknown, the transparent and the opaque part of our psyche. The ability to live in many worlds at the same time is essential for us to gain a truly integral and complete knowledge of reality. The concept of Abiku resonates well with the integral four worlds of research-to-innovation. Learning to live creatively in the four worlds is an art urgently needed by the modern world. The Abiku reminds us all that we indeed live in a symbiotic cosmos.

Conclusion

This chapter explored the missing depths in my complex topography, which embraces the Yoruba cultural heritage in which I grew up, the local community of Ewu and the monastic community where I live, as well as the Paxherbal enterprise-in-community, where I work with others. Following the tenets of phenomenology, which is the research method for this foundational level of my research, I described the different dimensions of life in my context, going beyond the surface to explore the core images, bedrock, subsoil and topsoil. All these point to different layers of being and existence, and how they influence, both consciously and unconsciously, the worldviews and orientation of the people in my community.

Describing my context is essential as a foundation for the next part of this research work, where I engage with a group of co-creators and co-researchers to explore existing knowledge and analyse current theories of health, economics and enterprise to generate new knowledge.

References

Abimbola, W. (1977). Ifa divination system. *Nigeria Magazine* 35: 122–123.

Abram, D. (2011). *Becoming animal: An earthly cosmology.* London: Vintage.

Ajayi, O. S. (1998). *Yoruba dance: The semiotics of movement and Yoruba body attitude.* Lawrenceville, NJ: Africa World Press.

Awolalu, J. O. (1979). *Yoruba beliefs and sacrificial rites.* London: Longman.

Awolalu, J. O. and Dopamu, P. A. (1979). *West African traditional religion.* Ibadan, Nigeria: Onibonoje Press.

Beti, M. (2005). *The poor Christ of Bomba.* Long Grove, IL: Waveland Press.

Cox, H. (1970). *The feast of fools.* New York: Harper & Row.

Eisenstein, C. (2013). *The ascent of humanity: Civilization and the human sense of self.* Berkeley, CA: Evolver Editions.

Fadipe, N. A. (1979). *The sociology of the Yoruba.* Lagos, Nigeria: Ibadan University Press.

Frobenius, L. (1980). *The voice of Africa.* New York: Arno Press.

Green, E. C. (1999). *Indigenous theories of contagious disease.* London: AltaMira press.

Hountondji, P. (1983). *African philosophy: Myth and reality.* London: Hutchinson.

Ijimere, O. (1966). *The imprisonment of Obatala and other plays.* London: Heinemann.

Keen, S. (1970). *To a dancing god.* New York: Harper & Row.

Kierkegaard, S. (1980). *The sickness unto death.* Trans. Hong, H. and Hong, E. Princeton, NJ: Princeton University Press.

Kung, H. (1990). *Theology for the third millennium: An ecumenical view.* New York: Anchor Books.

Ladele, T. A., Mustapha, O., Aworinde, I. A., Oyerinde, O. and Oladapo, O. (1986). *Akojopo Iwadii Ijinle Asa Yoruba.* Ibadan, Nigeria: Macmillan.

Lessem, R. and Schieffer, A. (2010). *Integral research and innovation: Transforming enterprise and society.* Farnham, UK: Gower.

Lessem, R., Schieffer, A., Tong, J. and Rima, S. (2013). *Integral dynamics: Political economy, cultural dynamics and the future of the university.* Farnham, UK: Gower.

Mazrui, A. (1986). *The Africans: A triple heritage.* London: BBC.

Moltmann, J. (1967). *Theology of hope.* New York: Harper & Row.

Neimark, P. (1993). *The way of the orisa: Empowering your life through the ancient African religion of Ifa.* New York: HarperCollins.

Ogunbowale, P. O. (1978). *Awon Irunmale ile Yoruba.* Ibadan, Nigeria: Onibonoje Press.

Okri, B. (1992). *The famished road.* New York: Vintage.

Oruka, H. O. (1990). *Trends in contemporary African philosophy.* Nairobi: Shirikon.

Otto, R. (1959). *The idea of the holy.* London: Penguin.

Patton, A. (1996). *Physicians, colonial racism, and diaspora in West Africa.* Gainesville: University Press of Florida.

Pieper, J. (2009). *Leisure: The basis of culture.* New York: Ignatius Press.

Schatzman, A. (1965). *What is the kingdom of God?* Nashville, TN: Parthenon Press.

Soyinka, W. (2003). *The credo of being and nothingness.* Ibadan, Nigeria: Spectrum Books.

Tillich, P. (2014). *The courage to be.* New Haven, CT: Yale University Press.

wa Thiong'O, N. (1965). *The river between.* Nairobi: Heinemann.

Wiredu, K. (1980). *Philosophy and an African culture.* New York: Cambridge University Press.

Worgul, G. S. (1980). *From magic to metaphor.* Mahweh, NJ: Paulist Press.

World Health Organization. (1977). 'The selection of essential drugs'. Report of a WHO Expert Committee. Technical Report Series, no. 615. Geneva.

Yvonne, D. (2005). *Dancing wisdom: Embodied knowledge in Haitian Vodou, Cuban Yoruba, and Bahian Candomble.* Champaign: University of Illinois Press.

Part IV

Co-creation

When you educate a man, you educate an individual, but when you educate a woman, you educate a nation.
—African proverb

6 Emancipatory critique

Introduction to feminism in an African context

Introduction

In the first part of this research work, I described my inner desire as a search for the truth as a tool of healing for my community, my society and myself. I identified my outer call as promoting integral healing in my immediate community of Ewu and the larger society of Nigeria and Africa, if not also the global world. In Part 2 I employed phenomenology as my research method to explore and describe my particular context (described in Part 3) with a view to uncovering the imbalances and thereafter work towards alleviating them. In this co-creation part, which is about the third of the 4Cs, I employ feminism as my research methodology.

According to Lessem and Schieffer (2015), the key feature of feminism, born out of the feminist movement, is the focus on the reflexive self or the situated knower. Feminism draws attention to the fact that much of what has passed for authentic knowledge in our male-dominated, androcentric society is in fact a one-sided, distorted knowledge. It is a worldview in favour of the masculine, heavily biased against the feminine in every aspect. Feminism argues against a research methodology, which creates a dichotomy between the knowledge and the knower, between the subject and the object. Holistic knowledge, for feminism, embraces both the human and suprahuman or more-than-human dimensions.

Co-creation refers to an unfolding of the integral research trajectory where the researcher now transcends self to work with others both locally and translocally. Co-creation is a process of institutionalizing research-to-innovation to ensure sustainability and community involvement. I will draw on the tenets of feminist theory as I co-evolve my co-creative ecosystem. I will begin with the location of feminism in its religious origins, and thereafter connect with the indigenous origins as a model of indigenous feminism in Africa.

Introduction to feminism as a theory

Kira Cochrane's (2010) book *Forty Years of Feminism* shows the preference of some feminist historians to limit the term to only modern feminists. The majority, however, would seem to prefer to consider all movements that work to obtain women's rights as feminist. The history of the modern feminist movements has been divided into three stages or epochs, each dealing with different aspects of the feminist movement. The first is the women's suffrage movements of the nineteenth and twentieth centuries, which involved active, often violent struggle to assert women's right to vote. The second stage involved more intellectual engagement and articulation of theories during the women's liberation movement of the 1960s. The third stage, which began in the 1990s, is a further evolution of the feminism of the 1960s, focusing especially on correcting some of the shortcomings of the second stage (Ruether, 2007). The feminism of the 1990s includes neocolonial feminism, liberation feminism and others.

Walters (2005) acknowledged that feminism is not just a twentieth-century phenomenon. In fact, the association of feminism with a neo-liberal, individualistic western society may distort its deeper meaning. According to Walters, reluctant as the secular society may be to acknowledge it, feminism actually had its origin in religion.

The religious origins of feminism

A Benedictine nun, Hildegard of Bingen (1098–1179) could be described as one of the early religious feminists (Maddocks, 2013). At a time when women were regarded as people only to be seen and not heard, except of course when in the kitchen, Hildegard not only wrote spiritual treatises but also composed poems, music and songs. Pope Benedict XVI declared her a doctor of the Church in 2012 in recognition of her significance as an authority on theology, spirituality and natural medicine. Her canonization could also be seen as an official endorsement of her teaching on the equality of men and women. Hildegard is celebrated in Catholic tradition as the patron saint of natural healers.

Hildegard wrote two books on medicine, *Scivias* and *Causae et Curae* (Cause and Cure), as well as numerous other writings about herbalism, botany, geology and biographies of saints. She wrote plays and poetry and wrote/directed the first operas. She went on four preaching tours, each lasting several years at a time, when it was illegal for women to preach. She refused to allow the Church to treat women as subservient to men; she rejected negative stereotypes of women as evil seductresses, and taught that every woman was created in the image and likeness of God (Fox, 2012).

Hildegard's main teaching can be summarized as follows:

- In the inner being of God, there exists an almost erotic relationship of feminine and masculine. That is mirrored in the complementary relationship of men and women.
- Since Jesus took his body from a woman, woman rather than man best represents the humanity of the Son of God.
- Contrary to the clear position of St Paul, man was made for woman just as equally as woman was made for man.
- In opposition to St Augustine's doctrine, sexual pleasure is not a result of sin, and should not be equated with guilt, as it would have been present in Paradise before the fall.
- Eve was far more the victim of Satan's cunning than the cause of Adam's sin and the fall from Grace.
- Menstruation in no way renders a woman unclean. Rather, the shedding of blood in warfare most certainly renders a soldier unclean (de Gruchy, 2012).

As a writer, composer, philosopher, mystic, abbess, healer, artist, feminist and student of science, Hildegard seemed to be ahead of her time. Her controversial ideas resulted in her being reprimanded by other clergy, but because the pope respected her as a seer, she went unpunished (Schipperges, 1997).

Julian of Norwich (1342–1416), an English anchoress and Christian mystic, is another notable religious feminist. Her work *Revelations of Divine Love*, published in 1395, is credited as being the first book in the English language to have been written by a woman

(Beer, 1992). Julian's theology was unique in three aspects: her view of sin as not the centre of our life, her belief in God as a loving and feminine God, without aggression and bitterness, and her view of Christ as mother (Turner, 2001).

Julian's teaching of God as mother was both controversial and unusual for her time. For Julian, God is both our mother and our father. Here, we find a foundation for one of the core tenets of feminism: to transcend gender bias in society, leading to the liberation of the oppressed and marginalized (Upjohn, 1989). Feminism, then, is not about war or conflict between male and female, the feminine and the masculine, but the promotion of liberation for all the oppressed, both men and women. Julian's affirmation of the maternal aspect of Christ is both literal and metaphoric (Beer, 1992). For Julian, Jesus is our mother, sister and brother. Julian's optimism at a time when people were prone to a gloomy view of life because of the Black Death was exceptional. She believed that 'all manner of things shall be well,' an expression that was repeated in later years in the work of T. S. Eliot, one of the most influential poets of the twentieth century.

Feminism in African context: Yoruba indigenous origins

The idea of the 'gods', or deities, which in Yoruba culture are called orisa, is common to African traditional religious cultures. In this section, I will trace the origin of feminism by focusing on the orisa as archetypes of different dimensions of life as it is experienced and lived in Africa. This will be a model of an indigenous feminist emancipatory critique method that can be applied by every traditional society, be it in Nigeria, Senegal, Ghana, Zimbabwe, South Africa or Kenya.

Moremi: Yoruba archetype of a woman of character

Moremi is the wife of Oranmiyan, a one-time king of Ile-Ife who later founded the Oyo Kingdom in Western Nigeria and became its first king as Alaafin of Oyo. Oranmiyan, a grandson of Oduduwa, the fabled father of the Yoruba race, was a very adventurous and dynamic warrior. Legend has it that he raised and trained a strong army and expanded the Ile-Ife dynasty into a strong empire. His expansionist skill led to the creation of the Oyo Kingdom.

As the story goes, Oranmiyan married a young, dynamic and beautiful woman named Moremi. Moremi was the youngest of Oranmiyan's wives. It is said there was a period during the reign of Oranmiyan when Ile-Ife was a victim of persistent attacks and invasion by enemies from a nearby kingdom. Each time the invaders came they killed, maimed and plundered Ile-Ife, leaving trails of woe, pain and suffering. This went on for years and the king was extremely worried, for his armies were unable to defeat the invaders, who were believed to be spirits and extraterrestrial beings (Ragan, 2000).

They consulted the oracle and were told that the people of Ile-Ife could defeat the invaders only through the bravery and intervention of an unnamed woman. When Moremi heard this she, like other women in Ile-Ife, wondered who this woman-saviour would be. She went to consult the *Esimirin* oracle and promised that she would offer herself to be conquered by the invaders if that would save her people from the agony of persistent attacks from the invaders. She vowed that if she came back alive with the knowledge of how to overcome the invaders, she would offer to the oracle any gift the oracle may demand of her.

One fateful day, Moremi was coming back from the market when suddenly the invaders attacked, and as promised, Moremi allowed herself to be kidnapped. The invaders took her to the king, and the king loved her at first sight, made her his favourite wife and always granted her wishes. One day Moremi, after cooking a delicious bowl of pounded yam for her stranger-husband, asked him to tell her the secret of the invaders' success over the Ile-Ife people. He confided in Moremi that the invaders were actually mere mortals and not spirits. They simply disguised themselves as extraterrestrial beings by wearing costumes made from dried grass, and the only way they could be defeated was if they were attacked with fire sticks, as the dried grass was highly flammable.

Having discovered this secret, Moremi escaped to Ile-Ife and gave her people the vital information, and so the people of Ile-Ife prepared themselves with sticks to set afire. When the invaders came shortly after, the people resisted them and pestered them with fire sticks. They were all burnt to death, and so victory was achieved over the enemies.

There was jubilation in Ile-Ife and a sense of liberation never before experienced. A woman, Moremi, became the liberator of her people, and the people revered her. Moremi informed the people of Ile-Ife about her promise to the river oracle to make a big and worthwhile sacrifice if she came back alive from captivity, and asked her towns-people to join her in making this sacrifice. Alas, on getting to the river, Moremi was told by the oracle that she must sacrifice her only son, *Ela*, and nothing else. Moremi was dev-astated. However, she had no option other than to fulfil her promise, for she was a woman of dignity and credibility. Therefore, she tied up her son and brought him to the *Esimirin* shrine to be sacrificed.

The story of Moremi has inspired generations of Yoruba men and women, especially young women, who strive to emulate her virtues of boldness, courage, self-sacrifice, loy-alty and care for the common good. In order to perpetuate the memory of Moremi, the Oyo people celebrate the feast of Edi every year until today. Moremi is a model of the ideal Yoruba woman: bold, courageous, strong-willed and principled. In modern times, monuments have been erected in her honour at the University of Lagos and Obafemi Awolowo University, Ile-Ife. A high school within the premises of the Obafemi Awolowo University, Moremi High School, is named after her. The sterling quality of Moremi is *iwa*. *Iwa* in Yoruba means 'character'. Good character is regarded as the foundation of a community, and without good character, there cannot be a stable community. That is why Moremi is regarded as the *orisa* of good character.

Yemoja: archetype of the protective role of women

Yemoja is the orisa of the sea and the moon. Unlike the other female orisa that are often depicted as young and beautiful, Yemoja seems to transcend physical beauty and is regarded more as a grandmother, one who has acquired wisdom based on life's experi-ences. Indeed, she is revered as a great mother, grandmother and queen of all the orisa. The name Yemoja means 'mother whose children are as many as the fish of the ocean' (Otero and Falola, 2014). Yemoja is the mother of humanity, and she looks after the sustenance of the earth. She is venerated as patron of fertility, fecundity and female empowerment. Like the sea, Yemoja has memories of past civilizations, and people go to her, including the other orisa, for knowledge and wisdom, enlightenment and clarity.

The meekness and gentleness attributed to Yemoja are not because of weakness but rather of strength graciously under control. Her calmness is based on knowledge. She is a symbol of comfort to the oppressed and suppressed, and an assurance that they will triumph, provided they hold on to their convictions. This stability or consistency is an important virtue.

Oya: Yoruba archetype of creativity and knowledge for liberation

Oya is the Yoruba orisa of creativity, inventiveness and knowledge seeking, the warrior goddess of wind, fire and thunder. She is the rationalist, strategist and scientist, and the first wife of Sango, the orisa of thunder, whom we spoke about in Chapter 5. Oya is often depicted as a beautiful woman, calm, composed, dark-skinned and serious-minded. Oya means 'she tears', one who can dispel, tear into pieces, destroy and dissolve.

As the myth goes, Sango and Oya loved each other, but Osun was in love with Sango. Sango and Osun had been courting each other, and Oya knew about it. Osun was a good dancer but a bad cook, while Oya was an excellent cook but not a good dancer. In addition, Sango loved dance and delicious food. Sango made it clear to Osun that he loved Oya, not only for her beauty but also for her creative and strong personality and for her inventiveness in cooking, trading and management of things and people.

Osun knew that if only she could learn to cook like Oya, she would completely win over Sango's heart. So one day, Osun met with Oya and asked her to teach her how to cook. Specifically, she wanted Oya to share her recipes for cooking Sango's favourite food – pounded yam, bush meat and egusi soup. Because Oya had always suspected that Osun was having an affair with her husband, now was her turn for payback. She agreed to share her cooking recipes with Osun, and instructed her she would need to put a part of her body, such as her ear, in the soup to achieve maximum good taste to please Sango.

Osun went to cut off one ear and then the second ear, and added them into the soup. When she brought the food to Sango, she kept her head covered with a scarf to hide her severed ears. Sango noticed a strange-looking piece of meat in the soup and asked what it could be. When Sango tasted the food, he thought the taste was horrible, and he was very angry. He stared hard at Osun and asked why she had to cover her head and ears with a scarf, which was not her usual way of dressing. Sango pulled off Oya's scarf and was horrified to see Osun's ugly new look without her ears. Osun told Sango that she cut off her ears to make soup for Sango in order to please him, based on the advice of Oya. Sango shivered with anger and revenge, and there was heavy rainfall, thunder and lightning all over the universe. Being an orisa of justice, and to spite Oya, Sango decided to bring Osun into his home and make her his wife.

It was said that Oya was the only one capable of standing up to Sango to challenge his anger. Because of her superior and inventive skills, especially in rational argument, Sango respected Oya and always listened to her advice. Thus Oya is the archetype of the strong-willed, independent-minded woman in a culture that tends to see the 'good' woman as unambitious and reticent.

Osun: archetype of enterprise and economic liberation in Yoruba culture

Osun is one of the three wives of Sango. She is the river goddess, the orisa of beauty, fertility, pleasure, enterprise and prosperity. She is faithful and loyal but not stupid. She typifies the qualities of diplomacy, ambition, adventure and purposefulness. It is no wonder that men and women approach Osun for strength of character and determination. In Yoruba mythology, Osun is the business executive *par excellence*, the entrepreneur: skilful with both negative and positive qualities. Osun is the orisa in charge of all markets and places of selling and buying. While Yemoja is the orisa of motherly love, Osun is the orisa of erotic, sensual love. While Yemoja is reserved and inward-looking, Osun is extroverted, social and outgoing, generous and loving. Osun is the archetype of the economically successful woman: she knows what she wants and then goes for it. Her eagerness to get whatever she wants could make her selfish and greedy and get her into trouble, as we saw in the story of her dealings with Oya.

Osun typifies an aspect of feminism that tends to be overlooked in favour of 'giving voice to the marginalized'. The marginalized and the oppressed must first of all cultivate a radical consciousness of their situation, interpret it and then confront the oppressor. Osun adds a strong dimension to feminism in Africa – that it is not enough to fight for the poor or to speak for the poor. The poor and marginalized should be brought to a consciousness of their condition so they can fight for their own rights. The poor do not love being poor. So long as justice for the poor depends on the benevolence of the rich, then there is no hope. According to an African proverb, '*Dogs do not actually prefer bones to meat; it is just that no one ever gives them meat.*' Giving money to the poor is like giving them bone. Giving them knowledge is like giving them meat. When the poor are empowered through knowledge, they will resist oppression. That is the message of Osun, the protector of the poor and orphans and all subjugated people (McKenzie, 1997).

The festival of Osun is celebrated in Osogbo, present-day Osun State in Western Nigeria. Osogbo is the capital of Osun State, a modern Nigeria state named after Osun. The festival takes place in August every year. Thousands of pilgrims, devotees and tourists within Nigeria and the diaspora throng to the ancient Osun Grove, a vast forest declared a world heritage site by the United Nations Education Scientific and Cultural Organization (UNESCO) in 2005. The devotees from all occupations come to ask for spiritual blessings and solutions to their problems, which they believe can be solved by the intervention of Osun. Osun is believed by her adherents to have enormous healing powers and can make infertile women fertile, and make businesses prosper.

Osun is believed to be the custodian of the key to economic success, which is why many of the devotees who throng to the Osun Grove every year are entrepreneurs looking for success in their businesses. Since Osun is the custodian of the market, all involved in the business of selling and buying must approach her for blessing and protection. Osun's negotiating skill was displayed in her ability to convince her rival Oya to give her the cooking recipes to entice Sango. That her encounter with Oya led to disastrous results shows the importance of having good intentions in business transactions. In other words, good character and loyalty, *iwa*, so well exemplified in Moremi, the orisa of good character, are essential tools of business administration. We now look at feminism in contemporary, postcolonial Africa.

Feminism in contemporary African context: exogenous origins

Nigerian political scientist Claude Ake (1995) identified three periods in African political development. The first was the pre-colonial period, when Africans fought a common enemy, which was the colonial power and the apartheid system in South Africa. This period witnessed the emergence of several liberation movements, nationalist movements and revolutionary movements, all united in achieving the common goal of gaining political freedom and independence. Incidentally, most African countries gained political independence in the 1960s and 1970s.

Historically, feminism in Africa has its root in the independence struggles in the colonial era. The experience provided fertile ground for the thoughts of African philosophers and statesmen, such as Senegal's Senghor (1964), Ghana's Nkrumah (1970) and Tanzania's Nyerere (1979). They all sought to practise 'African socialism', in contrast with the European colonial-style capitalism, which they associated with domination and exploitation of the African people. While they did not use the term feminism to describe their perspectives, their thoughts reflect the tenets of feminism.

In South Africa, philosopher Steve Biko (1946–1977) introduced the concept of black consciousness as part of a theoretical search for freedom and identity in South Africa. Biko (Briley, 2011) founded the black consciousness movement (BCM) in the 1960s at a time when the anti-apartheid political party, the African National Congress, had already been banned.

The aim of the BCM was to mobilize and empower the black population, especially the urban dwellers, to resist the evil of apartheid not just politically but also mentally. For Biko, there are two aspects to the liberation struggle: psychological or mental liberation and physical liberation (Biko, 1987). Like feminism, the BCM has its origin in religion. The Anglican Church had in 1966 convened a gathering of young Christians, which gave rise to the formation of the university Christian movement, of which Biko, then a medical student, was an active member. The university Christian movement eventually evolved into the BCM.

Unlike the African National Congress (ANC), which embraced multiracialism, the BCM promoted a distinct sense of 'black power', arguing that black people must take up positions of power and authority politically, and should not be content with solely being visible or recognized. The movement argued that a sense of pride in being black is essential to black identity. The group aroused in many blacks the consciousness of the cultural and psychological realities of apartheid, and the fact that genuine liberation for the black people must be integral, embracing the cultural, political and psychological.

Over the past two centuries, Africa has been an experimental ground for all sorts of political and economic theories, from capitalism to socialism, communism, Marxism and a host of others, often through the medium of Christianity. African thinkers and philosophers have tried to evolve their own brand of socialism and communism, often in opposition to colonial-style capitalism, but with devastating results (Mazrui, 1986). In Burkina Faso, military president Thomas Sankara introduced practical feminist ideas into government with admirable but short-lived success.

Thomas Sankara: from Marxism to African state feminism

Thomas Sankara, military president of Burkina Faso, a small West African country, is often described as one of Africa's lost heroes. A Marxist revolutionary, Pan-Africanist, anti-imperialist and a feminist, Sankara made improvement in women's status and liberation one of the central focuses of his government. For Sankara, liberation for the nation, and the African continent, is not possible without liberation for women (Harsch, 2014).

As a demonstration of his conviction of the important role of women in societal transformation, Sankara included an unprecedented number of women in his government, becoming the first African leader to appoint women into major cabinet positions and recruiting them into the military. He banned forced marriages, polygamy, genital mutilation and all sorts of domestic violence against women. He dismantled the long-held belief that women should work only in the home by implementing policies that encouraged women to work outside the home. He made laws that permitted pregnant women to stay in school throughout their pregnancy (Harsch, 2014). In a deeply patriarchal society such as Burkina Faso, these initiatives were nothing short of a revolution, psychologically and politically.

One of Sankara's most revolutionary initiatives was the introduction of the powerfully symbolic Women Solidarity Day. On the Wednesday of every week, men took over all domestic work usually done by women: cooking, washing, cleaning and running errands in the market, to allow men to experience the enormous pressures women endure at home. Such a policy also aimed to correct the patriarchal belief that regarded house chores as inferior to office work. In his famous address to thousands of Burkinabe women on March 8, 1987, a few months before his assassination, Sankara outlined his goal for women's emancipation in Africa, which was to establish new social relations and unsettle the relations of authority between men and women, forcing each to rethink the nature of both (Sankara, 2007). Three years earlier, Sankara had changed the name of the West African country from the colonial Upper Volta to Burkina Faso, which means 'land of upright people'.

During his four-year reign as president, Sankara initiated one of the most ambitious and successful socio-economic policies ever undertaken by any African government. To set a personal example, he slashed his salary and that of his ministers, and sold off the fleet of luxury cars he inherited from the president's convoy, opting for the Renault brand, which was the cheapest available in the country. Sankara limited his personal possessions to a car, four bikes, a freezer and three guitars. He refused to use the air conditioning in his office, since most of his fellow country people did not have access to the same. His salary was a paltry $450 per month, and he forbade his portrait from being hung in public places (Harsch, 2014). Sankara demonstrated that to be successful, a true revolution must have both subjective and objective, personal and official, as well as emotional and rational, characteristics.

His economic policy was indigenous rather than exogenous. In other words, Sankara promoted an inward-looking economic policy that uncovered, unveiled and activated the creative *gene* or spirit of his society. His government declined all foreign aid, for example, and nationalized all land and mineral wealth and gave a wide berth to neo-liberal organizations, such as the International Monetary Fund (IMF) and the World Bank.

Within three years, with no foreign support, an unprecedented 2.5 million children were vaccinated, and infant mortality rate reduced from 280 deaths per 1,000 births to 145 deaths per 1,000 births – not the ideal but a vast improvement from previous years. In the same period, Burkina Faso was becoming self-sufficient in food production and construction of massive housing and infrastructural projects, such as over 700 kilometres of rail through local initiatives without foreign aid, and illiteracy was vastly reduced, making Burkina Faso a model of Afrocentric economic transformation in Africa (Harsch, 2014).

Like Steve Biko of South Africa, Sankara was murdered in his thirties, depriving Africa of one of her great revolutionary heroes. Even more unfortunate is the attempt of subsequent African leaders to bury the memory of Sankara, as his actions and legacy pose a direct challenge to today's African leaders. The uniqueness of Sankara's Pan Africanism and liberation struggle lies in his feminist orientation. Women's liberation was at the forefront of his struggle. That his best friend cut his reign short through a military coup will remain one of the great tragedies of Africa, and the conspiracy of silence from the colonial superpowers, especially France, is a sad reflection of the hypocrisy and self-centredness of western policies in Africa. That his policies could not be sustained after his death also shows that they were not well grounded in local communities, and not sufficiently institutionalized. Such policies, if they are to be sustainable, must be grounded in nature, culture and community.

Secular feminism

Mary Wollstonecraft (1759–1797), though not a religious figure like Hildegard and Julian, played a prominent role in the eighteenth century in laying a solid foundation for the theory of feminism through her work titled *A Vindication of the Rights of Woman*, regarded as a classic of feminist history (Walters, 2005). Her argument is focused mainly on the right of women to have proper education. For Wollstonecraft, women should have the right to the same education as men. Education is key to complete emancipation, and without education, genuine freedom is not possible. She argued against limiting women's role only to domestic life while not dismissing its importance. Domestic life and public life are intrinsically connected, and creating a dichotomy between the two is part of the tendency of men to suppress the rights of women. Wollstonecraft's writings had great influence on feminism as it evolved in later centuries.

Feminism in the nineteenth and early twentieth centuries was focused on the fight for women's equality in terms of the right to vote, especially in the United Kingdom, Canada, Australia, the United States and the Netherlands, with inspiration from the work of Mary Wollstonecraft.

Feminist theory refers to the application of feminist principles in a variety of disciplines: sociology, economics, history, psychology, anthropology, education, music, art, literature and so on. The key concepts are that men and women should have access to the same standard of education, that nobody should be relegated to a second-class status because of sex.

In sociology, feminist theory builds on the conflict theory of Karl Marx, which posits that capitalism is not just an economic system but also a powerful tool in the hands of the rich and powerful to keep the means of social control in their grip so as to preserve the status quo (Chafetz, 1990). While such artificial means of control may work for some time, Marx posits that it will eventually self-destruct. Marx advocated violent revolution if need be, so long as this oppressive system was overthrown. Feminist social theory examines gender in its relation to power within social structure. It posits that societies are structured to ensure systematic oppression of women, a phenomenon termed 'patriarchy' (Abbott and Wallace, 1990).

In anthropology, feminism seeks to expose and reduce male bias in research findings and draws attention to how patriarchy has permeated most research findings, disciplines and social policies. Modern feminist theorists, such as Warren (2009), Dobson (2014) and Mies and Shiva (2014), are keen to point out the danger of limiting the liberating and emancipatory role of feminism to just women's empowerment. Feminism is about liberation for all the oppressed: plants, animals and human beings – hence the term ecofeminism, first coined in 1974 by Francoise d'Eaubonne (Cudworth, 2005).

The core contents of the theory of ecofeminism affirms that there are connections between the oppression of women and the oppression of nature, and understanding these connections is essential to any adequate understanding of this oppression. One such understanding is the fact that the association between women and nature has been historically used to exploit women.

For Mies and Shiva (2014), it is important that we become aware of, and resist, the tendency to limit the whole of reality to reason alone, the masculine, to the neglect of feelings and emotions, the feminine. The thinking being, so to speak, is often identified with the masculine, a symbol of strength, power and knowledge. The feeling or emotional being is identified with the feminine, a symbol of weakness, affection and passivity. History has been constructed to maintain this mindset and accept it as an intrinsic part of our social structure.

Feminist critique of feminism

Feminism itself has to be content with a criticism of itself as a discipline, especially in the postcolonial era. This criticism gave rise to what is now called postcolonial feminism, also called Third-World feminism. The basic argument of postcolonial feminism is that feminism seemed to be occupied solely with experiences of white, middle-class women in western cultures rather than of all women, especially women in the developing countries (Lionnet, 1995). Postcolonial feminists argued that feminism did not account for the effects of ethnicity and the history of colonialism. They wondered why issues of racism and the inadequacy of colonial education and policies hardly featured in feminist writings. The postcolonial feminist perspective emphasizes the uniqueness and particularity of every group of women based on their social environment. While the subjugation of women is a universal phenomenon, the experience of each group is unique and differs based on such factors as ethnicity, class and culture, and therefore it is not appropriate to use the term 'women' as a category of analysis. To this effect, postcolonial feminism wonders if the experience of women in western culture has in fact been universalized while that of women in the Third World or developing countries has been neglected (Joseph and Mirza, 2012).

Feminism as applied to my context

As indicated in Chapter 1, the question at this co-creation stage of my research is, 'What kind of concrete institution can we (my ecosystem) put in place to integrally develop and transform Africa educationally, economically, spiritually, socially and politically and health-wise?' How do we employ the CARE model, alongside the 4Cs research trajectory, to bring about societal transformation?

The 4Cs and CARE form a dual-rhythm research dynamism of integral research-to-innovation. While the 4Cs focus on the individual researcher's innovation drive in his or her particular context, the CARE aspect of the twin-rhythm research focuses on the institutionalization of my integral process towards a self-sustaining, dynamic and ongoing development. CARE is the acronym employed by Lessem and Schieffer (Mamukwa, Lessem and Schieffer, 2014) to describe this aspect of 'CARE-ing' for the society. Co-creation refers to how I intend to correct the imbalances already identified in my context – Ewu village, Edo State and Nigeria as a whole – and develop an integral model to apply to the rest of Africa as well as to contribute to the rest of the world. In terms of integral research-to-innovation, I am no longer an individual researcher but part of an energized ecosystem that applies research methods and methodologies in a particular context or polity to understand, critique and work towards changing the existing social structure, not by violence but through knowledge. In fact, such a focus on knowledge as a tool for inner and outer liberation is one of the key tenets of feminism. It is important to situate science as a tool for communal healing and societal integration. To that effect, feminism insists that science does not become a new religion, a god or an all-knowing master but rather a servant to the community. Science's role is not just to speak to the society but also to listen to, and be shaped by, the community (Lessem and Schieffer, 2015).

In the next subsection, I will propose the theory of communitalism as an alternative to the defects of previous theories.

From feminism to communitalism

This research work argues that Marxism, capitalism, socialism and communism, while focusing on economics, technology and enterprise, failed to build their concepts on nature and culture, thus leading to unsustainable and imbalanced development. An integral approach, which takes account of the totality of the foregoing, set within a particular African society, building up from nature and community, and embracing culture, politics, economics, spirituality and enterprise, is a surer path to sustainable and integral development in Africa. Such an approach is what I term communitalism. Communitalism, as opposed to capitalism or communism, is an integral approach to knowledge creation and development that is grounded in a particular enterprise-in- community, ultimately affecting a whole society, emerging indigenously and exogenously as such. Such a new African philosophy-in-practise, moreover, has been developed in and around a particular enterprise-in-community, Paxherbal in Edo State, and African Centre for Integral Research and Development (ACIRD), in Edo State, which I will cover further in this chapter.

ACIRD firstly develops, and continually enhances, a research-to-innovation process that leads to social innovation, in theory and in practise, while at the same time focusing on the systematic documentation and dissemination of such. Secondly, it continually co-evolves, together with others both within Africa and without, an approach to communitalism, transcending the prevailing approaches to capitalism and communism, which have caused chaos rather than harmony and underdevelopment rather than development in Africa.

The uniqueness of the theory of communitalism is its grounding in a particular, visible context. We call it a philosophy-in-action, or research-to-innovation, a combination of indigenous (local) with exogenous (global) knowledge through

*   southern **C**ommunity activation
*   eastern **A**wakening of individual and societal consciousness
*   northern innovation-driven institutionalized **R**esearch
*   western transformative **E**ducation.

Communitalism is the release of individual and communal, organizational and societal genius of a particular nature, culture, technology and economy, and societal transformation. How this is done will be the subject of the next four chapters.

From CARE-ing to healing: towards a Pax Africana

The central concept of this research work is healing – physical, mental, spiritual and communal. Chapters 4 and 5 were devoted to making a diagnosis of the 'diseases' (or imbalance) in Ewu community, Edo State and Nigeria. There is in fact a close connection, both metaphorically and literally, between the words 'disease' and 'imbalance'. Diseases occur because of imbalances. Chapters 4 and 5 explored the imbalances in my immediate context on four levels: imbalanced worldviews (transcultural), disciplinary imbalances (transdisciplinary), individual overemphasis (transpersonal) and missing depths (transformational). The four dimensions of Pax – Communis, Spiritus, Scientia and Economia – are the foundations of my theory of communitalism, which evolves from feminism.

In Table 6.1, I identify the female orisa in Yoruba mythology associated with each of the four paxes.

Figure 6.1 summarizes the whole theory of communitalism.

Table 6.1 CARE-ing for my society

South	East	North	West
Pax Communis Community activation (c)	*Pax Spiritus Awakening of consciousness via innovation ecosystem (a)* Orisa: *Yemoja*	*Pax Scientia Research-to-innovation in institutionalized form (r)* Orisa: Oya	*Pax Economia Embodiment via transformative education (e)* Orisa: Osun
Institution Ewu Development and Educational Multipurpose Cooperative Society (EDEMCS)	Institution St Benedict Monastery, Ewu, Edo State	Institutions Africa Centre for Integral Research and Development, Nigeria(ACIRD) Centre for Integral Socio-economic Research, Nigeria (CISER) Trans4m Centre for Integral Development – Institute of African Studies, University of Ibadan, Nigeria	Institution Pax Herbal Clinic and Research Laboratories

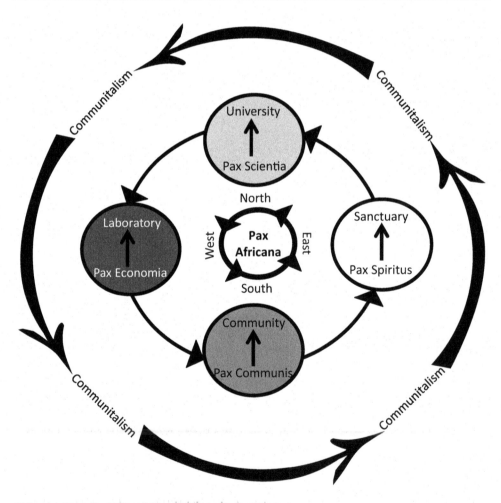

Figure 6.1 Communitalism: integral philosophy-in-action

The four paxes (4Ps): towards an integral CARE-ing society

The concepts of caring, healing and wholeness, integrally, are the foundations of the key tenets of feminism: giving the marginalized a voice through co-creation between science (research methodology) and society (enterprise and economy). Co-creation, within my context, is based on four institutionalized bodies, described ahead, each representing, in theory and practise, a letter of the CARE alphabets: 'C' for communal activation, 'A' for awakening of consciousness, 'R' for institutionalized research, or research-to-innovation, and 'E' for transformative enterprise.

Pax Communis: 'community': communal activation (C)

Communis is a Latin word from which the Latin word 'communitas', 'community' in English, is derived. *Communis* means things held in common, a fellowship, an organized group bonded together by complex relationships and a moral core. Such a concept of community, according to American writer Raymond Williams (2010), is utterly different from the modern understanding of community. For Williams, 'community', in its original meaning, is distinct from and even opposed to the modern-day understanding of an organized, individualistic, capitalist society.

Pax Communis and Moremi: reviving community spirit

Communal activation in Pax Communis is done by connecting with the ancestors indigenously, in my case with the orisa, as a foundation for a new spirit of community in the modern world, exogenously, leading towards communitalism.

We connect with the image of Moremi as the archetype of the good person in a community. In African aesthetics, goodness and beauty are moral issues (Nwoko, 1979). For the Yoruba, to be good is to have *iwa*. The word *iwa* is a summary of Yoruba ethics, and means 'character' or 'virtue'. The person of good *iwa* is a human being in the full sense of the term. Such a person has attained a certain disposition to act in accordance with his or her *eri-okon* (conscience) and act as the ancestors acted. The constant advice to every Yoruba child is: '*maaa se rere, se rere ko ba Ie ye o*' ('learn to do good, be good so that it may be well with you'). A child without character is seen as acting more like a beast. Such a person is described as *alai-ni-Iwa*, a person of no character. Thus in Yoruba, 'character' and 'being' are spelled and pronounced in the same way – *iwa* (Jacobs, 1977).

The person of character is honest, kind, obedient, considerate, tolerant and hospitable. According to Sofola (1978), the key characteristics or virtues of the typical African personality are having a wholesome relationship with others, respect for elders, community solidarity and generosity of heart. In Yoruba culture and in African culture generally, the good is the beautiful (Nwoko, 1979). Unlike in the English language, where there is a clear difference between 'good', which describes moral or religious qualities, and 'beautiful', which describes physical attractiveness, most African languages equate the good with the beautiful. In the African usage, 'goodness' is an absolute quality. A beautiful thing can be so only on the outside. For this reason, Africans lay emphasis on the good, not the beautiful (Nwoko, 1979; Euba, 1986).

The Yoruba word for 'good' is *dara*, which is a combination of *da* (to create) and *ra* (well, in good state, attractive). The notion of creation implies beauty. When we say that something is created we are also saying '*O dara*' – that is, it is good. The word *buruku* is a negation of *iwa*. *Buru* means 'bad', 'unattractive', 'not charming'; thus, *iwa buruku is* 'bad existence', 'bad spiritual life', 'evil character'. A person who has *iwa buruku* is *aburewa* (*buruku ewa*): ugly, not charming. This is expressed in various African proverbs, such as '*Ugliness with a good character is better than beauty*' and '*If there is character, ugliness becomes beauty; if there is none, beauty becomes ugliness.*' Another adage says, '*Judge not your beauty by the number of people who look at you, but rather by the number of people who smile at you.*'

The story of Moremi shows in practical, real-life terms, how the qualities of *iwa* and *dara*, goodness, are lived. Pax Communis aims to revive, albeit in modern guise, the original meaning of community. The starting point, for me, is to apply the tenets of feminism, inwardly and outwardly, by activating the existing local community (the 'C' of the CARE acronym) towards integral community and societal transformation.

In 2015 I gathered a group of local farmers, mostly women, some young people and market men and women to discuss the idea of 'self' and community development. In the true communis, listening is an important virtue. It is not enough to give the marginalized a voice. Equally important is putting appropriate structures in place to ensure each voice is heard. Human beings do not just have the right to free speech. Being listened to is also a right.

From the small group of local farmers who are passionate about development emerged a group called *Ewu Development Educational Multipurpose Cooperative Society* (EDEMCS), whose goal and objective is, among others, to explore the potentials inherent in the local community and build on them. The distinguishing feature of EDEMCS is that the local community is building on their own traditional systems, structure and worldview in order to create a better world for themselves. This bottom-up approach is a key element of sustainable development. The institutional expression of Pax Communis is discussed in detail in the next chapter.

Pax Spiritus: 'sanctuary': awakening consciousness via innovation ecosystem (A)

In Chapter 7, I argue that the root cause of the lack of identity and chaos in the world today is the exclusion of the 'sanctuary' from social life. While the separation of state and church in the so-called age of renaissance helped to set the stage for rapid economic and scientific growth, it also set the scene for a dichotomy between the holy and the profane, the sacred and the secular, nature and science, as well as economics and politics. It became an androcentric, male-dominated epistemological world with a penchant for not accommodating divergent views (Shepherd, 2007). Pax Spiritus refers to the spiritual dimension of the communitalist perspective, which insists that the spirit must not be set against the physical as opposites, but rather as part of an integral whole comprising the four paxes (4Ps). Once again, we begin by connecting with the indigenous core concepts of the sanctuary, using the Yoruba orisa concepts as our model.

Pax Spiritus: connecting with the indigenous image of Yemoja

Yemoja is the archetype of my indigenous image of spiritus – reconnecting with our inner self. Yemoja, the orisa of the sea and the moon, typifies those qualities of the sea that are often taken for granted. For example, we use water every day – drink it, cook with it, bathe with it – and yet we take it for granted, just as we take the air we breathe for granted. Yemoja represents the power of women: the power of resilience, patience, endurance, profundity and wisdom. On the negative side, she represents a destructive power. Just as the ocean is often calm and peaceful, it also has extremely destructive power, as during a storm.

Pax Spiritus: from orisa indigenous origination to Benedictine exogenous foundation

The Benedictines were pioneers in agricultural techniques all over Europe. They developed Sweden's corn trade, Ireland's salmon fish business and Italy's cheese-making factories. They invented new techniques of cattle breeding, and wine and champagne factories in France. In architecture, they made innovations. A Benedictine monk made the first modern clock in AD 996. In AD 1200, a Benedictine monk built and tested a glider that went 600 feet, a precursor to aircraft innovation (Woods, 2012). While some tend to think of monasteries as being shut away from the world, that is a narrow view of monastic life and does not portray how monastic life affects and enhances the wider community. Benedictine monasteries were, and still are, places of beauty, hospitality and learning, models of a caring community, a hospital in the true sense of the word. After all, the word 'hospital' is derived from 'hospitality'.

Defined as an option for the weak and marginalized as well as an option for equality and symbiosis between all people irrespective of race and class, the *Rule of St Benedict* is well qualified to be called a feminist document. The *Rule of St Benedict* was in the sixth century a short guide for establishing a simple, orderly and fraternal Christian community. St Benedict did not set out to write a treatise for publication but was writing for a particular community based on his own practical experience and study. Such experience included an attempt on his life by the same disciples who asked him to be their spiritual head or abbot. Benedict eventually ran for dear life and settled down in a new monastery that he founded on Monte Casino in Italy.

The book is St Benedict's guideline for peaceful and orderly community living. His emphasis is on simplicity, orderliness and humility, apart from silence, hospitality and respect for all God's creatures: plants, animals and human beings. St Benedict was himself a layman, and he emphasized the fact that respect should be shown to all, irrespective of sex, age or title.

In Chapter 35 of the seventy-three-chapter book, he insists that all brothers perform kitchen duty, unless sick or at a more urgent task. For him, taking part in kitchen work and other household functions is sharing in God's creative work. He strictly warned the abbot that the son of a nobleman or freeman must give the son of a slave who became a monk equal respect. For him, wealth is being in touch with oneself and with one's neighbour. An African proverb expresses it thus: '*To be without a friend is to be poor indeed.*'

The strength and power of monastic life through the centuries are that it offers an alternative to the modern materialistic, capitalist world. A former prime minister of the United Kingdom, Margaret Thatcher, was once reported to have said, 'There is no alternative' (TINA) to capitalism. For me, Benedictine monasticism is a perennial rebuttal to TINA, and affirmation that 'There is an alternative' (TIAA).

For Benedict, the real wealth and strength of a community lie in its ability to be detached from the things of this world in order to be more integrally involved in them. This is an emphasis on the real wealth of a people: solidarity, brotherliness, Ubuntu, respect for nature and people. The following African proverbs express these points very well: '*The wealth which enslaves the owner isn't wealth*' and '*If you eat alone then you will die alone.*'

In Chapter 53 of his *Rule*, Benedict instructs that all guests are to be welcomed as Christ, irrespective of sex, religion or race. In fact, the so-called unbelievers, the poor and the weak are to be given special courtesy, respect and attention, since they have nothing to give in return (Jamison, 2010).

In Chapter 57, all artisans in the monastery are enjoined to practise their skill with humility and honesty. They should sell their goods a bit cheaper than the conventional rate. The overriding idea in the *Rule of St Benedict* is that little things matter a lot (Chittister, 1991). For St Benedict, the key to greatness is to do little things with attention and dedication. Finding meaning in the little things of daily life, in the daily struggles, the daily challenges of being human, may well be the greatest challenge for us in the modern world. A key tenet of feminist emancipatory critique and co-creation is to represent and accommodate human diversity, both individually and organizationally.

A rediscovery of the 'sanctuary', represented in my case by the monastery, is essential to the discovery of our sense of identity, both for Africa and for the world at large. This rediscovery will take different shapes and forms in different parts of the world. However, a rediscovery of a society's sense of identity or meaning must be based on a rediscovery of its moral core, or spirituality.

We now look at the third dimension of Pax Africana, which we call Pax Scientia, embracing knowledge creation in the Nigerian context.

Pax Scientia: 'university': origination of indigenous communiversity concepts via Oya (R)

There is a close relationship between Oya (Scientia) and Osun (Economia), a relationship, in our integral communitalist terms, between the 'university' and the 'laboratory', between theory and practise. Both Osun (the orisa of pleasure, attraction and prosperity) and Oya are wives of Sango, the orisa of thunder and lightning.

In the story of Oya and Osun, Oya is depicted as the calculative and pragmatic other, not given to bursts of emotion and passion. Oya knows Osun is having an affair with Sango, her husband, and she waits patiently to handle the matter in her own way. Oya is secure in her skill and expertise. She does not need to struggle with anybody. She has recipes for cooking to retain the love of Sango. When the opportunity comes to punish Osun, she does so calculatedly. Unlike Osun, Oya is well in control of her emotions and feelings, and she knows what she wants. Oya is depicted as a goddess of transformation that comes from knowledge. However, knowledge is a two-edged sword: it can create and destroy. Oya is ready to let go and embrace new ways of doing things. Her cooking skill demonstrates her technical skill, and Oya has leadership qualities; hence, she is consulted when new kings, chiefs and leaders are being selected. She is the rationalist, with ability to analyse and interpret. It is for these reasons that Oya is the archetype of the researcher in our context of Pax Scientia, and is connected with our *Africa Centre for Integral Research and Development* (ACIRD).

Pax Economia: 'laboratory': Osun as Yoruba archetype of transformative enterprise (E)

Osun is regarded as a model of loyalty, determination, diplomacy and courage. She typifies those qualities needed by entrepreneurs to excel and succeed. Such qualities include ambition, skilfulness, the ability to take risks and the virtue of hard work. In Yoruba mythology, Osun is the patroness of business executives, market leaders and individuals who love to work and make profits. There is a tendency to stereotype rich and successful people as selfish and self-centred. Sometimes it appears that the rich are being blamed for the poverty of the poor. Here we have a lot to learn from Osun about the importance of balance and moderation. Material success and profit must go hand-in-hand with responsibility for the welfare of other people, the community and the environment.

A successful business model embraces care for oneself, for others, for the community and for the environment. In other words, once the desire for profit overshadows concern for the common good, it leads to conflict and disharmony. This is exemplified in the story of Osun, whose eagerness to get whatever she wanted often got her into trouble and caused conflict, as we saw in her encounter with Oya.

Skill, hard work and passion for success need to be balanced with *iwa*, good character, as exemplified in the life of Moremi. The entrepreneur of the future is one who can maintain a balance between individual ambition and communal progress. *Iwa* is one of the most important forms of capital in running an integral enterprise. Without good character, business enterprise loses its transformative impact. The market, or 'laboratory', must be a place where a sense of community and honesty is created and nurtured (Communis), 'a school of the Lords' service' as described in the *Rule* (1980) (Spiritus) and finally a communiversity of knowledge (Scientia).

Osun and Paxherbal: from indigenous archetype of enterprise to local-global (indigenous-exogenous) transformative enterprise

A lot has already been said about Paxherbal, a centre for scientific identification, cultivation and promotion of African herbal medicine. Paxherbal challenges the separations often created between the mind, body and soul, or in the local Nigerian context, between spirituality, politics, economy and medicine. Such separation is a product of a mis-education (Fanon, 2001; Woodson, 2010), which has contributed to a gross imbalanced worldview among many Africans.

Over the past decade, the Paxherbal approach to healing has grown beyond an exclusive focus on biological health to embrace holistic healing, or integral healing in the context of this research work. The question is to define what profit really means. In the language of liberal capitalism, profit means to acquire as much capital as possible for oneself. Capital could be in the form of exclusive ownership of property or money. 'Good' business, then, is the one that brings as much profit as possible for the individual or cooperation.

For Eisler (2007), conventional economic theories, policies and practices give only scant attention to important human actions such as caring and loving, simply because they cannot be monetized. Eisler argues that a radical orientation of economic policies is urgently needed, policies that give primacy of place to the economics of caregiving, empathy and loving. In fact, for Eisler, our survival in the next century depends on such reorientation. Such economics of happiness, as Anielski (2007) puts it, takes into consideration human feelings, emotions, loyalty and care for oneself, one's community and also one's environment.

Conclusion

This chapter served as a general introduction to the third part of this research work, which is based on emancipatory critique. I introduced feminism and critical theory as my emancipatory research critique methodologies. The central concept of feminism and critical theory was described as giving voice to the marginalized, which in my context includes not just women but also the indigenous, cultural, social, political, educational, religious and healing systems. I therefore connected with Yoruba mythology to surface the image of four prominent female orisa, each serving as the archetype of the dynamics of each of the four paxes (4Ps): Moremi (Pax Communis), Yemoja (Pax Spiritus), Oya (Pax Scientia) and

Osun (Pax Economia). I then went on to introduce my co-creative ecosystem, the aim of which is to bring about institutionalized innovative research towards the transformation of my society, guided by the overriding concept of CARE.

Having navigated feminism historically and discussed the relevant theoretical concepts, including the shortcomings, I introduced the theory of communitalism, which will be further developed in the next chapter as expressed institutionally in Ewu community of Edo State, Nigeria. Communitalism builds on feminism to evolve an integral system of emancipatory critique leading to sustainable social transformation. In the next chapter, I will focus on how each of the four aspects of my ecosystem relates to each other to form an integrated method of socio-economic research and innovation: communitalism in action, CARE-ing for the society in an integral and transformative way.

References

Abbott, P. and Wallace, C. (1990). *An introduction to sociology: Feminist perspectives*. London: Routledge.

Ake, C. (1995). *Democracy and development in Africa*. Washington, DC: Brookings Institution Press.

Anielski, M. (2007). *Economics of happiness: Building genuine wealth*. British Columbia: New Society.

Beer, F. (1992). *Women and mystical experience in the Middle Ages*. Suffolk, UK: Boydell Press.

Biko, S. (1987). *I write what I like: A selection of writings*. Portsmouth, NH: Heinemann.

Briley, J. (2011). *Cry freedom: The legendary true story of Steve Biko and the friendship that defied apartheid*. London: Penguin.

Chafetz, J. S. (1990). *Gender equity: An integrated theory of stability and change*. Newbury Park, CA: SAGE.

Chittister, J. D. (1991). *Wisdom distilled from the daily: Living the Rule of St. Benedict today*. New York: HarperCollins.

Cochrane, K. (2010). *Women of revolution: Forty years of feminism*. New York: Guardian Books.

Cudworth, E. (2005). *Developing ecofeminist theory: The complexity of difference*. New York: Palgrave Macmillan.

Dobson, A. (2014). *Listening for democracy: Recognition, representation, reconciliation*. Oxford, UK: Oxford University Press.

Eisler, R. (2007). *The real wealth of nations: Creating a caring economics*. Oakland, CA: Berret-Koehler.

Euba, T. (1986). The human image: Some aspects of Yoruba canons of art and beauty. *Nigeria Magazine* *54*(4): 9.

Fanon, F. (2001). *The wretched of the earth*. London: Penguin.

Fox, M. (2012). *Hildegard of Bingen: A saint for our times: Unleashing her power in the 21st century*. Vancouver: Namaste.

Gruchy, I. de. (2012). *Making all things well: Finding spiritual strength with Julian of Norwich*. Norwich, UK: Canterbury Press.

Harsch, E. (2014). *Thomas Sankara: An African revolutionary*. Athens: Ohio University Press.

Jacobs, A. (1977). *A textbook of West African traditional religion*. Ibadan, Nigeria: Aromolaran.

Jamison, C. (2010). *Finding sanctuary: Monastic steps for everyday life*. London: W&N.

Joseph, C. and Mirza, H. (2012). *Black and postcolonial feminism in new times*. London: Routledge.

Lessem, R. and Schieffer, A. (2015). *Integral renewal: A relational and renewal perspective*. Farnham, UK: Gower.

Lionnet, F. (1995). *Postcolonial representations: Women, literature, identity*. Ithaca, NY: Cornell University Press.

Maddocks, F. (2013). *Hildegard of Bingen: The woman of her age*. London: Faber and Faber.

Mamukwa, E., Lessem, R. and Schieffer, A. (2014). *Integral green Zimbabwe: An African phoenix rising*. London: Routledge.

Mazrui, A. (1986). *The Africans: A triple heritage*. London: BBC.

McKenzie, P. (1997). *Hail orisha!: Phenomenology of a West African religion in the mid-nineteenth century*. Boston, MA: Brill.

Mies, M. and Shiva, V. (2014). *Ecofeminism (Critique. Influence. Change)*. London: Zed Books.

Nkrumah, K. (1970). *Conscientism*. New York: Monthly Review Press.

Nwoko, D. (1979). Basic elements of aesthetic experience. *New Culture* 1(3): 3–5.

Nyerere, J. (1979). *Crusade for liberation*. Tanzania: Oxford University Press.

Otero, S. and Falola, T. (2014). *Yemoja: Gender, sexuality, and creativity in the Latino and Afro-Atlantic diasporas*. Albany: State University of New York Press.

Ragan, K. (2000). *Fearless girls, wise women and beloved sisters: Heroines in folktales from around the world*. London: W. W. Norton.

Ruether, R. (2007). *Feminist theologies: Legacy and prospect*. Minneapolis, MN: Fortress Press.

Rule of St Benedict. (1980). Trans. Fry, T. Collegeville, MN: Liturgical Press.

Sankara, T. (2007). *Women's liberation and the African freedom struggle*. Atlanta: Pathfinder.

Schipperges, H. (1997). *Hildegard von Bingen: Healing and the nature of cosmos*. Princeton, NJ: Markus.

Senghor, L. (1964). *On African socialism*. Santa Barbara, CA: Praeger.

Shepherd, L. (2007). *Lifting the veil: The feminine face of science*. Lincoln, NE: iUniverse.

Sofola, J. (1978). *African culture and the African personality*. Accra, Ghana: African Resource.

Turner, D. (2011). *Julian of Norwich, theologian*. London: Yale University Press.

Upjohn, S. (1989). *In search of Julian of Norwich*. London: Darton, Longman and Todd.

Walters, M. (2005). *Feminism: A very short introduction*. New York: Oxford University Press.

Warren, K. (2009). *An unconventional history of western philosophy: Conversations between men and women philosophers*. Lanham, MD: Rowman and Littlefield.

Williams, R. (2010). *Keywords: A vocabulary of culture and society*. London: Fourth Estate.

Woods, T. (2012). *How the Catholic Church built western civilization*. Washington, DC: Regnery.

Woodson, C. (2010). *The mis-education of the Negro*. London: CreateSpace.

7 Towards a true Pax Africana

Communitalism as an approach to health, community and enterprise in Ewu, Edo State, Nigeria

Introduction

The previous chapter focused on research methodology. I introduced feminism as my emancipatory research critique, based on my southern relational path. I discussed the evolution of feminist thought from its indigenous origination via, in my case, the Yoruba orisa, and then through the Middle Ages and to modern times. I introduced Benedictine feminism as well as colonial, postcolonial and African feminism as the exogenous background to my theory of communitalism. Communitalism, as I defined it, is an approach to sustainable and integral development in Africa, set within a particular African society, that builds up from nature and community, embracing culture, politics, economics, spirituality and enterprise. I discussed the indigenous as well as the exogenous evolution of communitalism by looking at feminism as inspired by Christianity and Benedictine monasticism.

I built my theory of communitalism on the four paxes (4Ps), nicknamed Pax Africana: Communis (Community), Spiritus (Sanctuary), Scientia (University) and Economia (Laboratory). This is a distinctly feminism perspective in an African context, which can be described as philosophy-in-practise, research-to-innovation or transformative education-to-enterprise, grounded on indigenous Yoruba core images of the four female orisa, each representing the different dimensions of pax. In this chapter, I will discuss the theory of communitalism in action, as it is applied through the institutions emerging from each of the 4Ps.

The grand failure: why western theories failed in Africa

The failure of most theories or policies is that they are often not founded and grounded on indigenous core images and culture (Lessem, Muchineripi and Kada, 2012). Western-style democracy, capitalism, socialism, communism and neo-liberalism are in fact products of their respective cultures. Most often, new theories from the North are globalized and then imposed unilaterally on weaker and poorer nations without any regard for existing traditions and cultures. According to Ake (1995), this neglect of existing traditions and culture is responsible for why development, political and economic strategies failed in Africa.

Culture, nature and community have been largely ignored in development, economic and political policies in Africa. African culture has fiercely resisted and threatened every project that fails to come to terms with it, even as it is acted upon and changed (Ake, 1995). The more the resistance of African culture became evident, the more the agents of development and economic policies treated it with hostility; and soon enough, they construed everything traditional, including the rural people, nega- tively. They castigated peasants for being bound to tradition, for being conservative and suspicious of change, for being irrational, unenterprising, superstitious and too subjective and emotional in their attitudes. The impression was given that Africans, particularly the rural people, are, by virtue of being themselves, enemies of progress, including their own progress.

Because the development paradigm as well as economic and political policies tends to have a negative view of the people and their culture, the so-called development agents are not able to accept the people on their own terms. Their point of departure, according to Ake, is not what is but what ought to be. The paradigm focuses on the possibility of Africa's becoming what it is not and probably can never be. It discour- ages any belief in the integrity and validity of African societies and offers the notion that African societies can find validity only in their total transformation – that is, their self-alienation.

On a practical level, these policies give credence to the notion that foreign-made goods are better, that foreign experts know better and that the major business of Africa, indeed the only business, is catching up with industrialized nations (Chinweizu, 1975). This research work argues that a Pax Africana, grounded in the communitalist perspective introduced in the last chapter, offers a better approach to integral development in Nigeria.

The term 'communitalism' is different from 'communalism' or, indeed, 'commu- nism'. Communitalism affirms that some aspects of capitalism, such as individual inventiveness, are worth pursuing and supporting, but such inventiveness must be put at the service of the community so that both the individual and the community prosper. The key philosophy of communitalism is 'we are either happy together as a prosperous community or unhappy together' and thereby unprosperous. For com- munitalism, the health and prosperity of the individual cannot be separated from the health and prosperity of the local community. Global health must newly start from the global south, so to speak, re-searching local health, not the other way round. In the process the link between individual, community, enterprise and wholeness, integrally so to speak, will be made.

Although many of us buy and use products from China, for example, capitalism does not ask us to think about the conditions of the workers who make these items. Those committed to communitalism would enquire about these people, not just the products. They would want to know who assembles the products and whether they are being treated fairly. We must think about justice not only for workers in our local communities but also for those who work for other companies and in other countries. Communitalism is a global concept. It requires capitalism to do more: to have a conscience, to care for the environment and for local communities.

Pax Africana: towards an indigenous communitalist theory in Edo State, Nigeria

Once again, we look at the four dimensions of pax as discussed in Chapter 6, and how each of them, building on the indigenous archetype of the Yoruba orisa, is institutionalized in Edo State, Nigeria, through a dynamic indigenous-exogenous, local-global interaction (Table 7.1).

Table 7.1 Pax Africana

Pax Communis South Community activation Orisa: *Moremi*	*Pax Spiritus East* Awakening of consciousness via innovation ecosystem Orisa: *Yemoja*	*Pax Scientia North* Institutionalized research-to-innovation Orisa: Oya	*Pax Economia* West Embodiment via transformative education / enterprise Orisa: Osun
Institution Ewu Development and Educational Multipurpose Cooperative Society (EDEMCS)	Institution St Benedict Monastery, Ewu, Edo State	Institution Africa Centre for Integral Research and Development, Nigeria (ACIRD) Centre for Integral Socio-economic Research, Nigeria (CISER) Trans4m Centre for Integral Development Nigeria Natural Medicine Development Agency (NNMDA) Institute of African Studies, University of Ibadan, Nigeria	Institution Pax Herbal Clinic and Research Laboratories

Ewu development and educational multipurpose cooperative society

In the last chapter, I introduced the Ewu local village cooperative association thus:

> From the small group of local farmers who are passionate about development emerged a group called *Ewu Development Educational Multipurpose Cooperative Society* (EDEMCS), whose goal and objective are, among others, to explore the potentials inherent in the local community and build on it. The distinguishing feature of EDEMCS is that the local community is building on their own traditional systems, structure and worldview in order to create a better world for themselves. This bottom-up approach is a key element of sustainable development.

The association cuts across all the villages that make up the Ewu kingdom. EDEMCS aims to identify the key potentials and resources in the local communities so as to develop them in a systematic and strategic way to lead to self-sufficiency, wealth creation and general transformation of the whole community, Edo State and Nigeria at large. The key concepts of EDEMCS are innovation and creativity and the belief that development and wealth can be attained and sustained only when they are grounded in local culture and worldview while open to modern changes.

EDEMCS's sphere of influence covers all aspects of the life of the people: agriculture, small business enterprises, skill acquisition, teaching, youth empowerment and business management. Whatever brings development and progress to the community is of special interest to the association. The motto of EDEMCS is 'United we stand. Divided we fall.'

The executive membership of the association comprises five elected representatives from the seven communities that make up Ewu Kingdom – namely, Eguare, Idunwele,

Ehanlen, Uzogholo, Eko, Ihienwen and Okhiodu. In addition, a group of proactive persons, which include one each from the five elected representatives, were elected to form an executive think tank, whose duty is to think outside the box and propel the association with new ideas, innovative thinking and practical action plans.

The major officials of the association are Rt Hon. David Iyoha, an economist and former speaker of Edo State House of Assembly. David is passionate about community development and brings the young people of Ewu local community together to discuss how to create employment in the community. Vice President Hon. Mukfhar, a member of the Ewu youth association, has a master's degree in community development. Mufkar is a politician who believes in letting the people be at the forefront of development. The patron of EDEMCS, His Royal Highness Abdul Rassaq Ojeifo, is the king of Ewu Kingdom, which comprises seven communities, each with a minimum population of twenty thousand. As the traditional ruler, he is the custodian of the community's age-old tradition. A trained lawyer, he is well respected in the community because of his interest in co-evolving the people into a community that is faithful to its tradition and history yet open to the good influence of modernity.

EDEMCS members also comprise many active local women, who are the driving force behind the association. Among them are Esther Otoide, a traditional taxonomist, who is renowned for her ability to identify different species of local herbs and their historical use. It is alarming that the local communities in Ewu and all over Nigeria are fast losing knowledge of the local names of medicinal plants as the old men and women have died, while the young people are heading for the cities. Esther works with other women to collaborate with Paxherbal in documenting the local names of medicinal plants and flora in Ewu and Edo State. Through monthly meetings, the farmers are gaining new insights into traditional farming techniques and its often hidden potentials.

Within EDEMCS are three active subgroups. The youth group comprises mainly artisans: mechanics, electricians, carpenters, hairdressers, artists, painters, musicians, drummers and so forth. The second group is the entrepreneurs, comprising owners of supermarkets, restaurants, drinking joints and market women who sell agricultural products and clothing. The third group is the agricultural group, comprising farmers, both male and female. Mrs Okoloise is head of the female farmers in Ewu community while Chief Idiagi is head of the male farmers. Within the agricultural division of EDEMCS is another subgroup called the Ewu Association of Medicinal Plants Cultivators. They specialize in growing medicinal plants for the Paxherbal factory, a good example of Pax Communis integrating with Pax Economia. This is part of the key tenets of feminist emancipation, which ensures that the local communities are involved in both production and marketing processes and see the enterprise as their own rather than as a foreign entity in the community.

St Benedict Monastery as an institutionalized expression of 'sanctuary'

Pax Spiritus refers to the spiritual, more-than-human aspect of the theory of communitalism. An exploration of the core Yoruba images connects us to the origination of the indigenous concept of Pax Spiritus, symbolized by Yemoja, the orisa of the sea, as one of the foundations of communitalism. Communitalism resonates with Eisler's (2007) concepts of the need to consider values such as good character, orderliness, housekeeping, community living and honesty as capitals, which should be taken into account in financial reporting and strategies. We refer to this perspective, in terms of Pax Spiritus, as bringing the 'sanctuary' into daily secular life.

In Chapter 2, I explained why I opted to join the St Benedict Monastery in Ewu, Edo State. I joined the monastery with the hope that it would help me to unravel the mystery of life and death. In other words, I was searching for a deeper meaning in life, beyond the struggle for power, wealth, prestige and material comfort. Monasteries have played this role of providing a model of an alternative way of life over many centuries. The St Benedict Monastery in Ewu, Edo State, has established itself as a model of how to bring nature, community and enterprise together integrally, for the benefit of all. In faithfulness to the Benedictine motto of work and prayer, the Benedictine monks have been able to maintain a balance between work as part of God's creative work and prayer as being at one with God, with nature, with the community and with oneself.

Pax Scientia: ACIRD as an institutionalized expression of 'university'

The *Africa Centre for Integral Research and Development* (ACIRD), nicknamed Pax Africana, is an evolution of Paxherbal from an organization which deals mainly with traditional medicine as an alternative and complementary practise to allopathic medicine to Pax Africana, a centre that explores healing beyond biological or physical health to integral healing. For centuries, we were a people spoken about, spoken for and spoken against by foreigners. We read about who we are from what others said and wrote about us. ACIRD seeks to assert the right of Africans to speak in their own language and metaphors. We must reclaim our right to cognitive freedom if we truly seek to be free. Africa must be aware of, and fight against the coloniality of knowledge and epistemicide, which are modern forms of colonization, by evolving and educing its own research methods and research methodologies suited to and geared towards African epistemological emancipation. To this effect, ACIRD is on the way to becoming a serious and genuine research-to-innovation centre, a university that will set new models for an Afrocentric education, in partnership with other integral research communities across Africa.

The journey to genuine freedom begins only when Africa takes control of her educational apparatus, the administration, curricula and systems of knowledge creation. Communitalism, an indigenous theory of knowledge creation in Africa, embracing CARE-ing for self, community and society through ACIRD, hopes to set new templates for doing research in and for Africa. The starting point, of course, is to unravel the missing depths, thereby reconnecting, based on our cosmologies, with our original foundation stories.

The liberating power of story

It could be argued that modern men and women are gradually losing the ability to tell and retell their stories in a liberating way. For American priest and theologian John Dunne (1972), story is the tool by which we pass over from one life to the other and then come back to rediscover ourselves.

Storytelling is not just a past-time in African societies. Storytelling is a means of gaining self-knowledge and self-identity. In times of crisis and doubt, stories help to reconnect one with one's origin and ultimate meaning. Every person has a story. To be alive is to have a story. Just as each of us has a story, so does the universe have its own story. The plants, animals and the entire cosmic system all have their own peculiar stories. Myth, in its original sense of *mythos*, means a tale, a story, a narrative (Dunne, 1973).

What story are you?

In Chapter 2 I narrated the story of my inner and outer calls. For me, telling my story is not just an intellectual exercise. The very act of telling the story itself is creative, recreative and liberating. Storytelling is a healing art. Canadian author William Randall (2014) explains how each of us strives to find meaning in life through the different categories of storytelling, such as plot, character, conflict and style. By weaving these categories into our own life stories, we simultaneously play the role of storyteller, listener, actor and reader. As an individual, it is not just the stories I tell about myself that affect the shape and direction of my self-creation, but also the stories others tell about me. These stories help to create the social climate in which my life is lived and determine the range of options and opportunities by which it is bound. Insofar as I am a social being, what others say about me is as important as what I say about myself. In other words, I cannot separate *my* story from the story of my community.

Randall (2014) identifies four layers or levels of storytelling – namely: existence, experience, expression and impression.

- *Existence*: This is the outside story. This refers to the story of my life as an individual with a past. The story of my life at this level is simply the sum total of everything I have ever done, said, thought or felt, in all the different dimensions of my life: the verbal, the emotional, the intellectual, the interpersonal, the conscious, the unconscious, the behavioural and the physical, even the biochemical, the molecular and the atomic. It is the story of my every saying and every cell, every movement and every molecule, every embrace and every breath. It is my story, my life in the sense of the facts.
- *Experience*: This is referred to as the inside story. On this level of experience, the whole story of my life becomes accessible to me. It becomes accessible not as a story in itself but only as it is taken up within me and interpreted by me. It is my autobiography. It is my inner story as I can remember and narrate it. Insofar as it depends on my memory, my inside story is partial and does not embody the whole of my reality. My inner story is not the sum total of what actually happened but only of my memories or impressions of it, of events I have personally experienced. My inside story is my understanding and interpretation of my outside story.
- *Expression*: This next level is called the inside-out story. This refers to the version of my inside story that I convey to the outside world. It is my story, my life, in the sense of what I present or project to the world, as it *emerges* from me.
- *Impression*: The fourth level is called the outside-in story. It refers to the stories that are 'read' into my life by those who know me or encounter me in any way. It is my life in the sense of what others have made of me. In short, my outside-in story is my biography, much in the same way that my inside-out story is my autobiography.

The story I am becoming

In terms of Randall's fourfold levels of storytelling, cognitive liberation involves liberating the individual human mind. For me, this liberation is expressed in the ability to connect with the multifaceted story of my life, to understand, embrace and retell my story.

For Randall (2014), the stories we tell ourselves determine the story we are and the stories we will become. They are based on what we know of ourselves and what others say about us. If the story of Africa is told by a non-African, such a story will reflect and will in fact be conditioned by the epistemological mode of the narrator, who will storytype (stereotype) the narratives based on his intention and motive.

The issue of epistemological emancipation is of utmost importance in the study of African history. As a child, my favourite song was 'Amazing Grace', described as one of the world's most loved and famous songs. 'Amazing Grace' is a testimony to the fierce evangelical fervour and piety of nineteenth-century Europe:

> *Amazing Grace,*
> *How sweet the sound,*
> *That saved a wretch like me.*
> *I once was lost, but now am found,*
> *Was blind but now I see.*

Paradoxically, the 'Amazing Grace' century was also the golden age of colonialism as a profitable business venture, an age when the whole of Africa fell under complete domination and control of the European powers, especially Britain. The composer of that popular song, John Newton, was a British evangelical pastor who, shortly after his conversion and the spiritual experience which inspired the composition of that song, became a full-time slave trader (Ferguson, 2004). For six years he shipped thousands of Africans, with intense brutality, across the Atlantic from Sierra Leone to the Caribbean without any qualm of conscience, and made huge profits from his exploits. The implicit foundation of the slave trade is the conviction that Africans were inferior to Europeans. European slavers were so brutal because they did not consider Africans humans.

My history teachers did not tell me about the exploits of Newton probably because they also did not know. And why did they not know? Because their history curriculum did not feature that aspect of African history. As African children, our history teachers told us about one evil man called Hitler, who killed six million Jews. It was part of our history curriculum to learn about Hitler. As an adult, I later read about one King Leopold II of Belgium, who was the sole owner of the colony of the Congo, a country rich in vegetation, especially rubber, and three times bigger than Belgium. King Leopold managed the vast African country of over fifty million people like a private empire, subjecting the whole population to brutal slavery. King Leopold was responsible for the death of 10–15 million Congolese people, and made a huge fortune from exploitation of rubber from the Congo. King Leopold was in fact a 'good Catholic', and was given a very Catholic burial, attended by bishops and church elites. To crown it all, he was buried in a royal crypt under a Catholic church near the royal palace in Laeken, Brussels, initially built by his father Leopold I as a mausoleum for his wife, Queen Louise-Marie (Hochschild, 1999).

Why is a man who killed six million Jews called 'evil' and known all over Africa, and it was part of our history curriculum to learn about him, while a man who killed 10–15 million Congolese people is not called 'evil' and his story of greed and brutality is completely excluded from our history curriculum? The answer, of course, lies in who tells the story.

The storyteller decides the cast, arranges the scene and decides which scenes to leave out. For Africans, economic freedom and social freedom are not enough. Contrary to what Ake (1995) opined, political freedom is not even enough. The most important freedom, in my view, is cognitive freedom. Cognitive freedom is the freedom of Africans to tell their own stories based on their own experiences, so as to understand the present in light of the past. Africans must *own* the story they tell, and take control of telling it in their own language and metaphors. We need cognitive freedom to help us resist the danger of being storytyped again, as our ancestors were. This is what ACIRD, as an institutionalized entity, a knowledge-creating university, sets out to do.

This research work argues that the path to emancipation in today's Africa is for the common people of Africa to free themselves from their own leaders. African leaders, from Zimbabwe to Uganda, Cameroon, Liberia, Burundi, Togo, Nigeria, Ivory coast, Senegal to Benin Republic, Kenya and the Democratic Republic of Congo, to mention a few, have obviously betrayed the trust of their people. They have succeeded in amassing state wealth to their own private pockets and lacked the will, skill and sincerity to govern and transform their countries. It is therefore obvious that Africans should not expect much from their leaders, and must now learn to free themselves from the greed of their leaders. The challenge for today's Africans, then, is for the commons, the majority of the people, to free themselves from their own leaders. Civil wars or violent protests, as we saw in the so-called Tunisian and Egyptian uprisings, cannot make this happen. This research work posits that a more systematic approach that evolves from the ground up, naturally and culturally, technologically and economically, within a functional polity (in our case Ewu, Edo State, Nigeria), through the CARE model, is a more efficient and sustainable way to transform Africa, thereby setting an example for the rest of the world.

Paxherbal as an institutionalized expression of an indigenous-exogenous knowledge enterprise: the 'laboratory'

Paxherbal is built on the core image of the Yoruba archetype of enterprise and adventure (Osun), in terms of origination. From origination, it is further consolidated by its foundation on Christian and monastic principles. It was indeed not easy for the company to find its feet at the beginning. The first task was to change the negative perception of traditional medicine from that of a fetish, old-fashioned and 'pagan' practise to a local-global enterprise with huge developmental potential. Paxherbal is regarded in Edo State and beyond as a model of an integrated rural enterprise and an industry leader, about which the local community and the monastic community are very proud.

Communitalism: bringing all together

We have indeed gone far, having embarked on an intellectual, cultural and spiritual odyssey, touching base with the ancestors, whom Mazrui (1986) described as very angry – angry because they have been abandoned by their prodigal children in favour of foreign gods. The foreign gods, of course, include materialism, consumerism, neo-liberalism and preference for a western way of life over a traditional way of life. Africa's romance with the so-called foreign gods has been disastrous, despite the obvious benefits, such as globalization, education and modernization. However, for Chinweizu (1975), these 'benefits' are in reality the very tools by which Africans are being enslaved.

There is no shortage of criticism or works detailing, often with intense bitterness, the evils of colonization and western imperialism (Said, 1994; Fanon, 2001; Thiong'o, 2011; Afrika, 2013). This research work takes a more systematic approach by looking at the imbalances in the society, focusing on a particular community in Edo State and proposing solutions. This led to the theory of communitalism, a theory built on the four dimensions of pax: Communis, Spiritus, Scientia and Economia. The four paxes taken together, Pax Africana, express the integral nature of life. Each of the four paxes is associated with a female orisa and their attributes, as shown in Figure 7.1.

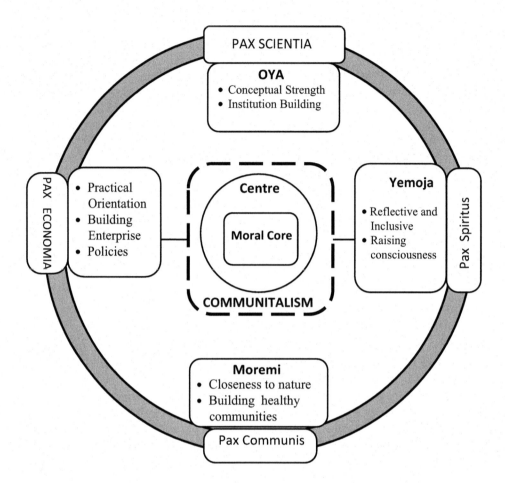

Figure 7.1 Yoruba orisa and the 4Ps (adapted from Lessem and Schieffer, 2010)

The four pax dimensions are brought together as a community of knowledge, bridging the gap between community, spirit, nature and reason. As previously indicated, a disintegrated way of knowledge production is characteristic of a conventional Mode 1 university (Etzkowitz and Leydesdorff, 2002; King, 2003). The chief characteristic of Mode 1 of knowledge production is its preoccupation with fundamental research with little or no interest in the application of the knowledge. Mode 1 universities are built on the concept of research as an objective search for truth, independent of nature, community and the environment. Gibbons, Limoges, Nowotny, Schwartzman, Scott and Trow (1994) have argued for a return to the Mode 2 way of knowledge production, which is interdisciplinary. It is a return because Mode 2, or a context-driven method of research, was the dominant way of knowledge creation until the nineteenth century (Nowotny, Scott and Gibbons, 2001).

ACIRD: towards context-driven research

In terms of research-to-innovation and knowledge production, we now turn specifically to ACIRD and its *communitalist* research perspective. The focus of ACIRD is the generation of community-based knowledge through Pax Africana (the four paxes). The local community was activated and motivated, through ACIRD, to form associations and cooperatives, which meet regularly to share ideas, analyse situations, conditions and challenges and proffer systematic solutions. The existing knowledge sharing system in the local community ensures that traditions and customs are preserved through storytelling, myths and folklore.

This chapter is replete with such examples of storytelling as a means of knowledge creation and knowledge sharing in the local community. The community development association, EDEMCS, is specifically formed to introduce an emancipatory, methodological if not political system into knowledge creation and knowledge sharing in the community. This is important to ensure that the community does not stagnate in past cultures and traditions, but is open to the continuous creative and dynamic interaction between tradition and modernity, individual and community, the indigenous and the exogenous. Such trans- and interdisciplinary interaction is the unique strength of the communitalist process of knowledge creation, leading to a true Pax Scientia.

Another characteristic of our university, within the context of ACIRD and the Ewu community, is the embrace of the spiritual, which we call the 'sanctuary'. Efforts of our so-called modern intellectuals to remove the sanctuary from the university have not been successful (Butler, Habermas, Taylor and West, 2011; Calhoun, Juergensmeyer and VanAntwerpen, 2011). Separating the spiritual from the secular is as absurd as separating teaching from research (Fuller, 2000). However, the greatest challenge for Nigeria is perhaps the ability to maintain a creative balance between piety, which is often mistaken for being spiritual, and science. The spiritual, within the context of Pax Spiritus, is not about going to church or external religious rituals. Such religiosity shares all the features of secularism, with an added slant of hypocrisy to it. The Nigerian political, economic and social space is thus occupied by such religiosity, which is often bereft of morality, or *iwa* – good character. This explains why despite the fact that churches are springing up everywhere and in every corner in Nigeria, antisocial activities, such as crime, theft and robberies as well as corruption, are also on the increase. Once religion loses touch with community (Communis) and with reason (Scientia), the result can be disastrous, as I expressed in Chapter 4:

> Excessive religionism and spiritualism may be one of the greatest obstacles to the progress of African nations. In addition, the greatest challenge facing Africa today is her ability to cultivate a mindset steeped in chemistry, mathematics and physics while still maintaining a reasonable and balanced approach to religion.

ACIRD is set up to research the relationship between nature, community and science, and their impact in the socio-economic development of the society. In this way, we overcome imbalanced worldviews (transcultural), alleviate disciplinary imbalances (transdisciplinary), unravel missing depths (transformational) and transcend individual overemphasis (transpersonal). Looking at the integral CARE model (CARE-ing for self and society) within the integral research system and the concept of integral health or healing in this research work, ACIRD serves as the institutionalized research-to-innovation centre. It will continue to evolve, research and conceptualize the theories of communitalism, integral healing, integral CARE and integral enterprise, all emerging from Ewu in Edo State, Nigeria, and evolving to embrace other centres in Nigeria, Africa and other parts of the world.

Conclusion

As stated in Chapter 1, the guiding question for this research work is to explore how the issues of indigenous-exogenous knowledge and value creation addressed by Paxherbal in the Ewu Village of Edo State can be focused on more widely in Nigeria, Africa and more generally in the wider world. How, specifically, could such a business, community health and social innovation be contextualized, evolved and conceptualized and thereafter be more widely and universally applied?

The issues of evolution and origination of the question were discussed in the first part, which is the first C (Call) of the four Cs. Contextualization, which is the second C (Context), was discussed in the second part. The last two chapters focused on the third C (Co-creation). As I stated in Chapter 1, co-creation means

> that one transcends the limitations of one's particular cultural context, and embarks on a transcultural journey through an exploration of research-to-innovation methods, existing theories and literatures. The guiding research question at this stage is, 'How can research and development be designed in such a way that they lead to social and technological innovation?' Such co-creation is significant in two ways. First, the relationship between academics and students is transformed into one of mutual co-creation, not to mention also the relationship between fellow researchers as co-creators across Africa. Second, the division between research method (methodology) and research work content (literature) is co-creatively transcended.

The two chapters on co-creation employed feminism as the emancipatory critique, with the objective of developing new theories, concepts and innovation techniques that will have a tangible and visible impact on the society. Rather than imposing global concepts and theories on local settings, which hitherto have been the trend, I joined voices with Lessem et al. (2012) to follow a local-global approach to theory building and activation.

Both Christianity and Islam, but most especially Christianity, waged a successful war against the traditional gods with iconoclastic fervour. The results are that traditional religions, practices, rituals and symbols were subjugated in favour of the imported ones. What is most evident on the surface in today's African societies, then, are not traditional sacred shrines, traditional religious monuments or traditional festivals. On the contrary, what we see are imposing churches and mosques, huge billboards advertising Christian religious crusades and flamboyant Christian evangelists on national television screens. In fact, there is a national church and national mosque built by the Nigerian government in Abuja, Nigeria's capital, as tribute to Nigeria's two major religions: Islam and Christianity. In this case, one can indeed question if Mazrui's 'African triple heritage' (1986), which refers to Islam, Christianity and traditional religion, is still valid today.

Having come to the conclusion of the fourth part of this research-to-innovation work, we now move on to the Part 5, which deals with contribution and transformation brought about by the four institutions, this time via ACIRD, towards the consolidation of an integral university in and for Africa. Indeed, the journey to a true Pax Africana has started.

References

Afrika, L. (2013). *Nutricide: The nutritional destruction of the black race.* Buffalo, NY: Eworld, Inc.
Ake, C. (1995). *Democracy and development in Africa.* Washington, DC: Brookings Institution Press.
Butler, J., Habermas, J., Taylor, C. and West, C. (2011). *The power of religion in the public sphere.* New York: Columbia University Press.

Calhoun, C., Juergensmeyer, M. and VanAntwerpen, J. (2011). *Rethinking secularism*. New York: Oxford University Press.

Chinweizu. (1975). *The West and the rest of us: White predators, black slavers, and the African Elite*. London: Random House.

Dunne, J. S. (1972). *The way of all the earth: Experiments in truth and religion*. New York: Macmillan.

Dunne, J. S. (1973). *Time and myth: A meditation on storytelling as an exploration of life and death*. New York: Doubleday.

Eisler, R. (2007). *The real wealth of nations: Creating a caring economics*. Oakland, CA: Berret-Koehler.

Etzkowitz, H. and Leydesdorff, L. (2002). *Universities and the global knowledge economy NIP: A triple helix of university-industry-government relations (science, technology and the international political economy)*. London: Continuum International.

Fanon, F. (2001). *The wretched of the earth*. London: Penguin.

Ferguson, N. (2004). *Empire: How Britain made the modern world*. London: Penguin Books.

Fuller, S. (2000). *The governance of science*. Buckingham: Open University Press.

Gibbons, M., Limoges, C., Nowotny, H., Schwartzman, S., Scott, P. and Trow, M. (1994). *The new production of knowledge: The dynamics of science and research in contemporary societies*. London: SAGE.

Hochschild, A. (1999). *King Leopold's ghost*. New York: First Mariner.

King, R. (2003). *The university in the Golden Age*. New York: Palgrave Macmillan.

Lessem, R., Muchineripi, P. and Kada, S. (2012). *Integral community: Political economy to social commons*. Farnham, UK: Gower.

Lessem, R. and Schieffer, A. (2010). *Integral research and innovation: Transforming enterprise and society*. Farnham, UK: Gower.

Mazrui, A. (1986). *The Africans: A triple heritage*. London: BBC.

Nowotny, H., Scott, P. and Gibbons, M. (2001). *Re-thinking science: Knowledge and the public in an age of uncertainty*. Cambridge, UK: Polity Press.

Randall, W. (2014). *The stories we are: An essay on self-creation*. Toronto: Toronto University Press.

Said, E. (1994). *Culture and imperialism*. London: Vintage.

wa Thiong'o, N. (2011). *Decolonising the mind: The politics of language in African literature*. Suffolk, UK: James Curry.

Part V

Contribution and transformation

If you think you are too small to make a difference, you haven't spent the night with a mosquito.
—*African proverb*

8 Participatory action research in an African context

The case of Ewu village, Edo State, Nigeria

Introduction

We now come to the fifth part of this research work, having journeyed through the integral research odyssey from Call to Context and Co-creation, and now to Contribution and Transformation. The uniqueness of the integral journey lies in its transformative, emancipatory and liberating quality. An integral PhD, according to Lessem and Schieffer (2010), should be not just an academic exercise but also a process of holistic development (PHD). The previous two chapters, jointly forming the part of co-creation, focused on my emancipatory critique along the relational research path. I applied the tenets of feminism as my critical methodology or research critique, beginning with an exploration of the Yoruba orisa mythology as the origination of indigenous feminist theory in my context. From there I explored feminism from the Christian religious perspective and monastic perspective and then secular feminism, colonial, postcolonial and modern African feminism. One consistent trend linking feminism in its various forms is the focus on liberation and emancipation. As I emphasized in the last two chapters, feminism aims to give voice to the marginalized and liberate the oppressed. I stressed the fact that an option for the weak and the oppressed has been an enduring part of the human struggle since the beginning of human civilization. It is therefore important not to limit the feminist perspective to the modern world. Feminism goes further back in human history.

My critique of feminism surfaced some of the limitations of existing theories, such as capitalism, socialism and communism, and how Africa has been a testing ground for such western theories imposed from outside. Such imposition of concepts and ideas are not only demeaning but also unsustainable and, according to my analysis and observations, serve only the selfish interests of the elite. One of the major defects of such exogenous theories is that they are not built on nature and community, and are not related to the people's culture and worldview. What is the way forward? Violent revolutions? Guerrilla warfare? Civil wars? History has shown that none of these has really produced sustainable outcomes. One of the arguments of this research work is the need to have a southern theory to serve as an alternative to the conventional theories. The majority of African intellectuals and activists, while criticizing existing theories, often do not provide alternative theories to correct the prevalent inadequacies entrenched in conventional social, political and economic systems.

Moghalu (2013) advocates a worldview-based approach to economics in Africa, by which Africans will pursue economic policies based on the worldview of Africans. However, he does not outline how this is to be done in any systematic way. Akhaine (2015) is also heavy on criticism of the World Bank, International Monetary Fund (IMF) and so on, but equally falls short of proposing any concrete and methodical alternative model. In this research work, I have proposed such an alternative model, which can be further developed by other researchers.

I proposed the theory of communitalism as a more indigenous, sustainable and integral approach to tackling the social, political, economic and developmental challenges of today's Africa. Such a communitalist perspective, also called Pax Africana, built on the four paxes (4Ps), addressed the four key dimensions of development, which I termed Community (Communis), Sanctuary (Spiritus), University (Scientia) and Laboratory (Economia). In Chapter 7, I described how the 4Ps are expressed concretely in Ewu rural community of Edo State, Nigeria, through four corresponding local institutions – namely, EDEMCS for Pax Communis, St Benedict Monastery for Pax Spiritus, ACIRD for Pax Scientia and Paxherbal for Pax Economia.

In this part, I describe how the application of communitalism, as expressed through the 4Ps, transforms the lives of the local community and Nigerian society. I will also describe what contribution the theory of communitalism is and will continue to make, not just to the local community in Edo State and Nigeria but also to Africa as a whole. Because of the complexity and dynamism of the 4Ps, I will employ two types of transformative action-research methodologies: participatory action research (PAR) and cooperative inquiry (CI). In this chapter, I shall focus on PAR, while CI is introduced in the following chapter. I begin with a brief introduction to action research in general.

Action research: working with and for people

Although the action research method in its modern western guise is attributed to American psychologist Kurt Lewin (1948), its origin goes far back in human intellectual history. Action research simply means what the term suggests: research-in-action, psychomotor research or researching and doing. Action research aims to move beyond the dichotomy between doing and thinking, between working and studying to balance problem solving with problem analysis. Action research challenges the tendency of conventional social science to arrogate to itself the ability to reflect on things and people and take this as the status quo for all cultures. It also challenges the dichotomy often created between action and research.

The dichotomy can be traced as far back as the Greek division between praxis (action) and theoria (research) (Waterfield, 1996; Barnes, 2001). Greek thinking tended to treat praxis and theoria as two separate, even opposing ways of life, each occupying separate positions on a hierarchical social status. In fact, the two most prominent Greek philosophers, Plato and Aristotle, saw theoria as the superior way of life, reserved for the intellectually refined and cultured members of society, the philosophers and kings, who are closer to the divine than the rest of the people (Barnes, 2000; Annas, 2003). Theoria involved contemplation on eternal principles, a detached focus on essential, intangible principles of the universe. Praxis, by contrast, was concerned with human affairs and the temporal and mundane things of the world. The preoccupation of praxis was said to be such that it contributed nothing of significance for the universe as a whole (Emery, 1996).

This dichotomy, imported from Greek thought, introduced an unhealthy dualism into Christian thinking, an influence which persisted until the late Middle Ages. It contrasted with the traditional biblical Jewish way of thinking, which conceived action and research as two sides of the same coin (Waterfield, 1996). The dichotomy later found expression in the monastic movement, with its emphasis on 'abandoning the world' and developing distaste for the things of the world. The things of the world included politics and economy. The monk became a symbol of theoria, one who is utterly detached from the world of praxis in order to focus on the superior life of contemplation on the eternal principles, on the Divine. So pervasive was the dichotomy that even within the monastic walls in the Middle Ages, a distinction was made between the 'choir monks' and the lay monks or working monks. The choir monks were known as the special ones, usually ordained priests, whose main work was the celebration of the sacred liturgy: the daily celebration of Mass, sacred chants and praying for 'the world'. The working monks or lay monks were non-ordained and occupied a lower rank in importance. Their work required preoccupation with mundane things – that is, praxis rather than theoria (Natou, Bonazzi and Benatouil, 2012).

It is a paradox that St Benedict, whose *Rule* moulded western monasticism in the Middle Ages up to the present time, would have found this dichotomy strange and contrary to the spirit of his *Rule*. In fact, one of the major goals that St Benedict, himself a non-ordained or lay monk, set out to achieve in his *Rule* was the eradication of this dichotomy between theoria and praxis (Clark, 2011). For Benedict, 'oratio' (prayer) and 'labora' (work) are important and complementary aspects of the monastic life. Prayer is not work and work is not prayer. Rather, prayer is prayer and work is work, and both form an integral, co-creative whole. This integral combination of oratio and labora is one unique characteristic of St Benedict Monastery, Ewu, Edo State, as reflected in a balanced interconnection of Communis (Community), Spiritus (Sanctuary), Scientia (University) and Economia (Laboratory). For St Benedict, this healthy balance is the virtue of moderation.

In the nineteenth and twentieth centuries, thinkers such as Newton (Janniak, 2015), Leibniz (Jolley, 2005) and Kant (2005) contributed in changing the tendency to view theoria as superior to praxis. Modern philosophies such as positivism, historicism, life philosophy and existentialism rejected the view of praxis as inferior to theoria (Scruton, 2001; Lefèvre, 2013). For Dewey (1998), founder of American pragmatism, research or inquiry should not be seen as the human mind or intellect passively observing and analysing the world. Rather, inquiry is a process of interaction between human beings and their environment in which each of them is affected in a symbiotic way (Dewey, 2012). Dewey argues that the Cartesian starting point, where the researcher separates and detaches himself from the world in order to seek objectivity in raising philosophical questions, is the wrong way to start a scientific inquiry. Scientific and philosophic inquiry, according to him, is always shaped by particular cultural contexts, and should feed back into society as part of an ongoing dynamic interaction. We now look at one variation of action research, called participatory action research (PAR).

What is participatory action research?

Participatory action research (PAR) is an action-oriented way of doing research towards the social transformation of a society, which includes the radical engagement of the community itself in defining the research goals and driving as well as owning the research process. It can be described as southern theory insofar as it has its roots in Africa, Latin America and Asia, the so-called neglected or economically weaker regions of the globe. PAR takes its inspiration from a combination of Nyereres's ujamaa socialism in Tanzania, liberation theology and neo-Marxist perspectives, especially in Latin America, and liberal human rights movements in Asia (Lessem and Schieffer, 2015). The distinguishing feature of PAR is that research projects are jointly owned by the community and the researcher.

In addition, the problems to be solved are identified and analysed by the community itself rather than by external experts, while the whole community (Carr and Kemmis, 1986) bases the actions taken on joint decisions.

PAR puts emphasis on communal inquiry and action grounded in experience and the social context of a people. Both the community and co-researchers are thus engaged in a creative movement of interaction geared towards participation (democracy), action (experience and history) and research (critical thinking and knowledge creation) (Chevalier and Buckles, 2013).

According to Baum, MacDougall and Smith (2006), PAR aims at not just understanding the world but also changing it. Its method is directly opposed to Galileo's mathematization of the world, his so-called scientific world, where the real properties of things are those that are measurable and quantifiable (Selener, 1997). In PAR, research is a

> collective, self-reflective inquiry that researchers and participants undertake, so they can understand and improve upon the practices in which they participate and the situations in which they find themselves. The reflective process is directly linked to action, influenced by understanding of history, culture, and local context and embedded in social relationships.
>
> (Baum et al., 2006, p. 854)

PAR aims to redefine democracy as power returning to the people rather than being lodged in the hands of the ruling elite. This inevitably leads to challenging the status quo, and confronting existing unjust structures (McNiff, 2013). The process of PAR is empowering the people and leading them to have increased control over their lives. Unlike conventional research, action in PAR 'is achieved through a reflective cycle, whereby participants collect and analyse data, then determine what action should follow. The resultant action is then further researched and an iterative reflective cycle perpetuates data collection, reflection, and action' (Baum et al., 2006, p. 854). The dynamic nature of PAR ensures that data and information are not removed from their contexts as often happens in conventional methods of research (Bessette, 2004; Reagan, 2004).

Participatory action research and its tenets

Lessem and Schieffer (2015, p. 171) summarized the tenets of PAR as shown in Table 8.1.

Both PAR and CI focus on action leading to research, or research-to-innovation in integral terms. The distinctive feature of PAR is that it involves animating a whole community at the periphery, and awakens in them the consciousness of their abilities, rights and power to change the course of events. As I argued in Chapter 6, one key path to emancipation in Africa is for the common people to challenge the status quo and the ruling elite, and free themselves from unjust social structure that puts them at perpetual disadvantage. Communitalism offers a methodical and peaceful way to do this as opposed to violent activism, which, as history has shown, hardly ever results in sustainable change.

According to Lessem and Schieffer (2015, p. 172),

> People then cannot be liberated by a consciousness and knowledge other than their own. It is therefore essential that people develop their own indigenous consciousness-raising and knowledge generation, and this requires the social power to assert this. The

Table 8.1 PAR tenets

The problem is defined, analysed and solved by the community, involving its full and **active participation** through **relational education.**

You are a committed participant, facilitator and learner in such, promoting an authentic **analysis of social reality.**

PAR creates awareness of the **people's own resources**, mobilizing the **freedom to be enterprising** for self-reliant community development.

The ultimate goal is the radical **transformation of social reality**, aimed at the exploited, the poor, the oppressed, the marginal.

---

scientific character or objectivity of knowledge rests on its social verifiability, and this depends on consensus as to the method of verification. All scientific knowledge is relative to the paradigm to which it belongs, and the verification system to which it is submitted. An immediate objective of PAR is to return to the people the control over their own verification systems.

It is not enough to engage in education. The structure of the education itself has to be examined and questioned. It is not enough to study scientific truths; how science arrived at such 'truths' has to be questioned. Science does not exist independently of its cultural context, despite its pretence to undiluted objectivity (Warren, Slikkerveer and Brokensha, 1995). While education can bring liberation, it can also be a means of keeping people in bondage. This theme has been well articulated by Freire (1970), de Sousa Santos (2014), Fanon (2008) and Chinweizu (1975). Education is what makes the difference between passive submission and active resistance to oppression. We now look at how the tenets of PAR are being applied in Ewu community of Edo State.

Participatory action research in Ewu, Edo State

The origin of the Ewu development association is rooted in this research work and in the cooperative inquiry group of Paxherbal, about which I will speak in detail in the next chapter. In 2014, I met with Rt Hon. David Iyoha, a politician who was a one-time speaker of the Edo State House of Assembly. David hails from Ehanlen, the largest of the seven villages that make up Ewu Kingdom. We discussed the challenges facing the local communities, such as unemployment, poor medical services, overly westernized education that is not rooted in the local culture, and loss of cultural identity. We also observed that there are many potentials in the local community which can be harnessed. We decided to follow a different path of problem solving. David, during his tenure as speaker of the Edo State House of Assembly, had initiated a number of projects which were meant to help the local community. However, the projects were based on a top-down approach to community development, characteristic of most government-sponsored projects. Such an approach, which I have already analysed in this research work, is, in most cases, not rooted in the people's culture and worldview. In addition, it follows the well-worn mentality of doing something for the people rather than engaging the people in a co-creative process of self-development.

Rather than 'doing a project' for the people, we resolved to animate the local community by encouraging the different communities to engage in regular dialogue to identify their challenges, and find a common ground to effectively proffer their own solutions rather than solutions from without. That then laid the foundation for our engagement with PAR at Ewu (Figure 8.1).

Figure 8.1 Participatory action research group with the Ewu king in his palace

Building consensus as part of community building

The first step was to share the idea of forming a local development cooperative with different members of the local community. We met with several individuals in the seven local communities in Ewu Kingdom. In every case, they were excited about being consulted even before an association was formed. They had hitherto been persuaded to join an already formed association, but this time, the idea was to seek their opinion about whether the association was worth forming in the first place. 'What you are doing is the right thing,' said a seventy-year-old woman during one of the meetings in appreciation of the fact that her opinion was being considered. A ninety-year-old man, the oldest (*ukodion*) in his village, told the group as a proverbial expression of support for our consensus-building efforts, 'When a king has good counsellors, his reign is peaceful.'

The next step was to inform the king of Ewu Kingdom, King Ojeifo. He was excited about the idea and contacted the eldest men in each of the seven local communities. This led to the formation of an initial group comprising these eldest men. The tradition in Esanland, as in other African communities, is that elderly men and women are respected and the eldest men and women are accorded special respect and reverence. They are seen as the custodians of traditions in the community. The eldest men are called 'ukodion'. In some communities, they are in their nineties and hundreds. When the eldest man is too old to act, as is the case in two of the communities in Ewu Kingdom, he appoints a younger person to represent him and act on his behalf.

The ukodions know the mindset of their people and are in direct contact with them. Part of their duty includes settling cases or disagreements among families and warring factions. Unlike the modern legal system, where justice means that one party wins and is rewarded while the guilty is punished, thereby creating permanent hatred and animosity, the local elders employ a separate system of justice. They opt for engagement, dialogue and settlement where each party acknowledges its own fault. Thereafter the elders will apportion blame to each party according to the gravity of the blame. The bottom line is that nobody is totally guiltless, and warring parties in a community should always strive for peaceful resolution and not depart as antagonists.

The ukodions are adept in sustaining this traditional justice system. When it is a case of theft where the culprit has been caught, he will be made to acknowledge his guilt, return the stolen goods to the owner and apologize to the victim. Thereafter he is given a penalty, which is often heavy, to serve as deterrence to others.

After a series of meetings and interactions with the elders, they all suggested that the village youth should be invited to join the association. Like the ukodions, each community has a village youth association. The group often elects the head of the association. The leaders of the youth associations in each of the seven villages were contacted, and they were excited to be a part of the emerging association. The village youth have associations of different artisan groups that act as pressure groups and meet from time to time to discuss issues of mutual interest. The associations include an Ewu association of car mechanics, Ewu association of motorcycle mechanics, Ewu association of carpenters, Ewu association of electricians and more. In fact, all artisans have their associations to which one must belong in order to be allowed to practise.

Figure 8.2 Hundreds of local women at an EDEMCS meeting in February 2015

Next were the powerful associations of local women (Figure 8.2). Once again, we contacted the female leaders in each of the seven villages in Ewu Kingdom. There were already in existence various associations, such as a women's farmers association, association of Ewu female traders, cassava sellers association and more. After due consultations, an initial group comprising three representatives, one of whom must be a woman, from each of the seven villages in Ewu Kingdom was formed. The twenty-one-member group would serve as a 'think-and-do-tank' for the emerging association. The group formulated some questions to guide their deliberations. These questions, listed ahead, are products of their own experience and not an imposition from without:

- Are we as a people more prosperous than our elders were ten or twenty years ago?
- Was there any time in our history when our communities lived in prosperity and abundance?
- Are we satisfied with the current socio-economic situations in our communities?
- If no, why and how can we make our lives better socially, economically, communally, politically and spiritually?

EDEMCS: creating awareness, mobilizing freedom to be enterprising in the community

As a researcher, I immersed myself fully into the daily life-world of the local community. I am not just a researcher but also a facilitator and learner. While members of the seven

Figure 8.3 Meeting with local farmers – 'Everybody is important'

villages hold allegiance to the king as their traditional head, relationships among the different communities can often be frosty, as they tend to be suspicious of each other. Bringing members of the seven communities together to discuss issues of mutual interest and agree on a common course of action requires considerable human management skills.

As one who has lived in the local communities for some twenty-nine years and is known as a spiritual figure as well as social activist, it was easy for the local communities to see me as a peacemaker, reconciler and bridge-builder. Already, through the activities of Paxherbal, which I founded and which has provided employment for many people in the communities, and the spiritual activities of the monastery, which I represent, a great deal of mutual trust and loyalty exists between me and the communities. 'We are here because Father Anselm invited us,' said a group of women from Eko-Ewu, one of the villages in Ewu Kingdom. They had trekked some 10 kilometres to attend the village meeting at the king's palace. Community development work is bound to fail without such mutual trust between the facilitator and the community.

After six months of intense engagement and dialogues involving series of meetings, the communities agreed on a name for the association: Ewu Development and Educational Multipurpose Cooperative Society (EDEMCS). The name was carefully chosen to embrace all segments of the community: youths, men, women, students, farmers and entrepreneurs. On February 21, 2015, EDEMCS was officially inaugurated at the palace of the king of Ewu Kingdom, with thousands of women, men and youths in attendance (see Figure 8.4). Also present were government officials and the local government authorities. An official goodwill message from the king of Ewu read as follows (see Figure 8.5).

Figure 8.4 Official inauguration of EDEMCS executives in February 2015

> ### Message from the throne of Ewu Kingdom
>
> *The establishment of St Benedict Monastery in Ewu has brought so much progress and development to Ewu Kingdom. Ewu is now globally known because of the popular Paxherbal products; our youths are now taken off the streets by the provision of employment.*
>
> *Today the St Benedict Monastery has initiated the **Ewu Development and Educational Multipurpose Cooperative Society (EDEMCS)**. The inauguration of this body today, which comprises reputable sons and daughters of Ewu, further attests to the fact that St Benedict Monastery is not only interested in the spiritual well-being of our people but also the economic and social development aspects. I want to assure the St Benedict Monastery that the good relationship existing between the community and the monastery will be sustained. Please accept my warmest regards.*
>
> **H.R.H. BARR. RAZAKY.I. OJEIFO III ONOJIE OF EWU KINGDOM**

Figure 8.5 Goodwill message from the king of Ewu

It was a unique gathering because the local communities had taken concrete steps to rediscover and mobilize themselves to use their own resources to develop themselves and question the existing status quo. During his speech, the president of the association, speaking on behalf of the thousand-member association, listed the practical short-term goals of the association:

- Demonstration farm with cassava processing facilities and an oil mill;
- Training for selected group of one hundred artisans on innovative and systems thinking;
- Support programme for small- and medium-sized enterprises (SMEs) through micro-finance loans;
- Training of local market women and traders in business and technology management;
- Youth empowerment through integral skill acquisition techniques.

Conclusion: Pax Africana: beyond theoria and praxis towards communitalism in action

This chapter argued that participatory action research (PAR) is more effective, sustainable and productive when it embraces research (theoria) and action (praxis), and then evolves

Figure 8.6 April 2015: sharing of ideas by local farmers and agricultural experts

Figure 8.7 Local farmers association after a meeting at EDEMCS office in 2015

further to embrace the 4Ps or Pax Africana: Communis, Spiritus, Scientia and Economia. This, I argued, is communitalism in action: an action–research method that transcends the conventional dichotomies of black and white, indigenous and exogenous, male and female and so on to embrace all dimensions of life, integrating the four worlds of South, East, North and West, a true Pax Africana.

I applied the tenets of PAR by first getting the local community fully and actively involved in defining, analysing and solving their own problems. As a committed participant, facilitator and researcher, I encouraged authentic analysis of social reality. As a result, PAR created an enabling atmosphere for the people to be aware of their own potentials and resources, thereby mobilizing the freedom to be enterprising for sustainable community development. Lastly, through PAR, EDEMCS became a movement for the radical transformation of social reality, giving power to the weak, oppressed and marginalized.

I argued that African intellectuals should go beyond critiquing conventional theories, be they economic, political, psychological or philosophical, to proposing alternative theories rooted in African culture and worldviews. Nigerian writer Chinua Achebe said during an interview in 1994, 'If you don't like someone's story, then write your own' (Brooks, 1994). A Malawian proverb also says, 'Until the lions have their own writers, the story of the hunt will always glorify the hunter.' African thinkers need to write their own stories. Retelling the African story is indeed what Paxherbal and ACIRD set out to do, both in theory and action, and beyond that, as Pax Africana.

In the next chapter, I will describe how Paxherbal and ACIRD apply the tenets of cooperative inquiry, which is another variety of action research, to the transformation of local communities in Edo State, Nigeria.

References

Akhaine, S. O. (2015). *Patrons of poverty: IMF/World Bank and Africa's problems.* Saarbrucken, Germany: Lap Lambert Academic.

Annas, J. (2003). *Plato: A very short introduction.* Oxford: Oxford University Press.

Barnes, J. (2000). *Aristotle: A very short introduction.* Oxford: Oxford University Press.

Barnes, J. (2001). *Early Greek philosophy.* London: Penguin.

Baum, F., MacDougall, C. and Smith, D. (2006). Participatory action research. *Journal of Epidemiology and Community Health* 60(10): 854–857.

Bessette, G. (2004). *Involving the community: A guide to participatory development communication.* Ottawa: International Development Research Centre.

Brooks, J. (1994). Chinua Achebe, the Art of Fiction No. 139. [online] *The Paris Review.* Available at: http://www.theparisreview.org/interviews/1720/the-art-of-fiction-no-139-chinua-achebe [Accessed 12 June 2015].

Carr, W. and Kemmis, S. (1986). *Becoming critical: Education knowledge and action research.* London: Falmer Press.

Chevalier, J. M. and Buckles, D. (2013). *Participatory action research: Theory and methods for engaged inquiry.* London: Routledge.

Chinweizu, I. (1975). *The West and the rest of us: White predators, black slavers, and the African Elite.* London: Random House.

Clark, J. G. (2011). *The Benedictines in the Middle Ages.* Suffolk, UK: Boydell Press.

Dewey, J. (1998). *Experience and nature.* Mineola, NY: Dover.

Dewey, J. (2012). *Human nature and conduct.* Lawrence, KS: Digireads.

Emery, K. (1996). *Monastic, scholastic, and mystical theologies from the later middle ages.* Rugby, UK: Variorum.

Fanon, F. (2008). *Black skin, white masks.* London: Pluto Press.

Freire, P. (1970). *Pedagogy of the oppressed*. New York: Herder and Herder.

Janniak, A. (2015). *Newton*. Hoboken, NJ: Wiley-Blackwell.

Jolley, N. (2005). *Leibniz*. London: Penguin.

Kant, I. (2005). *Critique of pure reason*. London: Penguin.

Lefèvre, W. (2013). *Between Leibniz, Newton, and Kant: Philosophy and science in the eighteenth century*. New York: Springer.

Lessem, R. and Schieffer, A. (2015). *Integral renewal: A relational and renewal perspective*. Farnham, UK: Gower.

Lewin, K. (1948). *Resolving social conflicts*. New York: Harper & Row.

McNiff, J. (2013). *Action research*. London: Routledge.

Moghalu, K. (2013). *Emerging Africa: How the global economy's 'last frontier' can prosper and matter*. Ibadan, Nigeria: Bookcraft.

Natou, T., Bonazzi, M. and Benatouil, T. (eds.). (2012). *Theoria, praxis, and the contemplative life after Plato and Aristotle*. Leiden, Netherlands: Brill.

Reagan, T. (2004). *Non-western educational traditions: Indigenous approaches to educational thought and practice*. London: Routledge.

Scruton, R. (2001). *A short history of modern philosophy: From Descartes to Wittgenstein*. London: Routledge.

Selener, J. (1997). *Participatory action research and social change: Approaches and critique*. New York: Cornell University Press.

Sousa Santos, B. de. (2014). *Epistemologies of the South: Justice against epistemicide*. London: Routledge.

Warren, D., Slikkerveer, L. and Brokensha, D. (eds.). (1995). *The cultural dimension of development: Indigenous knowledge systems*. London: ITDG.

Waterfield, R. (1996). *The first philosophers: The pre-Socratic and sophists*. Oxford: Oxford University Press.

9 Cooperative inquiry in an African context

The case of Paxherbal and ACIRD

Introduction

Having shared in the last chapter how the Ewu local community in Edo State, Nigeria, has been activated to rediscover and re-express itself through participatory action research, I will now describe the contribution and transformation being brought about by Pax-herbal and ACIRD as knowledge-creating entities. While Chapter 8 employed PAR as the appropriate action-research methodology for community engagement and transformation, this chapter will apply cooperative inquiry (CI) as the appropriate research methodology for this contribution and transformation stage. What, then, is cooperative inquiry?

Cooperative inquiry: co-creating action-knowledge together

John Heron (1996) proposed cooperative inquiry (CI) as a variation of action research with the aim, like participatory action research (PAR), to integrate action and research in such a way that one leads immediately to the other. Like PAR, one distinguishing feature of cooperative inquiry is its collaborative nature. In fact, another name for cooperative inquiry is collaborative inquiry. It is about working with people and ensuring that all participants are fully involved in research decisions as co-researchers and innovators (Reason, 1995).

Heron proposes a four-layered cycle of knowledge types, which forms the basis of cooperative inquiry. The first is experiential knowing. At this stage people with common interests come together, share and reflect on their experiences of some particular issues. It is at this reflection phase that topics and methods of inquiry are decided upon based on these shared experiences.

The second phase is when the group imaginably researches alternative ways of doing things and explores possibilities, opportunities and potentialities, correlates the imaginal ideas with the experiential, and keeps records of the new insights arising from the interaction of the imaginal with the experiential.

The third phase is the conceptual, which can be described as the nerve centre of the inquiry method. In this phase, members of the group become fully engaged with their action and experience and are open to new ideas, new ways of conceiving reality and even a new course of action. Their experience may see them shift away from their original ideas into new concepts, unpredicted actions and innovative insights. Finding oneself in such a new, unpredicted field of knowledge could be disconcerting and frightening. However, it is this creative tension between the known, unknown and the newly known that makes cooperative inquiry so unique and different from other research methods.

The fourth and final phase is the contribution stage, when the co-researchers come together to share their practical and presentational data in light of the original ideas at the experiential stage. This may lead them to reframe the ideas, develop new ones or even reject the ideas and pose new questions. At every stage, all active participants are fully involved in the research decisions as co-researchers (Reason and Bradbury-Huang, 2013).

Cooperative inquiry at Paxherbal: micro and macro contributions

We now look at the tenets of CI as described by Lessem and Schieffer (2015) (Table 9.1) and thereafter explain how these tenets are adapted and applied within the integral research model by Paxherbal in Edo State, Nigeria.

In October 2014, I initiated a cooperative inquiry group called *Pax CI Group*, made up of the following members listed in Table 9.2.

The group first met on October 7, 2014, with no agenda other than to come and talk. I, as the convener of the meeting, introduced the concept of cooperative inquiry and a brief history of its origin. As expected, the initial reaction was chaotic. In the first place, there was objection to why we needed to apply a western-made research method to an African indigenous setting like Paxherbal. We spent hours sharing and discussing the relevance of CI in our context. The breakthrough came when we traced the origin of cooperative inquiry method beyond Heron and Reading to its African origins. Then the group was able to connect with the concept of cooperative inquiry as an aspect of feminist emancipatory critique, giving voice to the marginalized and oppressed (see Chapters 6 and 7). In our discussions, we agreed that action research is not an invention of some western armchair scholars, but is rooted in the South (Africa) and East (Asia) and some parts of Latin America. Every member of the group was able to connect experientially with a deep-seated desire for authenticity. For us, the question of identity was not just theoretical; it was real. We felt Paxherbal

Table 9.1 CI tenets (source: Lessem and Schieffer, 2015)

You start experientially: restoring nature and promoting community.
Emergent knowing is imaginal: leading to conscious evolution.
The conceptual, building sociopolitical constructs, leads to knowledge creation.
The effective culmination is sustainable development and practical living economy.

Table 9.2 Pax CI Group members

Name	Designation
Fr Benedict Nkwuda	Deputy head of St Benedict Monastery
Fr Anselm Adodo	Director at Paxherbal
Br Bernard Mancha	Production/work manager at Paxherbal
Br Rufus Idehen	Assistant production/work manager at Paxherbal
Prof. Joseph OkOgun	Head of scientific R&D at Paxherbal
Dr Eric Okojie	Head solicitor at Paxherbal. Eric's PhD research work is titled 'Legal Framework for Traditional Medicine in Nigeria.'
Mr Yinka Olayiola	Scientist and administrative executive at Paxherbal

is an important tool for us to experience and express our African identity in a new, modern way. We love the past but are not stuck there: the past is essential to help us navigate the future successfully.

At the next meeting three weeks later, the issue of identity once again featured prominently in our discussions. We resolved to set some guiding questions for our subsequent discussions. We also agreed to meet once a month and set modalities for discussions. Sitting arrangements would be in a circle, and the group would appoint a chairman to moderate each meeting, with the understanding that every member would have an opportunity to be a chairman. The main duty of the chairman was to draw up an agenda for the meeting, which was to be circulated a week before the next meeting.

It was at the third meeting that the group was able to draw up guiding questions for further discussions. The questions were as follows:

- How have the clinical, administrative, business and community-oriented practices of Paxherbal in the past fifteen years, both within and without, impacted (negatively and positively) Ewu Monastery, the Ewu local community, Esanland, Edo State and Nigeria in general?
- Based on our past experience, how could Paxherbal's successes and learning in indigenous-exogenous knowledge and value creation in the Ewu Village of Edo State be applied more widely in Nigeria, Africa and, more generally, in the wider world? How, specifically, could such a business model, community health and social innovation be contextualized, evolved and conceptualized and thereafter be more widely and universally applied?
- How can Paxherbal effectively extend its role beyond that of a health care provider to other areas, such as education, agriculture, community development and sustainable business enterprise?

Cooperative inquiry at Paxherbal: from imaginal knowing to conscious evolution

The CI Group at Paxherbal, having passed through the turmoil of the experiential stage, reconnecting with their inner potentials and need for self-identity and proper grounding in one's culture and context, thereby promoting inner integration and self-sufficiency, was now able to move to the imaginal. In our discussions, we expressed satisfaction at the massive progress already made by Paxherbal, having grown from a small, unknown one-man factory to the biggest employer of labour in rural Edo State and a key player in the Nigerian health sector. The key questions at this stage were as follows:

- What sort of enterprise will Paxherbal be in five, ten and twenty years from now?
- How will Paxherbal activities affect the environment, nature and ecology in the next twenty years?
- Is it possible for Paxherbal as an indigenous herbal manufacturing enterprise to become a true model of an integral enterprise-in-community for the modern world, a true integral indigenous-exogenous knowledge-creating company?

During a series of meetings spanning many months, we decided to invite some external co-researchers to join in our conversations. This was our experimental stage of knowledge creation. Those not able to join physically were invited via Skype. Some of the external co-researchers are members of the Center for Integral Socio-Economic Research (CISER), based in Lagos, the founders of the Trans4m Centre for Integral Development, based in Switzerland, head of the taxonomy and botany department in nearby Ambrose Alli University and others. CISER is particularly interested in creating a new model of development banking that is well suited to the African context, using the Ewu community as a test case.

The group came to the realization that investing in large-scale cultivation of medicinal plants is essential to the sustenance of ongoing production of health supplements. The key to meeting the needs of millions of Nigerians who need our herbal products is to encourage large-scale cultivation. Our experience at this experimental stage led us to formulate the following questions:

- How do we acquire enough land for such large-scale cultivation?
- Can we afford the labour required to manage such large farmland?

The group initially saw this as a problem and was pessimistic about the prospects of expansion. The beauty of cooperative inquiry lies precisely in its ability to fire up the imagination of the co-researchers and open them to new possibilities. At the conceptual and third stage of the four modes of knowing, the group posed some critical questions to itself:

- Why does Paxherbal need to acquire and own vast farmland for cultivation all by itself?
- Why don't we involve the whole community who traditionally are owners of the land as partners in the cultivation business?
- Can we imagine the whole community becoming suppliers of raw materials to the company in such a way that they become an integral part of the Paxherbal enterprise?

From these questions, we arrived at a conscious evolution of what we should be and can be as an integral enterprise-in-community and, therefore, were able to move to the next stage in our cooperative inquiry, the conceptual. It was at this third mode that the idea of ACIRD was conceived and actualized.

ACIRD: fostering knowledge creation in the community

The group once again revisited the question asked earlier at the experiential stage:

> Based on our past experience, how could Paxherbal's successes and learning in indigenous–exogenous knowledge and value creation in the Ewu Village of Edo State be applied more widely in Nigeria, Africa and, more generally, in the wider world? How, specifically, could such a business model, community health and social innovation be contextualized, evolved and conceptualized and thereafter be more widely and universally applied?

For us, it was clear that we needed to move beyond individual research to institutionalized research through a centre that would focus on serious research in indigenous African knowledge systems, economics, history and other areas of the social sciences from the African point of view. In other words, action-theory, philosophy-in-action or research-to-innovation has been a missing link in institutionalized action research in Africa. This problem was described at the beginning of this research work, and the alleviation of the imbalance was proposed as one of the contributions of this research work. As I stated in Chapter 1,

> In many indigenous societies, when a knowledge bearer dies his knowledge dies with him. Indeed, a lot of knowledge is being lost, knowledge that appears to be worthless because it is not properly valued. Today we speak of protecting our environment from abuse and of protection for rare species of plants and animals. Equally important is the need to set up international efforts to protect and preserve indigenous knowledge. With each death of an old person in our villages, a whole library of books is lost. My final transformative practical contribution is geared towards a new model of business and enterprise based on nature, community and humanism, and finally, the foundation of a communiversity where authentic community-based participatory action research and knowledge creation, rather than mere accumulation of theoretical knowledge, are the focus.

The Africa Centre for Integral Research and Development (ACIRD) aims to institutionalize knowledge creation in Ewu village, Edo State, Nigeria and Africa as a whole. ACIRD is one of the practical answers to the question raised at the beginning of this subsection: How do we bridge the gap between research and innovation in Nigeria and Africa?

Becoming practical: towards a partnership for integral transformative education

ACIRD is in partnership with the Institute of African Studies (IAS) of the University of Ibadan, Nigeria's premier university. Together with the Trans4m Centre for Integral Development, Paxherbal, IAS, and ACIRD, which also embraces the Centre for Integral Socio-Economic Research (CISER), have teamed up to take on the challenge of integral transformative education in Africa, rooted in the Ewu local community indigenously while exogenously embracing new modern realities.

The organizations are working together to create new approaches to research and education in Nigeria and Africa as a whole. The burning question, for ACIRD, is to explore how community animation, awakening through conscientization, institutionalized research and transformative enterprise in Nigeria, can be a genuine vehicle for overall social innovation in Africa. ACIRD, in collaboration with local and international partners, seeks to set new templates for integral research-to-innovation, individually and collectively, to counteract the danger of ivory-tower institutions in Nigeria and Africa.

The goal of ACIRD is to continue to explore ways in which research can transform Africa. ACIRD seeks to be a centre for doing research *in* and *for* Africa, individually and institutionally. As discussed in Chapter 7, for centuries Africans were a people spoken about, spoken for and spoken against by foreigners. We learned about who we are from what others said and wrote about us. ACIRD seeks to assert the right of Africans to speak in their own language and metaphors. We must reclaim our right to cognitive freedom if we truly seek to be free. Africa must be aware of and fight against the coloniality of knowledge and epistemicide, modern forms of colonization, by evolving and e-ducing (from the word 'education') its own research methods and research methodologies *suited to* and *geared towards* African epistemological emancipation.

ACIRD is passionate about research, both processally and substantively, that leads to social, if not also technological, innovation in Africa – thereby addressing Africa's calling to ultimately contribute its unique gifts to the world. As mentioned in Chapter 4, there are firstly in Africa and other parts of the world brilliant individuals who have done marvellous research work and have produced excellent academic works in various fields of social research. Most of these individual researchers die unknown; some are frustrated due to lack of a platform to give flesh to their theories, while some simply lose interest in academic work and focus on 'more important things'. African intellectuals in diverse fields do research for the sake of research: research that contributes little or nothing to individual, and communal, organizational and societal development. Moreover, they fail to document, disseminate or indeed systematically analyse and ultimately institutionalize what African practitioners as exemplars of 'best practise' in the public, private, civic and environmental arenas have achieved. The result is that their research works end in beautifully, or not so beautifully, written dissertations and publications that only gather dust in libraries.

Trans4m was co-founded by Prof. Ronnie Lessem and Prof. Alexander Schieffer in 2006. Trans4m has developed the uniquely transformative 'integral worlds' approach to development that includes all aspects of a living human system: from nature and community to culture and spirituality to science and technology to enterprise and economics, altogether related to a particular world, that of Nigeria in Africa in this case. In recent years this approach has emerged as one of the most innovative and globally applicable approaches to individual, organizational and societal transformation in Africa, the Middle East, Near East and Europe as well as the Americas.

The ultimate aspiration of the integral worlds research approach is to support entire societies to bring about socially balanced and culturally authentic approaches to integral development. For this to happen, individuals, organizations and communities eager to advance their capacity to develop and to support societal development form a community of learning and practise to engage in a co-creative society-building process. To that end, the integral journey – Call, Context, Co-creation and Contribution – supports individual integral development, while the collective CARE process involves Community activation (C), Awakening consciousness (A), Research-to-innovation (R) and Embodiment via transformative education/enterprise (E).

ACIRD's research ecosystem also includes (CISER), co-founded by Dr Basheer Oshodi. The Centre aims to proffer practical solutions to the issues of poverty and economic inequality in Nigeria. CISER members comprise mostly bankers who are interested in evolving new perspectives on investment banking in Nigeria and how the banking system in Nigeria can be a genuine player in sustainable development in Nigeria. Both ACIRD and CISER work together as social innovation agents, using the integral research model.

Within our ecosystem is also the *Nigeria Natural Medicine Development Agency* (NNMDA), a parastatal of the Ministry of Science and Technology. It was established in 1997 to enable the ministry to actualize its critical and strategic mandate to research, develop, collate, document, preserve, conserve and promote the nation's indigenous (traditional) health care systems. It also aims to integrate into the National Healthcare Delivery System, as well as contribute to the nation's wealth and job creation, socio-economic growth, development effort, traditional medication and non-medication, healing arts, sciences and technologies.

The agency published the following information about itself on its website:

Mandate: Research, collate, document, develop and promote Nigeria's natural medicine defined as indigenous (traditional) health systems, medication and non-medication healing arts, science and technology to contribute to improved healthcare delivery, wealth and job creation and national economic growth and development.

Finally, ACIRD also collaborates with the Institute of African Studies (IAS) of the University of Ibadan. The IAS is based in the University of Ibadan, Nigeria's oldest and most highly rated university. The Institute offers postgraduate degree courses in African history, ethnomedicine and cultural studies. While NNMDA shares a lot in common in mission and vision with Paxherbal, the Institute of African Studies, a conventional academic institute, shares much in common with ACIRD. High-level meetings and interactions are currently going on between ACIRD and IAS with a view to completing a draft memorandum of understanding (MOU) to ensure proper institutionalized research and partnership between the two institutes. ACIRD and IAS plan to jointly organize and host an international conference on integral research and development.

The overall aims of ACIRD are as follows:

- To develop and institutionalize distinct Afrocentric research methods and research methodology interdependent with, rather than dependent upon, the dominant Eurocentric system;
- To research and develop the theory of communitalism, at both macro and micro levels, as the African antidote to the imbalances of rampant capitalism, relevant to particular societies and enterprises both within Africa and without.

The specific objectives are as follows:

- Giving voice to the oft-neglected voices from the peripheries, which account for 80 per cent of the world population;
- Revising the past and interpreting it in our own southern voice and metaphors as against the overly westernized narratives;
- Charting an individual, communal and institutional path through research to a sustainable socio-economic and political liberation of Africa, duly documented and disseminated, operating at both micro and macro levels;
- Developing the concept of cognitive justice as key to social, economic, political, mental and moral liberation of Africa.

The contributions/activities of ACIRD include but are not limited to the following:

- Publication of research work in the natural, medical and social sciences;
- Community activation through the association of Ewu Development and Educational Multipurpose Cooperative Society (EDEMCS), an independent, self-governing body owned by the local community in Ewu, Edo State;
- Development and institutionalization within a newly contextualized African university context, an ongoing evolution of the theory of communitalism;
- Dissemination of integral research knowledge through the local book series on innovation and transformation as well integral green economies and societies;
- Hosting of annual/biannual international conferences on African knowledge systems;
- Postgraduate degree programmes on integral research and development;
- Research and teaching partnership with universities worldwide.

Conclusion: another alternative is possible!

We have now come to the end of this exciting journey, following the 4C trajectory from Call to Context, Co-creation and Contribution. Alongside the 4Cs, we engaged in the fourfold CARE research trajectory (Community activation, Awakening of conscious-ness, Research-to-innovation, Embodiment via transformative education and enterprise). While the 4Cs focus on an individual researcher's particular innovation drive, CARE focuses on the institutionalization of an individual researcher's integral process towards a self-sustaining, dynamic and ongoing development. This institutionalization has been the focus of the last four chapters on co-creation and contribution.

The overriding theme of this research work is healing in the generic and integral sense of wholeness and harmonious living, from an African perspective. Building on the CARE metaphor, I argued that healing is more than an absence of biological or bodily pain. Genuine healing is integral by nature, embracing harmonious community living, a healthy ecosystem and a balanced socio-economic existence.

In Chapter 8 I described how the tenets of participatory action research are being applied in Ewu community through EDEMCS. With over four thousand local men and women who are financially empowered through the various self-development schemes of EDEMCS – such as the small-medium scale finance scheme for female farmers, local artisans and local artists, and the regular training in innovative thinking for the local youths – there is ample evidence that PAR is truly a transformative research venture.

In this chapter, the focus was on the application of the tenets of cooperative inquiry (CI) to the Paxherbal organization and its offshoot, ACIRD. The general guiding ques-tions guiding the two CI groups of Paxherbal and ACIRD were:

- What kind of concrete institution can we put in place to integrally develop and transform Africa educationally, economically, spiritually, socially and politically and health-wise?
- How do we institutionalize and concretize the concept of integral healing and com-munitalism in the short and long term?

The theory of communitalism, built on the four pillars of Pax Africana (Communis, Spiri-tus, Scientia and Economia), presents an alternative approach to the issues of health, medi-cine and enterprise in Africa. At first, one may wonder what the connections are between health, medicine, university and economics. Communitalism shows that the inability to see the connection between these different realms lies at the root of our modern sense of separation and identity crises. The message of communitalism is clear: another alternative is possible!

References

Heron, J. (1996). *Cooperative inquiry: Research into the human condition.* London: SAGE.

Lessem, R. and Schieffer, A. (2015). *Integral renewal: A relational and renewal perspective.* Farnham, UK: Gower.

Reason, P. (ed.). (1995). *Participation in human inquiry.* London: SAGE.

Reason, P. and Bradbury-Huang, H. (2013). *SAGE handbook of action research: Participatory inquiry and practice.* New York: SAGE.

Part VI

Distillation and conclusion of the integral journey

Until the lion learns how to write, every story will glorify the hunter.

—*African proverb*

10 CARE-ing for Nigeria

Towards an integral university in Africa

Introduction: beginning from the end

Having come to the end of this journey, I can now look back and see the way to the future. A Yoruba adage says that '*When a child falls flat on his belly, he looks at his front to see who will come and help him up, but when an elderly person falls down, he looks at his back to see who is observing him.*'When I started this project, I was a child looking ahead with a mix of uncertainty, ambivalence and hope. Now I can look back like an elder and see those who are watching me. I have evolved from a naïve seeker of truth to a social innovator, from an amateur healer to a healer of community and society. In a way, it is a journey which each of us must undertake, as individuals, as a community and as a society: a journey from me to us and back to me; from my community to our community; from my progress to our progress; from the subjective to the objective and back to the subjective. This is what communitalism is about, a Pax Africana where dichotomies are transcended, leading to integral development.

The complexity of my journey is reflected in the complex nature of this research work: combining conservative traditional ideals and principles with progressive and innovative community development initiatives and intense intellectual engagement leading to new research methodologies and theories. This has evolved into a full-fledged enterprise-in-community with a unique business model for Paxherbal, an active community development association for Ewu community, and a centre for integral research and development, embedded simultaneously in enterprise, community and society, altogether set within a particular local context in Edo State, Nigeria.

One of the major contributions of this research work is the demonstration of the relevant role of African voices, or southern theories, in the global intellectual space. Thomas Sankara (2007) once said that there could be no true liberation for Africa without the true liberation of women. In the same vein, there can be no integral development in the world without the contribution of the southern voice – precisely Africa. Former French president Nicolas Sarkozy, during an address in Dakar, Senegal, in 2012, infamously and cynically said, 'The tragedy of Africa is that the African has not fully entered into history . . . They have never really launched themselves into the future' (Ba, 2007).

Perhaps, the problem is that the western world is too obsessed with its own concepts, theories and stereotypes that it fails to see the contributions Africa has and is making to the world. The Igbo of Eastern Nigeria have a proverb that says, '*When something stands, another thing will stand beside it.*' It refers to openness to new ways of life, new ways of doing things and the fact that monoculturalism, mono–economics, mono–politics are not only against democracy but also against nature.

Pax Africana is the theory and practise of '*When something stands, another will stand beside it.*' We cannot separate community from spirituality, science from economics. This creative syncretism is what communitalism and Pax Africana are about. It is a worldview-based approach to sociopolitical development in Africa. The integral CARE model has been applied in a practical way to the Ewu local community in Edo State, Nigeria, with amazing results. As the integral research model is unique in its insistence on connecting theory to practise, the generic CARE concept has evolved into CARE-ing for Ewu, Edo State, Nigeria and Africa. This evolution led to two new institutions: *Ewu Development and Educational Multipurpose Cooperative Society* (EDEMCS), and *Africa Centre for Integral Research and Development* (ACIRD). While EDEMCS is based on the participatory action research model, the institutionalization and conceptualization of ACIRD are the result of cooperative inquiry. The two institutions are unique because they grew directly out of integral action research processes and provide excellent case stories of the relevant and transformative capacities of integral research and development.

ACIRD is set to carry on the mission of integrally CARE-ing for Nigeria through ongoing transformative research-to-innovation, in partnership with other institutions in Africa and beyond. The challenge for ACIRD and its research fellows is to remain true to its identity as a serious centre of research, not just an educational institution. A member of our integral ecosystem has expressed concerns about this danger. For ACIRD, however, such a tension between being a wholly research institution and overly educational institution is a challenge to greater creativity, flexibility and dynamism in the spirit of Pax Africana, and in line with the proverb cited earlier.

We now review the overall integral journey and see how it leads to CARE-ing for Nigeria.

Integral research and development: individually 4C-ing and institutionally CARE-ing for Nigeria

The research-to-innovation model, which formed the basis of this research work, is a dual, fourfold rhythm interweaving individual research, or a singular developmental initiative with institutionalized development. Integral research is also action research–oriented, focusing on the development not just of individuals but also of institutions. The uniqueness and transformative nature of these two parallel and interacting rhythms have been demonstrated in this research work. The integral dual-rhythm trajectory comprised the 4Cs (Call, Context, Co-creation, Contribution), 4C-ing development as individual or singular outreach. Closely aligned with the 4Cs is CARE, representing the four institutionalizing functions (Community activation, Awakening of consciousness, Research-to-innovation and Embodiment via transformative education and transformative enterprise). 4C-ing development and CARE-ing for Nigeria resonate well with integral healing, which is the overriding theme of this research work. In a country often divided along ethnic, religious and political lines, healing is the prerequisite for all social, economic, spiritual, political and educational development.

In the following two sections, I explain how the dual rhythms of the integral research-to-innovation trajectory build on each other to transform the society (see Figure 10.1).

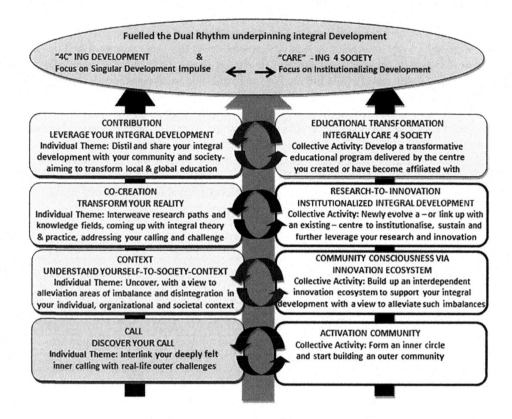

Figure 10.1 Integral rhythms

Individually 4C-ing development: overview of the 4Cs

The four phases of the 4C rhythm, from Call to Contribution, also interweave in such a creative and parallel way that one leads in and out of the other, as shown in Figure 10.1. It is a relationship between individual creativity and communal, institutionalized dynamism. This is well expressed in an African proverb that says that '*If you want to go fast, travel alone; but if you want to go far, travel with others.*' As an individual researcher, one can travel faster. However, what happens when one gets tired? It takes an institution to sustain an initiative. Institutionalized research is part of the 4C and CARE rhythm as well as Pax Africana, connecting community with spirituality, university and economics.

Call: *reconnecting with the inner self*

We all came from somewhere, and each of us is unique and special. 'Call' refers to this uniqueness and individuality of each person, and the need to first of all reconnect with this inner self, embrace it and discover what one's particular inner desire is. For me as an individual, my inner desire for truth led me to a deeper connection with my desire for healing. On the superficial level, one may not find a direct connection between truth and healing. For me, healing, in its deeper sense, is the discovery of the truth about myself, my community, my environment and my society, and finding my place within it. My inner desire for truth in the abstract sense led me to a concrete expression of my inner desire for healing of self, others and society. My inner calling was then energized by an outer challenge, which in my case was lack of knowledge in the local community. This lack of knowledge was expressed on different levels: medically, economically, politically and educationally. I described it as a poverty of the mind. The local communities are ravaged by common ailments, such as cough and malaria, when the land is filled with medicinal plants that can eradicate these ailments. Young people are malnourished when the land is filled with abundant fruits and vegetables. Unemployment is rampant in a land rich in natural resources and biodiversity. My outer challenge was connected to the burning issues in the wider community. To tackle these issues required going beyond my individual self to working with others institutionally. This led to the birth of Paxherbal, an enterprise-in-community, and Pax Africana, a centre for integral research and development, in this way 4C-ing integral development and CARE-ing for society.

Context: uncovering imbalances in self, organization and society

Understanding one's particular local context in order to surface the imbalances therein is central to the integral research model, leading to catalysation of research and development with a view to alleviating the imbalances. Action research does not stop at merely discovering and analysing problems or imbalances, but initiates concrete and practical actions that will lead to the alleviation of these imbalances. The imbalances in my local context of Ewu village and Edo State include a one-sided, overly westernized educational system that promotes a sense of alienation from local culture, tradition and worldview. An overemphasis on westernized education in the fields of medicine, for example, created a perennial interdisciplinary conflict between traditional medicine and western medicine, between economics and business management, and between the university and the factory, or laboratory. I proposed the theory of communitalism as an antidote to the imbalances in my local context, set against the backdrop of health alongside economics and enterprise.

Co-creation: transforming reality

One of the key tenets of co-creation is to combine research paths and knowledge fields in such a way that the researcher comes up with an alternative or complementary integral theory and practise, channelled towards one's particular calling and challenge. Whichever integral research path one chooses, be it relational, renewal, rational or pragmatic (Lessem and Schieffer, 2010), it invariably leads to innovation, in the process transforming oneself and one's society. This innovation-driven journey must be communal, or institutionalized, if it is to be sustainable. Following the southern relational path, I built on the existing platform of Paxherbal, an indigenous, community-based herbal medicine enterprise that aims to preserve African indigenous healing systems, and the platform of St Benedict Monastery, a community of monks following the *Rule of St Benedict*. These two institutions formed my initial ecosystem, from which emerged EDEMCS and ACIRD.

The four institutions represent the four dimensions of pax (the 4Ps), which I call in their entirety Pax Africana. Pax Africana is the basis of my theory of communitalism, a theory characterized by the interconnectedness of action and research, where community (communis) is represented by EDEMCS, spirituality (spiritus) is represented by St Benedict

Monastery, university (scientia) is represented by ACIRD, and laboratory (economia) is represented by Paxherbal. In a very real and concrete way, Pax Africana is transforming the local communities in Edo State and Nigeria, providing an excellent model of genuine and successful integral research-to-innovation in Africa. Following the integral CARE rhythm, EDEMCS emerged through Community activation (C); St Benedict Monastery became a catalyst for Awakening of consciousness (A); ACIRD emerged from Research-to-innovation in institutionalized form (R); and finally, Paxherbal became an Embodiment of transformative education and enterprise (E). In this way, transformative power, or 'people power', was restored in the communities.

Contribution: creating development

To create is to bring something new into being, or transform the old into something new. Beyond dreaming and planning, this final phase of the 4Cs deals with actual development: a development that follows from Call, Context and Co-creation, leading to Contribution. Development is systematic, deliberate, planned and sustainable because it is built on solid foundations. Another key feature of integral development is that the particular individual achievements and development impulse are further leveraged upon, and expanded by, others, leading to new educational curricula. In my particular case, ACIRD, the new integral research centre that grew out of this research work, is in partnership with the Institute of African Studies at the University of Ibadan and the Trans4m Centre for Integral Development, Geneva, to design a new master's and doctoral course on transformation studies. Such a course will be open to all students in the arts and social sciences to enable them to undergo tutelage in integral research-to-innovation methods and apply such theories in their respective areas of discipline.

However, the focus of ACIRD is to establish new models for doing research *in* and *for* Africa. ACIRD seeks to assert the right of Africans to speak in their own language and metaphors. Gradually, the modern world is beginning to recover the true meaning of research (*re-search*: to search for something that was once known but forgotten, to look again for what is missing). In fact, there is a connection between *re-search* (University, Scientia) and religion (Sanctuary, Spiritus), from the Latin word *religare* (to rebind, reunite, reconnect with a higher power). Science does not and cannot create *ab nihilo* (from nothing). Science only tries to rediscover, refine, reinterpret, redesign, reconfirm and re-search what is already there in nature. Whatever one calls it − chemistry, physics, botany, biology, anatomy, psychology, sociology, anthropology, economics − it still boils down to the same thing: *nature*.

We now turn from an overview of the 4Cs, which focused on particular developmental impulse, to the CARE functions, and the institutionalization of such an impulse, in order to ensure its long-term sustainable rooting in society.

The CARE functions: healing my society: towards institutionalized integral development

Introduction

Parallel to the 4Cs are the CARE functions, which build on the individual impulse of the 4Cs. The institutionalizing and collective activities of CARE aim at the ongoing building-up of communities and organizational structures that can not only sustain themselves but also give rise to new organizations. Thus, through cooperative inquiry, a small group of local think tanks in Ewu village evolved into EDEMCS, a local association of some thirty people. Within ten months, this group of thirty evolved further to embrace thousands of female farmers, artisans, youths, entrepreneurs and social innovators. EDEMCS has further evolved beyond a local association into a movement, a revolutionary social movement, if you like; the government can no longer ignore it. From a local group of marginalized and underrated people, EDEMCS is becoming a voice powerful enough to challenge the status quo and force a change in power relations in Edo State and Nigeria.

For so long, we were made to believe that power lies in the hands of those with guns. And they ruled over us with their guns. They terrorized us, intimidated us, stole our money and sold our God-given natural resources at giveaway prices, and we watched them helplessly because they had guns. They told us to vote, only to steal our votes and impose unknown candidates on us, and we watched them helplessly because they had guns. They told us to make sacrifices for the sake of national growth, while they revelled in obscene opulence and showered us with dust as they drove noisily in long convoys of armoured jeeps along our untarred market roads, and we watched them helplessly because they had guns. While the most educated and hard working of us earned peanuts as wages, they, the 'powers that be', approved for themselves outrageous allowances and privileges, and we watched them helplessly because they had guns.

For so long, they raised our hopes with sweet promises, and organized lavish conferences and symposia to get us talking. The more we talked, the happier they became. Before we knew it, we had become a nation of committees. In Nigeria, there are hundreds of seminars and conferences on every topic under the earth. If our roofs are leaking, we organize conferences before we mend them. If our houses are on fire, we first organize seminars on how to handle fire-outbreak before we quench the fire. If flood is wiping out our towns and villages, we summon a stakeholders' summit to discuss it even while our children are drowning.

As we were getting tired of their tactics, they employed religious and tribal sentiments to weaken our resolve, our focus and our will to resist. And to their relief, we willingly swallowed the bait, and began to fight with one another, insult one another and kill one another. The Muslims are fighting. The Christians are fighting. The Igbos, the Yorubas, the Hausas and hundreds of ethnic tribes that make up our vast Nigerian country are engaged in a fierce battle fuelled by fear, uncertainty, insecurity and suspicion. This is one of their tricks to keep the poor of Nigeria docile so they do not rise up with one voice to resist oppression by our leaders.

One day, rather sooner than later, the dead bones shall rise, and we – the commercial motorcycle riders, the wheelbarrow pushers, the palm-wine tapers, the shoemakers, the bricklayers, the banana sellers, the simple ordinary men and women of Edo State, of Nigeria, of Africa, struggling to earn our daily bread – we shall rise and liberate ourselves. We will no longer wait for any saviour, or depend on the goodwill and benevolence of the rich. We will be the ones to set ourselves free. And to set our country free. It may be hard, but one day, we will liberate our communities, our society, our country. We will frustrate them with our resilience and humiliate them by our determination. No amount of gun powder and bomb power can match our will, our determination, our dreams. Real power does not lie in the hands of those who hold the gun. Real power lies in the hands of men and women of ideas, of imagination and of will. It is these men and women who make up EDEMCS, a true participatory action research group, CARE-ing for the society and promoting healing and integral harmony. What, then, are the key functions of CARE that make it so unique?

Community activation: restoring nature and community via Pax Communis

The first of the CARE functions is Community activation. Pax Communis, which in CARE terms is called Community activation, corresponds to Call, leading to healing of the community and a happy and healthy coexistence through deeper consciousness of abilities, sense of self-worth and reconnection with nature and community. Institutionally, EDEMCS continues to serve as a rallying point for the local community of Ewu to rediscover itself and further realize its potentials. Such sense of empowerment has been further bolstered by the discovery of the economic potentials of *voacanga Africana*, a plant easily grown in the local communities of Ewu and its environs. *Voacanga* has a complex mixture of iboga alkaloids, such as *coacangine*, *voacamine* and *tabersonine* among others, which are pharmaceutically used to treat addictions and depression. Recently, a British entrepreneur, Jeremy Weate, working in partnership with American and South African pharmaceutical companies, contracted the cultivation of *voacanga* to the Ewu community through EDEMCS. To this effect, EDEMCS has mobilized the local farmers in the communities to engage in mass cultivation of *voacanga Africana*. The harvested plant will be collected and extracted by Paxherbal and then exported worldwide to a market worth \$20 million. The synergy and complementarity of EDEMCS (Community) and Paxherbal (Laboratory) are an excellent example of communitalism in action, an integral Pax Africana.

Awakening consciousness: regaining meaning via Pax Spiritus

Just as Community activation builds on Call, Awakening of consciousness via innovation ecosystem builds on Context. Within my context, Awakening is the building of a higher, religious consciousness, arousing a deeper sense of personhood, maturity, wholeness: a lifetime PHD (Process of Holistic Development) complementing the academic PhD. The St Benedict Monastery, to which I belong, is a symbol of openness, religious tolerance and is outstanding in bridging the divide between spirituality and secularism, or in integral terms, between the sanctuary and the market. It is no wonder that Paxherbal, an enterprise-in-community, and EDEMCS, a community development initiative, have their roots in the monastic spirituality of the monks, *ora et labora* (prayer and work), characteristic of Benedictine monasteries. At the end of the day, spirit is where culture is, and culture, in its liberating sense, is spiritual. In addition, catalysation involves transcending the dichotomy between spirit and body, *theoria* and *praxis*, indigenous and exogenous, the individual and the community, the personal and the interpersonal, uniting all things together, for me in Christ, or for another person in Allah, or any other representation of the ultimate, uniting source of being. Having been well rooted in an active community and catalytically grounded in a supportive ecosystem, a strong foundation has been laid for a rock-solid and sustainable institutionalization through research-to-innovation.

Research–to–innovation, institutionalized: reframing knowledge via Pax Scientia

We now come to the third CARE function, called Research-to-innovation, leading to the creation of a new centre to institutionalize and sustain the development agenda. Such institutionalization builds on the other preceding CARE functions, Activation and awakening of consciousness, as well as the final culminating function, education Embodiment/education enterprise, all interwoven rhythmically in a circular movement. In my case, the new institution that emerged is ACIRD, about which a lot has been written in this research work. ACIRD evolved from a cooperative inquiry group formed at Paxherbal two years ago. One of the main functions of ACIRD is to institutionalize and practicalize the theory of communitalism, Pax Africana, bridging the gap between research and innovation, knowing and doing, sanctuary and laboratory, community and university. How is this vision of ACIRD to be actualized? The answer is provided in the next subsection, which deals with the final function of care: Embodiment via transformative education and transformative enterprise.

Embodiment: rebuilding institutions and community via Pax Economia

Since knowledge, by its nature, is borderless and cannot be confined, the vision of ACIRD goes beyond the local community of Ewu in Edo State and Nigeria to embrace other research centres within and without, be they in Zimbabwe, South Africa, Egypt, Slovenia or the United Kingdom. In January 2016, ACIRD and Trans4m entered into a collaborative partnership with the Institute of African Studies of the University of Ibadan, Nigeria's premier and best-rated university, to design a new postgraduate curriculum on transformation studies in Africa.

The reader will observe that there is already a great overlap between the last subsection and the present section, between institutionalization of integral development and educational transformation. In fact, only a very thin line separates Pax Scientia (university) from Pax Economia (laboratory), as they are part of the same process. A university, in our integral use of the term, is also a laboratory, a place of action research, philosophy-in-action, where theories and action, dream and reality are dynamically merged. It is a place where knowledge is translated into capabilities and capabilities are translated into knowledge. In this case, ACIRD, representing Pax Scientia, and Paxherbal, representing Pax Economia, are intrinsically linked. Education, then, is not something that happens in isolation from one's community. Rather, education takes place in full embeddedness in the real life-world of one's community. This is the way of Pax Africana, communitalism in action, an African approach to integral healing via holistic understanding of enterprise-in-community, acting, in this integrated form, as a key driver for sustainable development of society as a whole.

Pax Africana: CARE-ing for Nigeria: an African alternative is possible!

As this research work draws to a conclusion, one cannot help but be excited at the transformation and development that have emerged out of this research work, a true model of how research can transform society. At the beginning of this research work, I described one of the burning issues this research work would address:

> Social research is built on a faulty foundation, a one-sided methodology that is heavily biased towards the West, and systematically neglects the South and East, if not also the North. Yet, the foundation and origin of civilization lie in the South. The only way forward is for research to go backwards to reconnect with the foundation story of humanity, in order to chart a meaningful path towards the future. A truly integral research therefore will embrace the four worlds of South, East, North and West, each with its own distinctive strengths and weaknesses.

As shown in Figure 10.2, I have adapted the generic integral four-world research approach to my local context. I developed an Afrocentric, communitalist perspective as a remedy to the one-sided, Eurocentric research methodology that has hitherto dominated the social science space. I argued that it is time for African thinkers and researchers to provide an alternative theory of development to complement, if not replace, the existing theories. The unique strength of the theory of communitalism is that it embraces, and builds on, nature and culture, rather than relegating them to the background. Such a worldview-based approach to development speaks directly to the aspirations of the people. In other words, development is not about doing something for the people; it is enabling people to discover their own creativity and genius, their capabilities and talents, and providing a solid platform for them to take charge of their lives.

Figure 10.3 shows the connection of the Yoruba female goddesses as archetypes of the different dimensions of pax, each one reflecting the qualities associated with each 'world'. After decades of imposed western development theories that have failed to make any meaningful impact on Africans, after spending over $3 trillion in developmental aid with-out any meaningful impact on the African continent (Easterly, 2006; Collier, 2008), Africa and the world need a fresh and new perspective on development. The world needs a new

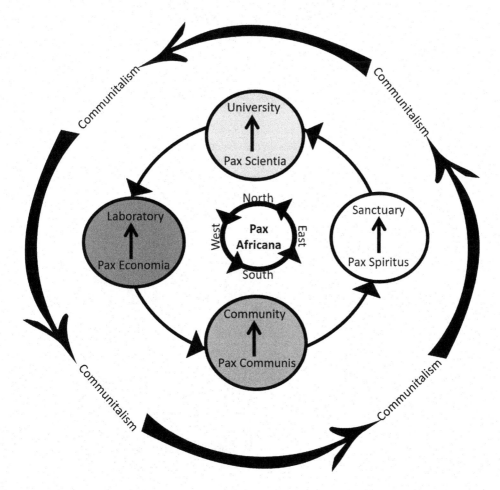

Figure 10.2 The communitalism model: the way of Pax Africana

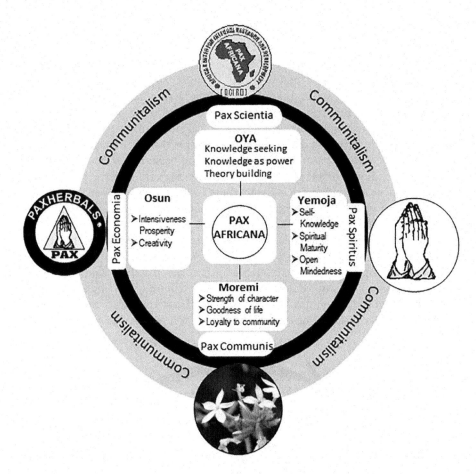

Figure 10.3 Pax Africana: grounding theory on indigenous worldview

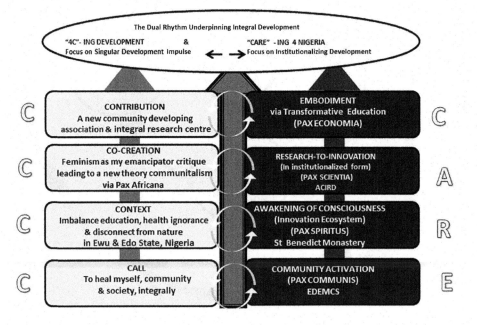

Figure 10.4 A contextualized dual-rhythm integral research trajectory (adapted from Lessem and Schieffer, 2010)

theory of development, a southern theory, as Comaroff and Comaroff (2012) put it. Pax Africana is one of such southern theories.

The uniqueness of the theory of communitalism, as I indicated in Chapter 6, is its grounding in a particular, visible context. Communitalism was described as a philosophy-in action, or research-to-innovation, a combination of indigenous (local) with exogenous (global) knowledge through CARE. Communitalism is the release of individual and communal, organizational and societal genius of a particular nature, culture, technology and economy and societal transformation. Communitalism, as opposed to capitalism or communism, is an integral approach to knowledge creation and development that is grounded in a particular enterprise-in-community, ultimately affecting a whole society, emerging indigenously and exogenously as such. Such a new African philosophy-in-practise has been developed in and around the four institutions of EDEMCS, St Benedict Monastery, ACIRD and Paxherbal. Together, they represent the four dimensions of pax, which I call Pax Africana. Figure 10.4 shows an indigenized and localized version of the original integral dual-rhythm research trajectory (Figure 1.1), embodying the 4Cs and CARE.

Decolonizing knowledge creation in Africa

For Ndlovu-Gatsheni (2013), the process of unifying Africans into a community to pursue common ideological, economic and political ends has been ceaseless. What is disturbing, for Ndlovu-Gatsheni, is that the pluralistic and civic nationalist traditions of the 1950s and 1960s had been increasingly degenerating into nativism, xenophobia and, in extreme cases, genocides. The roots of these negative aspects can be traced to an identity crisis brought about by the struggle to choose between being a distinct postcolonial state different from the preceding colonial political structure. The colonial state on which the postcolonial one is based was deeply racist. African nationalism followed in such exclusivist footsteps. What has worsened the degeneration of African nationalism into nativism and xenophobia, according to Ndlovu-Gatsheni, is the globalization process that provokes deep uncertainties. Deepening poverty and diminishing resources have heightened struggles over resources and also increased reliance of the poor on the state. As history has shown, such a top-bottom approach to development, characterized by a neglect and subjugation of nature, culture and community, does not and will never work in the African setting. Paradoxically, the African ruling elite is quite happy to sustain this doomed method of development because it benefits them and keeps the means of control in their grip. The ruling elite is scared of an economic model that gives power to the peasants and rural peripheries.

As I have argued in this research work, there is no evidence in Africa that violent revolutions have worked or will work. Therefore, while Marx and his African admirers, such as Frantz Fanon, Patrice Lumumba, Jerry Rawlings and Thomas Sakara, are right in their analysis of the sociology of oppression and exploitation engrained in African political systems, they could not offer sustainable and workable solutions. A call to arms often appears to be an appealing and practical step, but there is no example in Africa of a peaceful state emerging out of violent revolutions. Ghana may come up as an example of peace after violence revolutions, but one wonders if there is any real change in Ghana's political and economic system. The case of Ghana is simply a bold soldier, inspired by Marxist ideas and principles, killing some of the ruling elite and taking over power. But such taking over of power is still about control of state resources by the state, who now give out to the poor rural dwellers. While many Ghanaians are proud to refer to the Jerry Rawlings revolution as a decisive point in their history, the fact is that Ghana is still a victim of globalization, neo-liberal economic policies and a poor economic system like the rest of Africa. The Rawlings revolution, like the short-lived Thomas Sankara revolution, was not systematic and not built on culture, nature and community. According to Fanon (2008), the only language the ruling elite, be it in colonial or postcolonial Africa, understand is violence. Therefore, armed violence is essential to liberation and freedom. Let us assume for once that a group of liberation fighters or revolutionaries took over the reign of governance. How would they liberate the rural poor and the peasants? What economic model will be put in place to benefit the poor? How will the poor understand the language of the new revolutionaries? Fanon's ideal freedom state is probably what it is: a utopia, a dream.

For Ndlovu-Gatsheni (2013), a more fundamental and sustainable revolution that is urgently needed in twenty-first-century Africa is knowledge revolution, the revolution of the mind. Philosophically, under coloniality, the principle of Cartesian doubt – I think therefore I am – underwent a quick metamorphosis to *I conquer therefore I am*. The right of conquest became an important legitimizing value that authorized all sorts of violence deployed against the colonized.

The important challenge today is 'how to reconstruct the state and nation into an ethical community where wealth is fairly distributed, power is exercised in a responsible and caring manner, and society is united behind an integral national vision' (Mamukwa, Lessem and Schieffer, 2014, p. 31). There is need for a serious consideration of how peripheral societies can emerge into dynamic, innovative and forward-looking political entities that can thrive within a stifling and dominant western neo-liberal economic tradition. As events unfold in the modern world, it is obvious that capitalism, neo-liberalism, socialism and globalization have failed to protect the poor, the weak and the marginalized. The world needs a new model of development. Such models are not likely to come from the centre but rather from the peripheries, where the so-called bottom billion live. One characteristic of such a model is what I call the communitalism advantage.

The communitalism advantage

The communitalist perspective, which I developed in this research work, insists that material development must be accompanied by cognitive, spiritual and cultural development. Communities must first develop a consciousness of who they are and what they are as a people, and what they want to be. The communitalist perspective rejects the notion of some modern scholars, notably American sociologists, such as Lawrence Harrison and Samuel Huntington, who tend to blame culture as responsible for the backwardness of Africa and other poor countries. In other words, they blame the poor for being poor. The rich countries are rich, according to Harrison and Huntington (2000), because they have a culture of hard work, discipline, punctuality and individualism, and not least because they do not subscribe to the Catholic faith. The question now is, do the current moral and social values in the west – America, for example – represent the best of human civilization? Does the fact that some countries are rich economically mean that the citizens are more decent, honest, disciplined and hard-working than others? Perhaps more intelligent? Or do we now regard social vices such as drunkenness, night club violence, sexual licentiousness, gun toting, all of which are common features of 'developed' countries, as values to be emulated by the poorer countries so that their citizens can also be rich? Chang (2007, p. 186) observed that

> Culture-based explanations for economic development were popular up to the 1960s.
> But in the era of civil rights and decolonization, people began to feel that these

explanations had cultural-supremacist (if not necessarily racist) overtones. They fell into disrepute as a result. Such explanations have, however, made a comeback into fashion . . . just as the more dominant cultures (narrowly Anglo-American, more broadly European) have started to feel 'threatened' by other cultures.

The assumption of the culture-based explanation for economic development is that the Germans or the British or the American are doing well economically because they are sincere, trustworthy, hard-working and irreligious. The Africans are poor because they lack these virtues. And yet, according to Chang (2007), it was not so long ago that the British and the Germans were at each other's throats. While the French regarded the Germans as unpolished and lazy, British travellers described them as dishonest and lacking in enterprise skill and creativity. In the same vein, British travellers in Japan described the Japanese as having little capacity to think, while their Korean counterparts were described as dirty, religionless savages (Chang, 2007).

According to the doctrine of the culture-based economists and their African students, the Africans are poor because they love to dance, sing, play and pray about everything. Such a retrospective explanation seems appealing and consoling for those baffled by the complexity and paradox of Africa's persistent underdevelopment. In 2000, an African Cameroonian, Etounga-Manguelle (2000, p. 69), wrote at a conference in America,

> In traditional African society, which exalts the glorious past of ancestors through tales and fables, nothing is done to prepare for the future. The African, anchored in his ancestral culture, is so convinced that the past can only repeat itself that he worries only superficially about the future.

The message of neo-liberal, North–West capitalism for the past five decades is that Africa must modernize if it wants to be rich. In this perspective, to modernize means to westernize. Throngs of young Africans spent years at Harvard Business School and London School of Economics, just to mention two of the most prominent western schools of economic indoctrination, to learn that globalization and modernization are prerequisites for economic prosperity. For them, the way forward is for African countries to abandon much of their tradition and culture and replace them with the new neo-liberal culture of profits, individualism and rampant competition.

The neo-liberal theorists simply wished away the historical dimensions as the developed nations became developed all on their own without any external input. A culture of discipline and hard work was praised as being responsible for the success of the developed countries, while the underdeveloped countries were blamed for their laziness and lack of creativity. The underlying theory behind this is based on the assumption of the marathon fallacy theory and original sin theory (Onigbingbe, 2003). The marathon fallacy assumes that the issue of development and underdevelopment is like a marathon race between nations independent of one another whereby some are ahead of the others as a result of individual efforts without assistance from anybody. The assumption is that those trailing behind could catch up with the others with more hard work, training and discipline. This fallacy underlies much of the economic policies of global organizations, such as the World Bank, the International Monetary Fund (IMF) and funding agencies devoted to fighting poverty in Africa. The economists wrongly assumed that the underdeveloped nations are lagging behind in a global marathon contest on an equal, level field where all have equal opportunities. According to Onigbingbe (2003), the truth about the political economy of the modern world is that the economies of the developed countries and the underdeveloped countries are essentially mutually integrated and necessarily dependent on one another. However, instead of an international economic system where one works for the benefit of the other, what we do notice, according to Onigbingbe, is massive and systematic exploitation of one by the other:

> Exploitation in this case means, fundamentally, the movement of capital from one part of the world to another part of the same world. Thus, where capital is removed is now classified as underdeveloped and where the capital is removed to is classified as developed by the neo-classical economists of the western world. Social reality of the situation is that we do not have two conditions. What we have is a single socio-economic process. An underdeveloped country is not just a pre-capitalist society as a developed country once was, but a para-capitalist society. . . . A pre-capitalist society has not yet entered capitalism or subjected to it. Whereas a para-capitalist society has been exploited to make possible the development of capitalism.
>
> (Onigbingbe, 2003, p. 20)

While Onigbingbe tends to blame the so-called rich countries for the underdevelopment of the poor nations based on his political economy analysis, culture-based neo-liberal economist theorists tend to blame the poor nations for not having a culture that is conducive for capitalism to flourish. Between the extremes is communitalism, which proposes a more positive and integral approach to economics but looks beyond economics to embrace other vital aspects of human life: nature, community, spirituality, education and human capital. Surely economics or 'development', which is often mistakenly equated with being rich or 'developed', cannot be a dominant determinant of progress. For example, Chang (2007) argues that once the economy of a nation is good, every other thing will naturally fall into place: people will act in a more civilized manner, become more honest, be less prone to crime and so on. Such a simplistic view falls flat in the face of the social reality of our time. While the so-called developed countries cannot exonerate themselves from being responsible for creating the atmosphere which has led to the underdevelopment of the poor countries, it is a fact that the elite of the poor countries of Africa have ensured that Africa continues to remain poor. But how long must we continue the blame game – the rich blaming the poor and the poor blaming the rich? What is the way forward? The way forward is what this research work has discussed.

Communitalism argues that rather than reject or abandon their tradition and culture, a re-understanding, re-assimilation and reinterpretation is the way forward. Africa needs to codify those positive qualities in their culture and tradition, and arrange them into a system to power development. This is a task which only Africans can and must do. The key challenge, for Ndlovu-Gatsheni (2013), is how to articulate African problems in an authentic African voice without falling into nativism – how to talk and think about democracy without mimicking western liberal democracy. And from the African side it is clear that another world cannot be possible as long as the continent and its people are not fully decolonized and the snares of the postcolonial neo-colonized world are not broken (Mamukwa, Lessem and Schieffer, 2014).

The ideal of knowledge as espoused within this framework, according to Mamukwa et al. (2014), is not just about woven baskets, handicrafts for tourists or traditional dances. Rather, it is about excavating the technologies behind these practices and artefacts, and creating the right social, political and economic atmosphere to allow individual and communal creativity to bloom.

The communitalist perspective as described in this research work is that which sees the dynamic interaction between the indigenous and the exogenous as essential for authentic knowledge creation in Africa. For communitalism, the ideal is to transcend the dichotomies of West and East, South and North, and engage in innovative co-creation, where identities are preserved and respected. The big barrier is the arrogance and misplaced superiority complex of formal institutions that are determined to continue with their imposition of the one-sided logic of western epistemology. Sadly, most African universities have become accomplices and, in fact, major tools in the systematic mental colonization of Africans.

Rethinking education in and for Africa

Higher technical education is increasingly recognized as critical to development, especially with growing awareness of the role of science, technology and innovation in economic growth. Universities and research institutions are well placed to aid development through their involvement with local business industry and society. Universities and institutions in developing countries can aid development by focusing some of their technical training on specific development needs. Nigerian polytechnics were established precisely to meet the needs for technical training in various fields of expertise in order to hasten development. Unfortunately, the craze for university degrees and the prestige of being labelled a university graduate often makes polytechnic graduates feel inferior and less valued.

It is very important that universities in Africa focus on encouraging innovations and concentrate on building entrepreneurial skills among students to help them develop the capacity to transform ideas into business proposals, and actual products and services; otherwise these universities remain mere ivory towers with no impact on societal transformation. University education, as it is presently constituted in Nigeria and Africa, is geared towards producing graduates who are job seekers rather than job creators. Universities can also integrate into their local communities and help to promote local economic transformation. Communitalism demonstrates how important this is for Africa. The aim of the envisioned integral universities in Africa is to become communiversities that produce entrepreneurial graduates who are likely to generate jobs in their communities while adding to the growth of the economy. Such communiversities consciously recognize and transcend the embedded dichotomies in the conventional mode of knowledge creation.

The acquisition of western knowledge has been and is still invaluable to all, but, on its own, it has been incapable of responding adequately in the face of massive and intensifying disparities, uncontrolled exploitation of pharmacological and other genetic resources and rapid depletion of the earth's natural resources. In that context, a return to indigenous knowledge, cast in contemporary guise, is all important (Lessem, Schieffer, Tong and Rima, 2013).

Indigenous science recognizes no separation between the individual and society, between matter and spirit, between each of us and the whole of nature. Whereas Newtonian physics saw dichotomies, quantum physics perceives connectedness (Cajete, 2000; Lessem et al., 2013). The exogenous needs the indigenous just as the indigenous needs the exogenous.

Conclusion: towards an integral university: lessons for the world

We have now come to the end of this research work. This last chapter attempted to summarize in a few pages what integral action research, authentically applied to an African context, is in theory and practise. The foundation was the dual-rhythm research trajectory, which is described as the 4Cs and CARE. The 4Cs referred to individualized research, while the complementing CARE trajectory referred to institutionalized research. The two form an alternating, interwoven rhythm, 4C-ing development and CARE-ing for the society.

The most exciting aspect of this research work is that the end is like a beginning. The institutions that have emerged out of this research work have taken on a life of their own, and they will continue to expand and grow because they are built on solid foundations. The Ewu Development and Educational MultiPurpose Cooperation Society (EDEMCS) is expanding in scope and outreach. In January 2016, a group of local female farmers was presented with a cheque of $500 each to support them as they prepare for a new farming season (Figures 10.5 and 10.6). This group of female farmers was selected after a rigorous screening exercise. The money was presented to each farmer as a loan, which will be paid back within twelve months with 5 per cent interest. This is different from the conventional top-bottom, western system of bank-controlled loan giving. This is a development project initiated by the local communities themselves. The oldest man in her community, called the ukodion, and the king of Ewu, guaranteed each beneficiary. No other collateral is needed except the integrity of each beneficiary.

The loan for EDEMCS was made available through partnership between ACIRD, based in the rural community of Ewu, Edo State, and the Centre for Integral Socio-Economic Research, based in Lagos, Nigeria's commercial capital. As I explained in Chapter 9, CISER is made up of a group of young Nigerian bankers who are passionate about evolving a new model of development banking and entrepreneurship built on local culture, worldview and community. Such a model will be well suited to the African context

Figure 10.5 A female member of EDEMCS being presented with a cheque by the king of Ewu, in February 2016, witnessed by the ukodion of the village

Figure 10.6 Executive members of EDEMCS with female farmers after being presented with their cheques in February 2016

and tradition, rather than merely imitating the western model, using the Ewu community development association, EDEMCS, as a test case. Co-founder of CISER Basheer Oshodi in his book *An Integral Approach to Development Economics: Islamic Finance in an African Context* (2014) positions Islamic banking, or non-interest banking, within the context of Mazrui's 'triple African heritage' (1986), referring to Africa's triple heritage of indigenous culture, westernized Christianity and Islam. Oshodi argues that the principles of Islamic banking and finance can be adapted to and integrated with other elements of Africa's triple heritage to bring about authentic socio-economic development in Africa.

While EDEMCS is helping the local communities to look inwards to discover themselves, ACIRD is helping them to look outwards to embrace other cultures and worldviews. In 2015, Jamie Hitchen, a policy researcher at the London-based Africa Research Institute (ARI), spent two weeks at the Paxherbal office in Ewu, Edo State, to carry out field research into the activities of Paxherbal. ARI is an independent think tank that focuses on highlighting innovations, events, discoveries and ideas that have worked in Africa. For ARI, the story of Paxherbal and its community development initiatives is a success story that is worth telling to the wider world. During his stay in Edo and Lagos states, Jamie interviewed all stakeholders in the Paxherbal enterprise: wholesalers, health care providers, physicians, government officials and consumers of Paxherbal products. His report, titled *Modern Herbal Remedies: Herbal Medicine and Community Development in Nigeria*, was published in 2015 (Africa Research Institute, 2015). At the launch of the publication in April 2015, which was attended by a lively group comprising health professionals, policymakers, students, scholars, entrepreneurs and spiritual figures, I spoke passionately about the need for Africa to tell her own story. ACIRD is set to continue to tell and retell the African story in our own African symbols and metaphors, in line with the proverb quoted earlier: '*Until the lion learns how to write, every story will glorify the hunter.*'

The dynamism of integral development is this blend of the indigenous and the exogenous, the local and the global, the new and the old. While it is essential that we reconnect with our origins and our roots in order to discover our identity and originality, it is equally important that we reach out to other people, other cultures, other worldviews and other ways of doing things. This brings us once again to the Igbo proverb that we cited at the beginning of this chapter: '*When something stands, another thing will stand beside it.*' There is not one but many ways of knowing, doing, seeing and being. An integral university is a communiversity of knowledge, both local and global. An integral university helps to build an integral society where we all have a voice and where we all share in the same wisdom embodied in humanity's cultural heritage and diversity.

So long as we all breathe the same air, we will remain bonded together, both the living and the dead. This is the communitalist perspective on which this research work was based. Only a thin line separates the spiritual from the physical, spirit from matter, and life from death. The wisdom of the ancients is there in the molecules of the air around us, waiting to be tapped when we are open enough to perceive them.

The idea of the stranger, the unknown, is an illusion. We are all linked together in a symbiotic cosmos. What affects one affects all. Nobody is destined to be poor, or to be sick. Millions of men and women from all parts of the world are coming together to remind us that it is our human greed and selfishness, fuelled by our disconnect from nature, culture and spirit, rather than nuclear bombs, that constitute the greatest threat to human survival, human health and global peace.

In the integral university, we learn how to be human. We learn how to relate to the earth in a positive and productive way. The word 'humility' is derived from the Latin *humus*, which means earth, ground, earthliness, humanness. To be human is to be humble and see ourselves as part of, not the centre of, creation. To be human is to be healed by the earth, integrally bringing together the South, East, North and West.

This, indeed, is the way of a true Pax Africana.

References

Africa Research Institute. (2015). *Modern herbal remedies: Herbal medicine and community development in Nigeria* [online]. Available at: http://www.africaresearchinstitute.org/newsite/wp-content/uploads/2015/04/ARI-Policy-Voice-Pax-Herbal-download.pdf. [Accessed 10 Oct. 2015].

Ba, Diadie. (2007). Africans still seething over Sarkozy speech. [online] *Reuters.com*. Available at: http://uk.reuters.com/article/uk-africa-sarkozy-idUKL0513034620070905. [Accessed 3 Dec. 2015].

Cajete, G. (2000). *Native science: Natural laws of interdependence*. Santa Fe, NM: Clear Light.

Chang, H.-J. (2007). *Bad Samaritans: The guilty secrets of rich nations and the threat to global prosperity*. London: Random House.

Collier, P. (2008). *The bottom billion: Why the poorest countries are failing and what can be done about it*. Oxford: Oxford University Press.

Comaroff, J. and Comaroff, J. L. (2012). *Theory from the South: Or, how Euro-America is evolving toward Africa*. London: Routledge.

Easterly, W. (2006). *The white man's burden: Why the West's efforts to aid the rest have done so much ill and so little good*. London: Penguin Press.

Etounga-Manguelle, D. (2000). Does Africa need a cultural adjustment program? In: L. Harrison and S. Huntington, eds., *Culture matters*, 65–79. New York: Basic Books.

Fanon, F. (2008). *Black skin, white masks*. London: Pluto Press.

Harrison, L. and Huntington, S. (eds.). (2000). *Culture matters: How values shape human progress.* New York: Basic Books.

Lessem, R. and Schieffer, A. (2010). *Integral research and innovation: Transforming enterprise and society.* Farnham, UK: Gower.

Lessem, R., Schieffer, A., Tong, J. and Rima S. (2013). *Integral dynamics: Political economy, cultural dynamics and the future of the University.* Farnham, UK: Gower.

Mamukwa, E., Lessem, R. and Schieffer, A. (2014). *Integral green Zimbabwe: An African phoenix rising.* London: Routledge.

Mazrui, A. (1986). *The Africans: A triple heritage.* London: BBC.

Ndlovu-Gatsheni, S. (2013). *Coloniality of power in postcolonial Africa myths of decolonization.* Oxford, UK: African Books Collective.

Onigbingbe, A. (2003). *Development of underdevelopment: Conceptual issues in political economy.* Ibadan, Nigeria: Frontline Books.

Oshodi, B. (2014). *An integral approach to development economics: Islamic finance in an African context.* Farnham, UK: Gower.

Sankara, T. (2007). *Women's liberation and the African freedom struggle.* Atlanta: Pathfinder.

Index